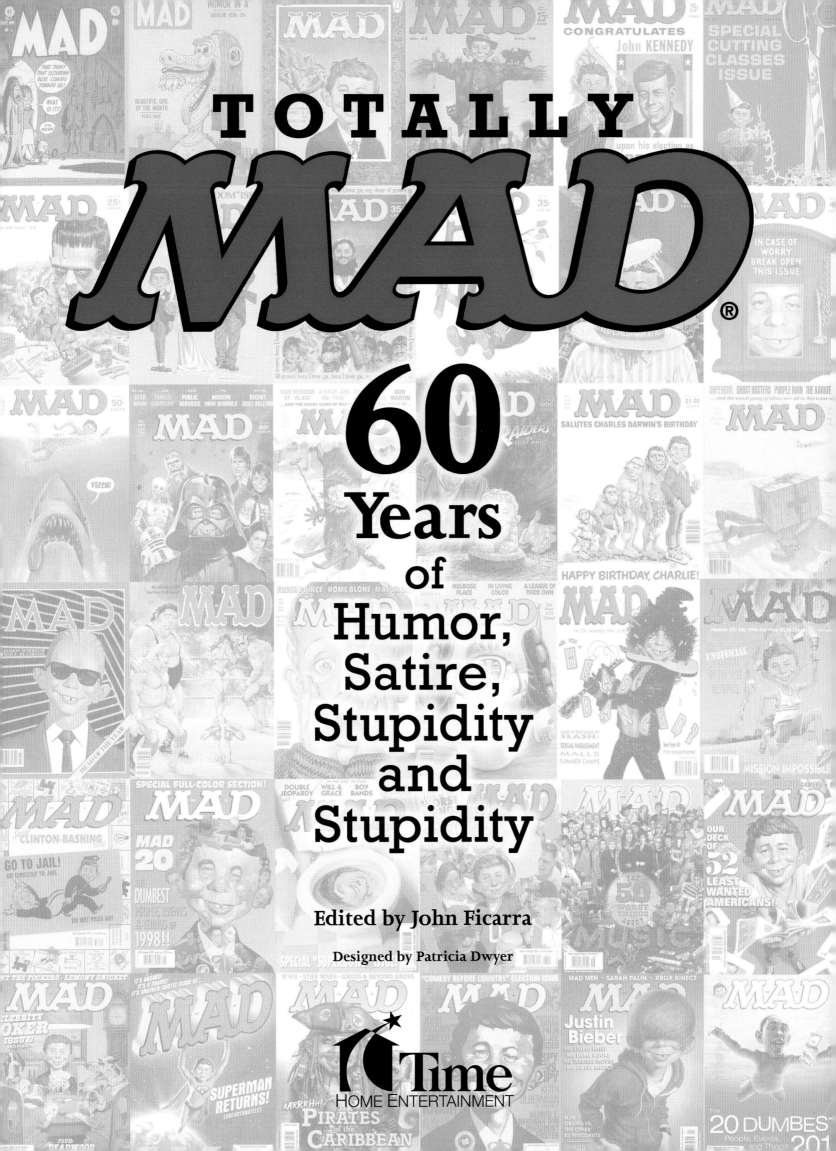

TOTALLY MAD

60 Years of Humor, Satire, Stupidity and Stupidity

Edited by John Ficarra

Designed by Patricia Dwyer

Time
HOME ENTERTAINMENT

In Memoriam

This book is dedicated to the memory of the thousands of jokes that have died on the pages of MAD over the past 60 years.

Introduction

By Stephen Colbert & Eric Drysdale

Hi. Stephen Colbert here. In an early episode of my hit television show *The Colbert Report*, I celebrated Al Jaffee's 85th birthday in a segment I wrote, written by a guy named Eric Drysdale. We immediately bonded over our mutual fondness for MAD, if only to the degree I allow myself to 'bond' with any employee. (VIACOM frowns on it, and I'm a company man.) So when the folks at MAD asked me to contribute a foreword to this collection, I didn't hesitate to ask Eric to do most of the work. Plus, I'm sure he will be fine with taking just the credit instead of the cash.

—Dr. Stephen T. Colbert, D.F.A

I was honored when Stephen asked me to participate in a dialogue with him about the enduring cultural impact of MAD magazine. Needless to say, I jumped at the opportunity to make use of those college Mass Comm theory classes I'm still paying for. Plus— and it's not unrelated—Stephen promised to split the fee.

—Eric Drysdale, B.S.

SAM VIVIANO

STEPHEN: Ha ha. B.S.! That's hilarious.

ERIC: No, that's actually my degree from Emerson College—Bachelor of Science, with a major in Mass Communication.

STEPHEN: And yet, you're employed! Let's talk about MAD. I loved it. I saved my allowance up for it every week and bought it after church on Sunday at The Book Bag. I remember hiding the "Middle Finger" issue from my parents…You remember that? 1973ish…We're about the same age, right?

ERIC: No, I'm much younger than you. However, I'm not sure that matters because the appeal of MAD is intergenerational. It was around for a full two decades before we even caught a glimpse of it, and has been around for four decades since. MAD's history lives along a continuum of popular lampoon, stretching from the comedies of the ancient Greeks to the psychedelic grotesqueries of [Adult Swim.]

STEPHEN: Uh-huh. So, like how much younger?

ERIC: What? Um, I think like five years.

STEPHEN: Uh-huh. Do you remember Fester Bestertester and his protégé Karbunkle? It was Don Martin. They were two guys who sort of had adventures/occupations that all ended incredibly violently. The first thing that ever made me laugh in MAD was Fester and Karbunkle moving a safe in a highrise for Mr. Boney…or Mr. Beanflurrrp or something. Anyway, the safe falls out a window and hits a man on the head. His tongue unrolls out of this mouth all the way across the street. I remember a parade marches over it. That was the first thing that really made me laugh.

ERIC: But it wasn't the first thing you saw in MAD?

STEPHEN: Well, my first MADs were the ones my older brothers left behind when they went to college. So the first stuff I saw was the 1950s Harvey Kurtzman and Bill Elder stuff, and I just didn't get the cultural references. So that kind of fits in with what you were saying about the different humoristic endeavor continuums in history and the like. Right?

ERIC: Sure. But let's explore why we kept reading even though we didn't understand it all.

STEPHEN: Definitely. You go first.

ERIC: Sure. Well, I think it's because no matter the level of sophistication you brought to MAD, there was always something dumb enough to keep your attention—if only the glorious weirdness of the pictures. And with any material that required deeper understanding, there was always a sense that you would get it eventually. It felt like being guided into a new, dangerous place—but in the good hands of fun-loving friends eager to share new and hilarious truths about the world.

STEPHEN: Oh! I think I understand what you said so let me talk. I remember I saw Nixon on TV a bunch when I was a kid, and I knew from how people talked about him that he was the President and was in some kind of trouble. But because I read MAD, I was able to piece together all of the information and eventually get to this moment of, "Oh! I get it now! He's the President of the United States…but look at his funny nose!"

ERIC: Well, sure. The nose is a good start, but I actually thought you were about to say something about your discovery of the fallibility of authority.

STEPHEN: Well, of course. I was going to say something about that, too.

ERIC: O.K.

STEPHEN: O.K.! So should I say that now?

ERIC: Please.

STEPHEN: Well...think about it. When did we see Nixon's nose the most? During the Watergate scandal, and that was a very bad thing for his authority, and I don't think that could have been a coincidence.

ERIC: Well. It was a moment at which you understood something new about Nixon, and you were rewarded for that understanding with laughter. In a way, your consciousness was raised, which creates a nice feedback loop. You're laughing along with MAD more and more often as you learn about the world and are able recognize more of its imperfections. Then, within the jokes you aren't getting, MAD is tipping you off about where to seek out the next imperfections. It functions as nothing short of an ongoing, transformative spiritual text.

STEPHEN: So, only 5 years younger than me? You look good.

ERIC: I run.

STEPHEN: I have bad knees. Sorry. You were talking about The Transformers?

ERIC: No. I said that MAD could be seen as a transformative spiritual text. Transformative, in that engagement with the text changes the reader's worldview. Spiritual, in that it concerns itself with the mysterious gap between the explainable and the unknown—especially as it relates to human interaction, love and death—The human condition.

STEPHEN: Exactly. "More than meets the eye." See? In a way you were talking about The Transformers. And you know who was transforming? We were.

ERIC: Well, we were transforming into guys who read MAD magazine. And in a way, we even got to transform into guys who wrote MAD magazine. Al Jaffee included a comedy writing exercise in every Snappy Answers to Stupid Questions—There was a blank space for you to write your own comebacks, which is probably where...

STEPHEN: Fonebone!

ERIC: What?

STEPHEN: Freenbean I. Fonebone! That was the guy who Bester Festertester and Karbunkle were moving the safe for. Well, This has been great.

ERIC: Wait? We're done? What about the structural subversions of Sergio Aragones' Marginals? What about Spy vs. Spy in the context of the Cold War? What about Dave Berg's unmasking of suburban hostility? Or the freneticism and pathos of Woodbridge? I had notes.

STEPHEN: Yeah, that all sounds good. But they're probably gonna cover a lot of that stuff in the book. So let's just say it was really funny, we learned a lot, and we wouldn't be who we are if we hadn't read it. O.k?

ERIC: So... It was transformative.

STEPHEN: Sure. And it still is.

ERIC: Are you sure you don't want to look at my notes and...

STEPHEN: I'm good.

Eric Drysdale and Stephen Colbert, New York City, 2012

Who Was Bill Gaines? Part One
By Frank Jacobs

With the untimely death of his father, Bill Gaines seemed unprepared to become the head of Educational Comics, often abbreviated as EC. He was naïve and inexperienced, but even he could see that the company, then $100,000 in the red, was in deep trouble. Its kiddie comics — "Bouncy Bunny in the Friendly Forest" was a typical title — had seen their day.

Gaines experimented, tapped his creative side, and a new breed of comic book emerged. Its name was horror. Gaines and writer/editor Al Feldstein hit the jackpot and begot an empire that would spawn the most fanatical cult in the history of the industry. EC now stood for Entertaining Comics, and with the changeover a new Bill Gaines gradually emerged: an efficient, determined, honest-to-goodness publisher and businessman.

A few years later, with the enormous success of MAD, the transformation was complete. Gaines became the prototype of a leader — unshaven, unkempt, and sometimes off the rails — but a leader nonetheless, and a father figure to many.

Longtime MAD art director John Putnam agreed. "He can be a warm friend and yet keeps a workable distance between himself and his employees. I'm never made to feel like an employee, but I'm not going to walk all over him — no one is."

The door to Gaines' office was almost always open and unless he was counting money or double-checking items on his daily calendar, he was available to anyone. He loved gossip and listened avidly to any tidbit, but almost never contributed a view of his own.

"Bill will listen and Bill will laugh," said Putnam, "but that's all. I've never heard him put anyone on the staff down."

Gaines' office was a museum of sentimental and macabre memorabilia. The first thing you saw was the gigantic presence of King Kong peering in a window. The papier-mâché, fur-covered gorilla was handcrafted by artist Sergio Aragonés and presented to Gaines as a Christmas gift from his staff and contributors. Hanging from the ceiling were zeppelins of various sizes — all gifts from MADmen — and the outlandish MAD Zeppelin, co-created by artist George Woodbridge and art

director John Putnam and later included as a bonus cut-out in a MAD Special.

On a cabinet sat an old peep-show nickelodeon — also a Christmas gift — in which one could view a flip-card film, interposed with photos of the MAD crew, each greeting Gaines with an obscene gesture. Nearby rested another gift, an ancient cash register that belonged to then-associate editor Nick Meglin's grandfather. Each key bore a peculiar face or phrase. Push down the key picturing then-assistant art director Lenny Brenner, and at the top a metal tab popped up, asking, "Whaddya want, ya fat bastard?" Push down a picture of omnipresent mascot Alfred E. Neuman, and up would pop "No Sale."

Gaines and his gift—a life-size King Kong head to call his own.

8

"Gaines was a very responsive person, and he inspired you to bigger and better gags," recalls Meglin. "You found yourself doing most anything to hear him laugh." Said Putnam, "There is no more musical sound in the world than Bill Gaines laughing."

Facing Gaines' desk was a glass-door cabinet, in which rested the dual-framed photographs of a man and a woman. Some visitors believed they were portraits of his parents, a supposition that Gaines often allowed to go uncorrected. In truth, they were photos of silent-screen star Fatty Arbuckle and starlet Virginia Rappe, whom Arbuckle was accused of molesting at a Hollywood orgy. "I thought it would be a nice gesture to link them forever," Gaines said.

On a door was a plaque with an inscription which used to adorn the walls of geisha houses:

> ### INSTRUCTIONS TO THE STAFF
> DO NOT FORGET THE BENEFITS
> YOU RECEIVE HERE
> AND DO NOT, THEREFORE,
> COMPLAIN OF ANYTHING
>
> DO NOT TELL LIES
>
> DO NOT BE UNREASONABLE
>
> HONOR YOUR ELDERS AND BETTERS
>
> BE GLAD YOU'RE ALIVE

Gaines checked his desk many times a day to make sure every item was in its proper place. Dwarfing everything was a circular rack on which hung 30 rubber stamps, nearly all of which he used regularly. Many bore the names and addresses of people he corresponded with often, thus saving him the time of inscribing outgoing mail by hand. He admitted that he needed more than 30 rubber stamps, but being a creature of habit, he made do with what he had.

Gaines' most cherished possession was his calendar on which, in a script only he could decipher, he notated his missions for the day. As each task was completed, he blackened out the mission with savage satisfaction. It was vital, important, even sacred for him to get every item crossed out.

Contrary to the size of his person, appetite, and bankroll, Gaines thought small—at least as publisher of MAD. *Playboy's* Hugh Hefner once asked him what new projects he was planning.

"None," Gaines replied.

"*None?*" Hefner asked incredulously.

Bill in his office circa 1982 at 485 MADison Avenue looking satisfied—he must have crossed everything off of his "to do" lists.

Some of Gaines' 30 rubber stamps. The name "Gaines" is not synonymous with hi-tech.

PHOTO: IRVING SCHILD

"It was like I was guilty of blasphemy," Gaines said later.

What one must realize is that Gaines was terrified of getting involved in an operation too big for him to handle personally. Therein lieth ruin — not for Hefner, perhaps, but assuredly for himself. He didn't seek to build an empire; MAD would provide him with a modest, quite profitable kingdom.

During his reign, the magazine changed hardly at all. It continued to contain 48 black-and-white pages printed on uncoated paper. There were no frills, no three-hour expense-account lunches, no feudal chain of command.

Yet MAD prospered, its circulation climbing to a top figure of slightly over two million. Cheap imitations abounded, aiming at MAD's audience. Only one survived, an ill-equipped pretender to the throne.

Gaines managed to achieve growth without really growing. Three times a year he published MAD Specials, each containing 80 pages of mostly reprinted material plus a bonus, such as a giant poster or a hangable MAD calendar. Then there were MAD's paperbacks, eight per year, some containing reprinted material, some completely original. The magazine was also

FROM THE PERSONAL COLLECTION OF ANNIE GAINES

Bill Gaines' idea of a strenuous workout.

he explained. "By making my own deposits, writing all the checks, making all the payrolls, even serving as stockroom clerk, there's nothing that goes on that escapes me. So I run my business in this insane way in which I handle every single thing, down to the tiniest detail.

"Being a compulsive, I must have my bills paid by the end of the month. If my suppliers don't send me their bills on time, I get very angry and call them up and scream at them because they haven't billed me yet."

Herewith the Gaines Formula: "Don't let your business expand to the point that you can't control it. Keep your staff intact and don't hire unnecessary people just because you're successful. Insist that the people who work for you are efficient. Provide incentives, such as bonuses and trips. Increase salaries regularly, but not capriciously. Provide a quality product for your customers at a price they can afford. Do not gouge them with spin-off merchandise. Make everything — your people, your offices, your operation — just big enough for success, but no bigger. The result: Happiness."

translated into seven languages — Swedish, Norwegian, Finnish, Dutch, Italian, German, and British. (Yes, British — "dollars" became "pounds" or "quid," "trucks" became "lorries," etc.)

Neither the paperbacks nor the foreign editions were published by Gaines, though he still regarded them as part of his flock. "I have only one big market and that's the United States," he said. "Everything else is for fun."

Fun? Well, sort of, as long as the overseas publishers played by Gaines' rules — like the time a British operation wanted to sell a poster of Alfred E. Neuman for about a dollar. Gaines, who detested merchandising gimmicks that soaked his readers, suggested that the poster should be sold for no more than 50 cents. The British publisher argued that there were many reasons for the higher price. Gaines gave grudging permission on the condition that he be allowed to see the poster before it was printed. The next thing he knew, however, the posters were being printed and sold. Gaines screamed via airmail:

"This is a perfect example of why it is difficult doing business with you. Since you have already printed 4,000 copies, what are you going to do if we decide to disapprove of the posters, which we very well may do?"

The British publisher apologized, but the affair was a *fait accompli*, leading Gaines, two years later, to inquire about sales. "Sorry to say," the British publisher admitted, "it has had a steady sale of two a week, and on a recent check-up I find that we have sold just under 500 copies."

Gaines' methods of doing business were arguably unique. "I do menial things no executive in his right mind would do,"

"Don't let your business expand to the point that you can't control it."

Bill Gaines, as remembered by everyone who met him: laughing uproariously and living life on his terms.

HORROR DEPT.: THE TALE WAS TOLD BY AN OLD SEA-FARING MAN, BABBLING IN DELIRIUM BEFORE HE DIED! BABBLING AMONGST THE FLOTSAM AND JETSAM TOSSED UPON THE CONEY ISLAND SHORE HE BABBLED... ABOUT A MYSTERIOUS ISLAND IN THE TROPICS... ABOUT THE LOST TRIBE OF THE OOKABOLAPONGA... ABOUT THEIR GOD...

PING PONG!

BILL ELDER

THE TROPICS!...SOMEWHERE IN THE LATITUDES, SOUTH OF THE SARGOSSA SEA, A PEA-SOUP FOG...SO THICK YOU COULD CUT IT WITH A KNIFE... HUGS THE OCEAN!

AND INSIDE THE FOG...A SHIP RIDES LIKE A GHOST...A BLACK SHIP WITH A GRIM-FACED FEARLESS CREW OF MEN... RIDING TO ITS DESTINY...WITH DEATH...WITH PONG!

Artist: Will Elder   Writer: Harvey Kurtzman

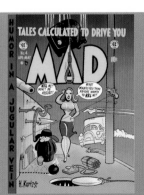

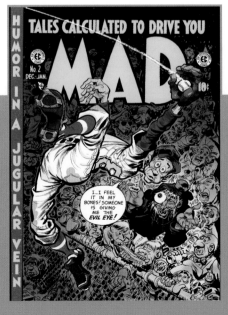

HERO WORSHIP DEPT.: FASTER THAN A SPEEDING BULLET! *KA-PWEENG!* MORE POWERFUL THAN A LOCOMOTIVE! ...CHUGACHUGACHUGA CHUG! ABLE TO LEAP TALL BUILDINGS IN A SINGLE BOUND!...*BOINNGSWOOOSH!* LOOK!... UP IN THE SKY!... IT'S A BIRD!... IT'S A PLANE!... IT'S...

SUPERDUPERMAN!

OUR STORY BEGINS HIGH UP IN THE OFFICES OF THAT FIGHTING NEWSPAPER, 'THE DAILY DIRT'!

AN INCREDIBLY MISERABLE AND EMACIATED LOOKING FIGURE SHUFFLES FROM SPITOON TO SPITOON!

FOR THIS IS THE ASSISTANT TO THE COPY BOY... CLARK BENT, WHO IS IN REALITY, *SUPERDUPERMAN!*

Artist: Wally Wood   Writer: Harvey Kurtzman

For most people, being reflective means spending hours in front of a mirror!

Writer: Harvey Kurtzman

Artist: Jack Davis

#8 DEC '53/JAN '54

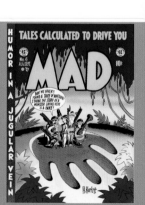 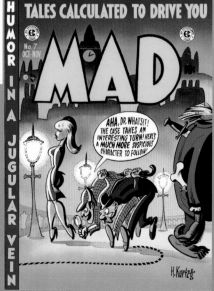   

Writer: Harvey Kurtzman

Artist: Wally Wood

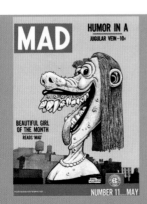

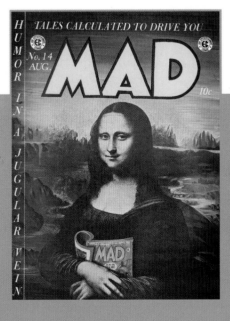

...a MAD tea party.

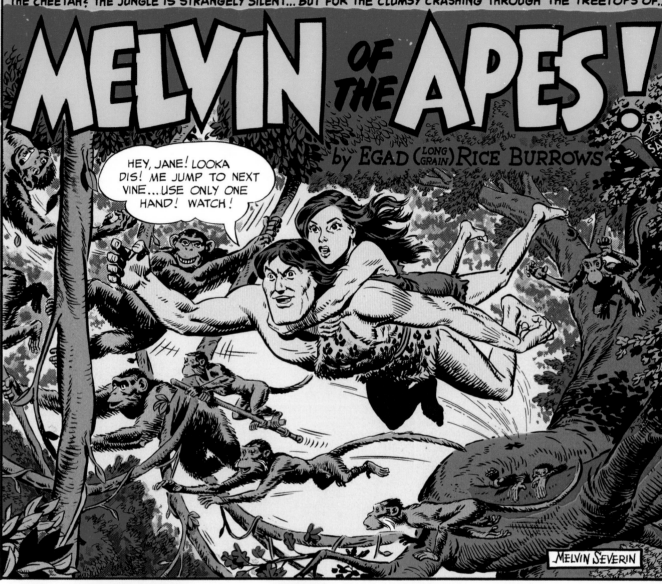

Artist: John Severin   Writer: Harvey Kurtzman

#6 AUG/SEP '53

SPECIAL FEATURE DEPT.: DEAR READERS!... THE FOLLOWING SIX PAGES ARE SO DISGUSTING... SO NAUSEATING, THEY'LL MAKE YOU SICK FOR DAYS TO COME!......NOW THAT WE'VE AROUSED YOUR INTEREST... HERE'S A FEATURE ABOUT SOMEONE YOU KNOW VERY WELL!...VERY VERY WELL! HERE IS A FEATURE ABOUT YOU...OUR...

MAD READER!

ON THIS AND THE FOLLOWING FIVE PAGES ARE VIEWS OF WHAT WE, THE EDITORS OF MAD, BELIEVE TO BE A CROSS-SECTION OF THE PEOPLE WHO READ MAD!... AND SO, WHILE YOU WANDER THROUGH THE FOLLOWING PAGES, SMIRKING GUFFAWING AND RETCHING AT WHAT YOU SEE... PAUSE A MOMENT! THE FACE YOU'RE RETCHING AT MAY BE YOUR OWN!

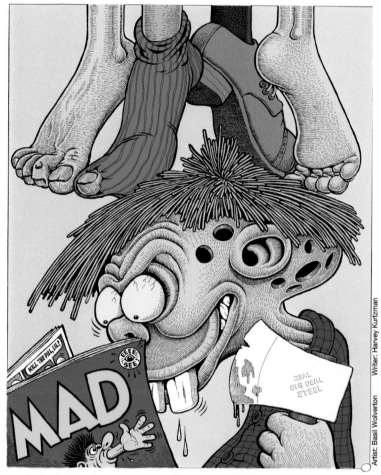

THE YOUNG MAD READER (WITH MOTHER AND FATHER): HERE IS A GOOD EXAMPLE OF THE CLEAN WHOLESOME AFFECT MAD HAS ON OUR YOUNG READERS! FOR INSTANCE, BEFORE READING MAD, THIS YOUNG MAN VERY OFTEN USED AN AXE ON HIS PLAYMATES! WHEN HE READ MAD, HE REALIZED HOW UGLY AND SORDID AXING HIS PLAYMATES WAS... SO NOW HE USES A PISTOL!

Artist: Basil Wolverton   Writer: Harvey Kurtzman

#11 MAY '54

MR. WEATHERNOT! SHAME ON YOU, CHASING SALONICA AND BIDDY AROUND YOUR DESK!

I CAN'T HELP IT I TELL YOU... I CAN'T HELP IT! THEY'RE DRAWN SO GOSH DARNED CUTE!

STARCHIE!... BOTTLE-NECK!... THE REASON I'VE CALLED YOU TO MY OFFICE IS TO TELL YOU YOU'VE FAILED THE EXAMS AND I'M LEAVING YOU BACK TO GRADE SCHOOL ...AGAIN!

MR. WEATHERNOT! YOU MUST UNDERSTAND...OUR MARKS WERE THE RESULTS OF THE USUAL TYPICAL TEEN-AGE PRANKS! SURELY IF YOU WILL LISTEN TO COLD LOGIC AND FACTS... MY LOGICAL REASONING WILL SHOW YOU SHOULD PASS US!

ER... STEP OUTSIDE, BOTTLENECK!

GIVE A BOOK TO A SERVICE MAN!

WHACK!

MR. WEA

CRASH! BAM! THUD

MR. W

THUD THUD THUD KERHAK

C'MON, BOTTLENECK!... MY COLD LOGIC AND FACTS... MY LOGICAL REASONING SHOWED MR. WEATHERNOT HE SHOULD PASS US!

...GAD THAT COLD LOGICAL REASONING PLAYS HOB WITH MY KNUCKLES!

SCHEDULE A LECTURE WILL BE GIVEN BY DR. KINSEY ON WHY STUDENTS CUT CLASS EVERY SPRING!

HERE COMES BIDDY!... YOU KNOW, STARCH!... I THINK SHE'S GOT A CRUSH ON YOU!

DON'T BE SILLY, BOTTLENECK!...JUST BECAUSE YOU SEE THOSE HEARTS FLOATING AROUND HER HEAD IT DOESN'T MEAN SHE'S GOT A CRUSH ON ME!...IN CARTOON LANGUAGE, THOSE HEARTS COULD MEAN PLATONIC FRIENDSHIP!

ZIP!

#12 JUN '54

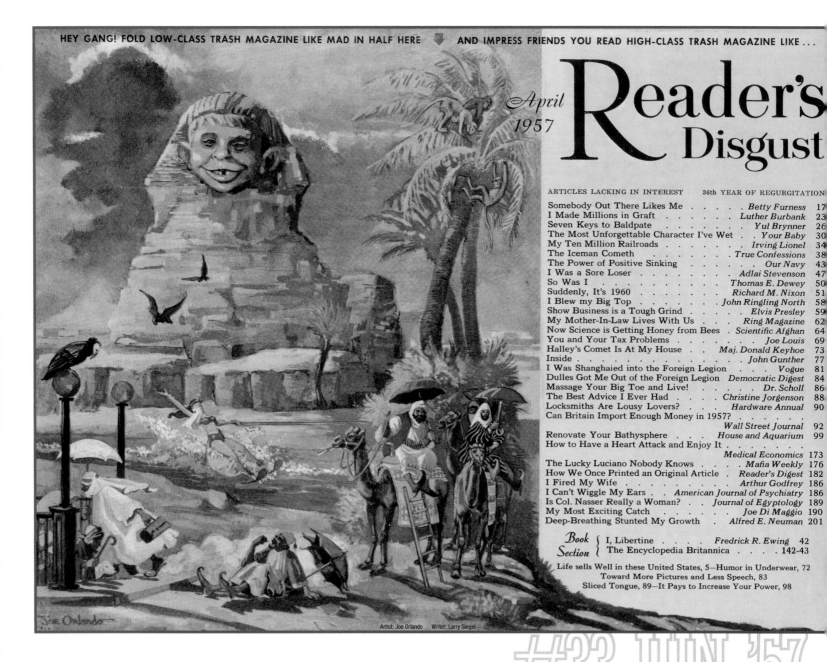
#33 JUN '57

"Look, Mom—no more cavities!"

Crust Gumpaste helps gums take the place of teeth by coating them with a hard white enamel finish! Just the thing for punks who get their teeth knocked out from running around with teen-age gangs.

Fluidsteel is a trademark for Proctor & Rumble's exclusive liquid metal gum-coater.
© 1958, The Proctor & Rumble Co.

Artist: Kelly Freas

"VISITING THE GRANDPARENTS" by William Elder. Number 1 in the series "Ol' Home Life."

While you are visiting—

What makes a glass of beer taste so good?

Malted barley—with important body minerals plus liquid matter. For thing that makes glass of beer taste so good is terrible thirst.

Tangy hops. Yes—visiting can be a series of tangy hops if you play your cards right. And you'd be surprised how good free beer tastes!

The way it "goes with everything"—makes beer this country's Beverage of Moderation—the way it fits into our friendly way of life—the way each glass makes us friendlier and friendlier and friendlier.

Beer Belongs—Enjoy It!

Artist: Will Elder Writer: Harvey Kurtzman

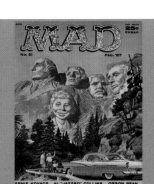

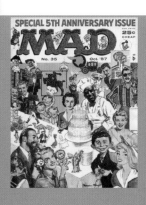

BOB

RAY

Noting the recent trend on the part of manufacturers to put their new products, no matter what they may be, into Push-Button Pressure Cans, MAD assigned Bob & Ray's ace roving correspondent, Wally Ballew, to investigate the behind-the-scenes story of this new packaging fad. So let's go out to the Blasst Pressure Can Company in Rumney, Vermont, for an educational, on-the-spot interview, as Mr. Ballew presents his

PRESSURE CAN REPORT

This is charming and talented Wally Ballew, four-time-winner of the "Elkart P. Loftus Award for Unimpressive Reporting," speaking to you direct from the "Filling Room" of the Blasst Pressure Can Company here in Rumney. And beside me is the president of the Blasst organization, Mr. Fenwick J. Finster. Tell me, Mr. Finster, just **what** goes on here in the "Filling Room"?

The little red button goes on here, Mr. Ballew!

ARTIST: MORT DRUCKER   WRITER: VIC COWEN

I . . . I beg your pardon?

You know . . . the little red button you press to squirt the stuff out of the can? Well, after the can is filled and pressurized, that little red button goes on here in this room!

Oh, I see! And what are these particular cans being filled with, Mr. Finster?

Well, right now we're running off a batch of Spray Insecticide, Wally. The chemical is sent to us in drums by the manufacturer and we put it into each individual can with that big soup ladle you see over there . . .

Then the top is screwed onto the can, and it goes over there to the compression department . . .

You mean where those hundred or so men are lined up, working . . .

That's right, Wally! They're called "The Blowers"! Each man attaches what looks like that straw to each can, and then he blows into it for all he's worth. When he can't get any more breath into it, he holds his finger over the hole, and slips one of those little red buttons onto it!

That's amazing! I was always under the impression that some kind of big **machine** shot gas into the can!

No . . . it's all done by my boys! They're a great bunch! They love to work under **pressure**! Heh-heh! That's a little joke we tell around here . . .

Yes, that's very funny! But tell me, Mr. Finster . . . Don't they get dizzy and headachey from blowing air into those cans all day long?

They did at first, but they all have lungs like elephants now! Take Eddie Zitzlaff, for instance . . . the third one from the left! He's our champion blower!

INSTANT SCOTCH

**THE SWEET SMELL OF SUCCESS—GONE WITH THE WIND

On his day off, he blows up Navy blimps . . . just to keep in trim!

I see! Do you ever get any complaints on your pressure cans from consumers, Mr. Finster?

Oh, we did at first! Folks would complain about strange smells coming from our cans. But we traced it to some of our boys who had eaten garlic or onions before they came to work! Now we make everybody **gargle** before they start!

PERFECT ACCIDENT RECORD

12 DEAD 4 SEC.8

#47 JUN '59

THE CAVEMEN

MAD's maddest artist, Don Martin, who is an expert in the art of love (drawing pictures of it, that is!), now offers his idea of ''romance'' as practiced by...

Hardly a day goes by that letters don't pour into MAD's palatial tenement offices from deficients all over the country asking: "Just who is this Alfred E. Neuman?" "Where did he come from?" "What does he want?" "Who cares, anyway?" etc. In answer to this great upsurge of interest in the subject, MAD has employed a Geneologist (who works cheap) to investigate Alfred's background and fill us in on

Alfred E. Neuman's FAMILY TREE

ARTIST: WALLACE WOOD   WRITER: TOM KOCH

NU MUN
2,538,391 B.C.-2,538,340 B.C.
First man to be convinced that invention of fire was just a passing fad.

TUT-ANKH-NU-MEN
6328 B.C.-6251 B.C.
Labored 27 years on pyramid of Ramses IX, regarded as eighth wonder of the world, which collapsed three days after its completion.

SOCRATES NUMANOS
508 B.C.-462 B.C.
Created classic philosophy calling for Greece to be ruled by an élite of clods.

NERO NUMINUS
51 A.D.-122 A.D.
Sold asbestos togas while Rome burned.

ALFRED THE HUN
453-513
Stayed home in Mongolia and operated a black market lichee nut shop, while Attila's hordes conquered the known world.

ALFRED THE CHICKEN-HEARTED
1193-1258
Started out on Second Crusade. Made mistake of trying to ford stream three miles from home with armor on.

JOHANNES NEUMANBERG
1417-1462
Attempted to print first book from moveable type. Gave up when he discovered he couldn't read.

CHRISTOPHER NUMUNBUS
1462-1513
Sailed Westward in 1492 searching for short route to Indies. Through poor navigation, discovered Sweden.

AMERIGO NUMANUCCI
1470-1526
Read of discoveries of kinsman Christopher Numunbus, was convinced it proved Earth was flat, and spent rest of life searching for edge.

MICHAELANEUMANO
1508-1562
Commissioned to paint ceiling of Sistine Chapel, mistakenly painted ceiling of building next door, which was condemned and torn down the following week.

ELDER NEUMAN
1584-1658
Convinced the "Mayflower" was unseaworthy, remained in England and went bankrupt in the Used Galoshes business.

SIR ISAAC NEUMAN
1602-1681
Disagreed with Newton's Law of Gravity, spent 45 years in futile effort to prove things could fall up.

BENJAMIN NEUMAN
1707-1793
Successfully flew a kite during a storm; and thereby proved the existence of wind.

GENERAL GEORGE NEUMAN
1732-1793
Crossed the Delaware with a ragged army, and passed Washington going the other way.

PAUL NEUMAN
1733-1781
Waited to bring the news to every Middlesex village and farm, then forgot whether two lamps meant by land or by sea, so he went home.

PATRICK NEUMAN
1742-1801
Seeking to avoid public censure, yet convinced the Colonies would lose The Revolution, became only man to sign the Declaration of Independence in disappearing ink.

You'll find the root of all this evil on the next page

ABRAHAM NEUMAN
1809-1865

Born in a log cabin, walked 20 miles to borrow racy French novels. Later lost bid for presidential nomination because he could only read French.

JEFFERSON DAVIS NEUMAN
1811-1870

Lost family fortune investing in fireworks factory, anticipating Confederate Victory Celebration.

NIKOLAI NUMANSKI
1856-1917

First man to predict Communists would never win control of Russia. First man to be sent to Siberia when they did.

TEDDY NEUMAN
1858-1919

Developed slogan "Speak loudly and carry a small stick!" Joined Rough Riders and soon discovered he was allergic to horses.

WILLIAM JENNINGS NEUMAN
1848-1922

Delivered stirring "Cross of Gold" speech at Democratic National Convention of 1896, but speech impediment made it impossible for delegates to understand what he said.

THOMAS ALVA NEUMAN
1867-1929

Failed in demonstrating that a jar of fireflies would provide a cheap, efficient form of illumination.

WHAT, ME WORRY?

ALFRED E. NEUMAN
194?-?

What—Me Worry?

READIN' AND WRITHIN' DEPT.

Some time ago (MAD No. 41), we voiced concern over the dullness of elementary school readers, and presented an up-to-date MAD PRIMER. Now, even the MAD PRIMER is outdated! The single most important thing in the lives of youngsters today is watching "horror movies"! And so, in order to help educate our early grade school kids properly in "horror movie appreciation," we feel schools should offer as required reading...

THE MAD HORROR PRIMER

ART—WALLACE WOOD   STORY—LARRY SIEGEL

LESSON 1.

See the man.
He is a doctor.
He is mixing formulas.
Mix, mix, mix.
He is also transplanting brains.
Transplant, transplant, transplant.
The doctor is building a monster.
The doctor will make a lot of money
    with his monster.
The doctor will save this money.
Soon, the doctor will be able to afford
    to go to medical school.

LESSON 2.

See the awful monster.
See the bolts in his head.
See how he kills people.
Kill, kill, kill.
The monster likes to kill.
Poor, poor monster.
The monster is sick.
Sick, sick, sick.
He wants to be cured.
The doctor cannot cure the monster.
The monster does not belong to Blue Cross.

LESSON 3.

This is a girl.
As if you couldn't tell.
See how her dress is torn.
See how pretty she is.
Pant, pant, pant.
Listen to her scream.
Eeek, eeek, eeek.
The doctor loves the girl.
The monster loves the girl.
The director hates the girl.
She is a terrible actress.
Even the monster is more articulate.

LESSON 4.

See the other girl.
She is a little girl.
She is not so pretty.
Her dress is not torn.
The monster will kidnap
    the little girl.
She will also scream.
Eeek, eeek, eeek.
She is also a terrible actress.
But she has an excuse.
She is only eight years old.
Then again, she is lucky.
She can always make a living
    writing horror movies.

**SLEEPING BEAUTY "... rousing and animated!"

Yoga is great practice for marriage — all you do is
bend over backwards when someone tells you to!
—Alfred E. Neuman

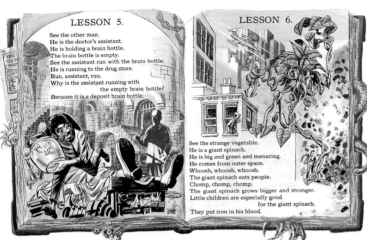

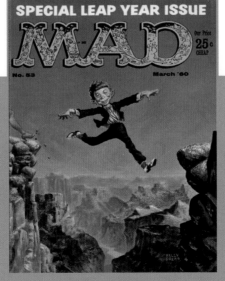

WESTERN DEPT.

AND NOW MAD PRESENTS ITS OWN VERSION OF THE REALISTIC WESTERN TV PROGRAM THAT BEGINS WITH AN UNUSUALLY REALISTIC WESTERN FLAVOR.

MAINLY, THIS PROGRAM BEGINS BY FIRST KILLING OFF THE TV AUDIENCE

Artist: Jack Davis   Writer: Harvey Kurtzman

GUNSMOKED

This here is Boot Hill. Many men are buried here. Some 'cause they were good, some 'cause they were bad. But all, 'cause they were dead, by George!

My name's Madd Dillinger. I'm DeSoto City's U.S. Marshal. I'm responsible for puttin' most of these men here in Boot Hill. Yuh see, I'm also DeSoto City's grave-digger.

Every week, I come up here t' Boot Hill, take off m' hat, look down, an' remember a story from the old days in DeSoto City. I look down an' I remember the story 'cause I got the script hid right here in the sweatband!

HOLLYWOOD DEPT.

Scenes We'd Like to See

Driving The Golden Spike

ART—GEORGE WOODBRIDGE   STORY BY EUGENE ST. JEAN

#51 DEC '59

PRESENTING THE BILL—reproduced here, is one of a series of original oil paintings, "Practising Medicine For Fun and Profit", commissioned by Park-David.

Great
Moments
in
Medicine

Once the crisis has passed . . . once the patient has regained his strength . . . once the family is relieved and grateful . . . that's the time when the physician experiences one of the great moments in medicine. In fact, the *greatest moment* in medicine! Mainly, the moment when he presents his bill! That's the time when all of the years of training and study and work seem worthwhile. And there's always the chance that the shock might mean more business for him!

Park-David scientists are proud of their place in the history of practicing medicine for fun and profit, helping to provide doctors with the materials that mean higher fees and bigger incomes. For example, our latest development . . . tranquilizer-impregnated bill paper . . . designed to eliminate the shock and hysteria that comes when the patient gets a look at your bill. Not only will he remain calm when he sees what you've charged . . . now he won't even *care!*

PARK-DAVID

. . . Pioneers in bigger medical bills

#48 JUL '59

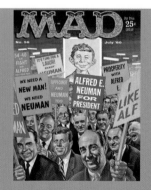

34

Who Is Alfred E. Neuman?

By Frank Jacobs

One day in the 1960s a letter was delivered to the MAD offices bearing no name or address. Other than a postage stamp, the envelope bore only a picture of the magazine's cover boy, Alfred E. Neuman.

Clearly, the gap-toothed face of the idiot kid had become iconic. Alfred and MAD, to use an overworked phrase, were joined at the hip. Already the grinning face had shown up in unlikely places: placards of him as a candidate — "You could do worse, you always have!" — were flaunted at political conventions. His features were sculpted in ice at a Dartmouth Winter Carnival. Fred Astaire danced in an Alfred mask during a TV special. A party of climbers planted a Neuman flag atop Mount Everest.

Alfred owes his place in history to four men. The first was MAD's first editor, Harvey Kurtzman, who glimpsed the grinning face, captioned "Me worry?" on a postcard in 1954.

"It was a kid that didn't have a care in the world, except mischief," Kurtzman recalled. The boy soon made his way into the pages of the magazine, though he was as yet unnamed.

Kurtzman had been using the Neuman name mostly because it had the ring of a nonentity — although there was a Hollywood composer named Alfred Newman. Misspelled, with the added "E," it too was integrated into the magazine.

When Al Feldstein replaced Kurtzman as editor, he decided to link "Alfred E. Neuman" with the face of the idiot kid. The idiot kid made his official debut in 1956 as a write-in candidate for President on the cover of MAD #30, and the magazine now had an official mascot and cover boy. In the next issue, Alfred made his second cover appearance pictured as an addition to Mount Rushmore.

Norman Mingo's classic Alfred.

Though others had their doubts, Nick Meglin, then an assistant editor, believed that MAD should continue to use Alfred as the magazine's cover boy. "You'll have to convince me," said publisher Bill Gaines, who had veto power over all MAD covers. Playing up to Gaines' interest in archaeology, Meglin submitted a rough sketch of Alfred in an Egyptian tomb (MAD #31) and one or two others that emerged as cover illustrations later. Having been convinced there were endless possibilities, Gaines agreed that Alfred should reign as the magazine's icon.

And so he has — in a fireworks display (#34), as a guru (#121), a Neumanized George Washington (#181), a California

ME WORRY?

1954 postcard of the "idiot kid."

Raisin (#281), a self-reproducing Xerox machine (#356). And posters — Alfred the Hun, Toulouse Neuman, Alfred von Richtofen, the Red Baron. Movie stardom was slow in coming. Alfred's first gig as an "actor" arrived on the cover of #86 as Lawrence of Arabia. He had to wait more than three years for his role as Robin to Adam West's Batman (#105), then two years more when he appeared with Bonnie and Clyde (#119). From then on, Alfred's show-biz career skyrocketed, especially when billboarding MAD's spoofs of the *Star Trek* and *Star Wars* films.

The Neuman face was created by Norman Mingo. Curiously, none of MAD's artists, though extremely versatile, has been able to render accurately the Mingo prototype. When Mingo died in 1980, his obituary in The New York Times identified him in its headline as the "Illustrator Behind 'Alfred E. Neuman' Face."

Several decades ago, Charles Winick, a psychologist, polled some 400 readers of MAD. He found that Alfred was liked especially by low achievers. "Less successful students," Winick observed, "are more likely to identify with Neuman because he conveys a feeling of failure, defeat, defensiveness, and uninvolvement. His non-worry slogan has a 'let the world collapse, I don't care' quality, and his appearance suggests stupidity."

Today, Winick might well change his views were he to examine many of the postings on the Internet. But he was right on one score: Alfred does suggest stupidity, which may lead to ill feeling on the part of a lad who is told he resembles MAD's mascot. Such a reaction occurred in 1958, the slighted youth apparently being Britain's Prince Charles. A photograph of the bonnie young heir to the throne, who was then nine years old, had been carried in newspapers throughout the United States. Prince Charles was smiling in the photograph, and his face, so thought many MAD readers who subsequently wrote in, bore a striking resemblance to Alfred E. Neuman.

MAD published several of the comments, along with the photo, on its letters page. A few weeks later arrived the following letter, postmarked London:

Dear Sirs,
No it isn't a bit — not the least little bit like me.
So jolly well stow it! See! Charles P.

Did the letter really come from Prince Charles? Art director John Putnam, who knew about such

things, analyzed it. The handwriting was typical of a well-educated nine-year-old. The stationery was triple cream-laid paper, bearing the copper-engraved crest of the Duke of Edinburgh, and would have been commercially impossible to duplicate. The signature, "Charles P," was eminently correct, the P standing for Princeps, which is how Charles would have likely signed his name. A contact at the British Embassy in New York City noted that the postmark revealed that the letter had been mailed within "a very short walking distance of Buckingham Palace."

Putnam weighed the evidence and pronounced that barring someone having pilfered the royal family's stationery, the letter was authentic.

What is the source of the "What — Me Worry?" Boy? MAD asked its readers to help out and was deluged by suggestions and theories. The kid was used in 1915 to advertise a patent medicine; he was a newspaperman named Old Jack; he was taken from a biology textbook as an example of a person who lacked iodine; he was a testimonial on advertisements for painless dentistry; he was originated by comedian Garry Moore; he was a greeting-card alcoholic named Hooey McManus; he was a Siamese boy named Watmi Worri. One reader dug up a 1909 German calendar bearing a version of the inane smiling face.

By far the most pertinent correspondence came from a lawyer representing a Vermont woman named Helen Pratt Stuff. She claimed that her late husband, Harry Stuff, had created the kid in 1914, naming him "The Eternal Optimist." Stuff's copyrighted drawing, she charged, was the source of

> I consider
> Mr. Neuman to
> be our trademark
> at this point.

It sure sounds like him! From MAD's archives, the letter that 9-year-old Prince Charles may have sent (L); "The Original Optimist," by Harry Stuff, who claimed to own the copyright on Alfred.

Alfred E. Neuman and she was taking MAD to court to prove it.

Thus began the great Alfred E. Neuman lawsuit. The stakes were not small. If MAD lost, it would be liable for millions of dollars in damages. And Alfred no longer would be permitted to show his worriless countenance in any MAD publication or property.

MAD's attorney, Martin Scheiman, hired tracers on both coasts to hunt for pictures of the idiot kid that had been published before 1914. A number of renderings popped up, several of them almost dead ringers for Harry Stuff's "Original Optimist." It became evident that portraits had been floating around the United States since before the turn of the century. But exact dates were hard to put down.

Mrs. Stuff had sued before and had won several cases. Scheiman argued that Stuff, in copyrighting his "Original Optimist," had not created an original face — that he had based his version of the idiot kid on pictures in the public domain. In other words, Stuff's illustration was not copyrightable. Also, there was no copyright notice on most copies of Stuff's drawings, making it impossible for MAD to know it was copyrighted.

The trial of the case in United States District Court was full of legal infighting, most of which would bore readers of this book to tears. Nevertheless, Neumanphiles could rejoice at the deference shown their idol. Alfred, for years the butt of a thousand jokes, was, for once, being treated with respect.

For example, this exchange between Mrs. Stuff's attorney, Samuel J. Stoll, and Gaines:

STOLL: Has any MAD issue appeared since the adoption of this character, Alfred Neuman, without Mr. Neuman appearing on one of its pages or cover page?

GAINES: I do not believe that any issue has come out without featuring him in some way, sometimes more prominently than others, but he would always be there.

STOLL: Would you consider Mr. Neuman to be a rather prominent and substantial part of your publication?

GAINES: I consider Mr. Neuman to be our trademark at this point, an identification with the magazine and, as such, very helpful.

After listening to some six thousand words of arguments and testimony, and poring over several hundred pictures of Alfred and his ancestors, Judge Lloyd F. MacMahon arrived at his decision. MAD, he opined, had not infringed on the Stuff copyright, mainly because the copyright notice was rarely included on copies of Stuff's picture. To put it another way, it was as if the grinning boy was a bastard orphan and that MAD had every legal right to adopt him, give him loving care, and provide him with a Christian name.

What — him worry?
No longer. The idiot kid was, at last, legitimate.

Alfred as rendered by MAD's current cover artist, Mark Fredrickson.

"The MAD Horror Primer" (Issue #49) received such a GREAT response from our readers (i.e. *"A GREAT disappointment!"*—B.F., Phila., Pa.; *"It would be GREAT if you discontinued this type feature!"*—L.D., Dallas, Tex.; *"Articles like that GRATE on my nerves!"*—F.H., Fresno, Calif.) that we've decided to present another primer. This one is for the benefit of any children under seven (in other words, ALL of our readers) who may possibly be interested in working in the advertising field when they grow up.

THE MAD MADISON AVENUE PRIMER

ARTIST: WALLACE WOOD · WRITER: LARRY SIEGEL

MY FIRST READER

(EDUCATION-WISE)

Rock-Bottom Slants for Little Group-Noodlers

By Batton, Barton, Durstine & Cowznofsky

Lesson 1

See the man.
He does advertising work.
He is called an "ad-man".
See his funny tight suit.
See his funny haircut.
Hear his funny stomach churn.
Churn, churn, churn.
The ad-man has a funny ulcer.
Most ad-men have funny ulcers.
But, then, some ad-men are lucky.
They do *not* have funny ulcers.
They have funny high blood pressure.

Lesson 2

See the ad-man run.
Run, ad-man, run.
The ad-man must catch the 8:02.
All ad-men must catch the 8:02.
It is a fast commuter train.
It is never more than two hours late.
And it has a club car.
"All aboard!" says the conductor.
"Chug, chug!" says the train.
"Gulp, gulp!" says the ad-man.
Wouldn't *you* like Bourbon for breakfast, too?

#55 JUN '60

Lesson 3

See the pretty street.
It is called "Madison Avenue".
All the ad-men work here.
They write "Winston tastes good . . ." here.
Write, write, write.
They write "Mr. Clean, Mr. Clean . . ." here.
Write, write, write.
Don't you wish you could write like that?
You can.
You're almost *seven* now.

Lesson 4

See the nice advertising agency.
400 nice people work here.
Let us count the 400 nice people.
Count, count, count.
Hmmm! 300 nice people are missing.
The nice advertising agency must have
lost another nice $4-million account.
Dear, dear, dear.
Where are the 300 nice people now?
At the nice Unemployment Insurance office.
Sign, sign, sign.
Isn't job security nice on Madison Avenue?

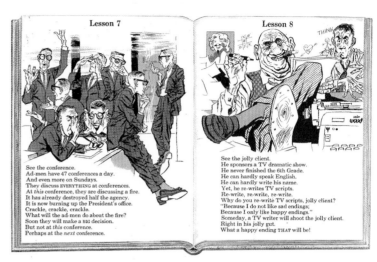

Lesson 7

See the conference.
Ad-men have 47 conferences a day.
And even more on Sundays.
They discuss EVERYTHING at conferences.
At *this* conference, they are discussing a fire.
It has already destroyed half the agency.
It is now burning up the President's office.
Crackle, crackle, crackle.
What will the ad-men do about the fire?
Soon they will make a BIG decision.
But not at *this* conference.
Perhaps at the *next* conference.

Lesson 8

See the jolly client.
He sponsors a TV dramatic show.
He never finished the 6th Grade.
He can hardly speak English.
He can hardly write his name.
Yet, he re-writes TV scripts.
Re-write, re-write, re-write.
Why do you re-write TV scripts, jolly client?
"Because I do not like sad endings;
Because I only like happy endings."
Someday, a TV writer will shoot the jolly client.
Right in his jolly gut.
What a happy ending THAT will be!

Lesson 5

See the kindly old man.
He is the President of the agency.
He has fired 132 people today.
And it isn't even lunch time yet.
Fire, fire, fire.
See the fine young man with him.
He will not be fired, today.
He is a fine ad-man.
He is a fine Vice-President of the agency.
He is a fine son of the President of the agency.

Lesson 6

See the Account Executive.
His accounts are Puffo Cigarettes,
Bubble Soap, and Flaky Cereal.
The agency loves and trusts him.
Kiss, kiss, kiss.
Trust, trust, trust.
Next week he will resign.
He will form his own agency.
He will have three accounts in his agency.
They will be Puffo Cigarettes,
Bubble Soap, and Flaky Cereal.
Bounce, bounce, bounce.
That's the way the ball bounces on Madison Avenue.

Lesson 9

See the man rate a TV show.
See how he arrives at a scientific rating.
First he makes 10 phone calls.
Then he puts 10 numbers in his hat.
Then he closes his eyes tight.
Then he picks the scientific rating out of his hat.
Oh-oh! This TV show's rating is 6⅜.
Ho-ho! He has made a scientific mistake.
He has picked his scientific *hat size.*
But it is too late.
It was such a nice TV show, too.
It cost three million dollars, too.
It might have remained on the air, too.
If the man had a bigger head.

Lesson 10

See the amazing average clod.
He is the Eighth Wonder of the World.
He has a 40-year-old body and a 10-year-old mind.
According to Madison Avenue.
So they write TV commercials especially for him.
And they write magazine ads especially for him.
If this keeps up, the amazing average clod will
become even more amazing.
He will no longer have a 40-year-old body and a
10-year-old mind.
He will have a 40-year-old body and a
FIVE-year-old mind.

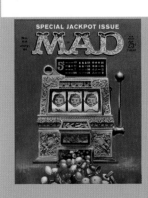

There seems to be a rash of new musicals slated for Broadway based on the "Madison Avenue" theme. Since one of the most successful musicals ever to hit Broadway was "My Fair Lady," based on the book by George Bernard Shaw, we figure it won't be long before we'll be seeing a hit "Madison Avenue" musical along the same lines and called . . .

My Fair Ad-Man

ARTIST: MORT DRUCKER

BASED ON THE BOOK "YOU'RE A PIG, MALLION" BY GEORGE BERNARD SCHWARTZ

WRITER: NICK MEGLIN

ACT 1, SCENE 1: EARLY MORNING ON MADISON AVENUE, OUTSIDE OFFICE BUILDING HOUSING BVD&O, A LARGE ADVERTISING AGENCY. ENTER OFFICER EINSFOOT . . .

ENTER HENRY HIGGENBOTTOM AND CHARLES PICKERWICK, BVD&O ACCOUNT EXECUTIVES ON THE WAY TO WORK . . . FOLLOWED SHORTLY BY IRVING MALLION, A BEATNIK . . .

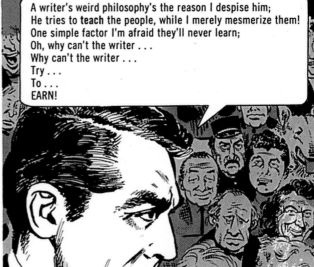

A judge is nothing more than a lawyer who's been benched.

A TURN FOR THE WORSE DEPT.

We know about "Russian Roulette" . . . the game where you have a six-shooter with one bullet and you keep pulling the trigger until somebody loses by getting killed. And we know about "Magazine Roulette" . . . the game where you have six magazines and you keep choosing one until somebody loses by picking MAD. But the most vicious game we know is the one that millions of Americans play every day. That's the game where you have six TV channels and you keep turning to each, trying to find some entertainment. The game starts when it's time for the commercial. Mainly, when you decide to switch it off. Because the TV networks are wise to this sneaky maneuver, and they've all scheduled their ads to come on at the same time. Here, then, is what it's like . . . when you're playing . . .

COMMERCIAL ROULETTE

ARTIST: BOB CLARKE

WRITER: GARY BELKIN

#59 DEC '60

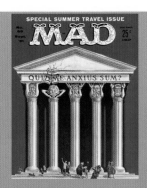
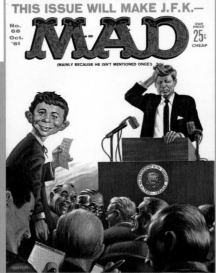

42

Antonio Prohias is a famous Cuban artist whose anti-Castro cartoons have appeared in such publications as Bohemia (largest circulation of any Spanish language magazine), the daily *Prensa Libre* (Free Press) *El Mundo,* and the Sunday *Oveja Negra* (Black Sheep). He has won the "Juan Gualberto Gomez" award (the equivalent of our Cartoon Society's "Ruben") six times. On May 1st, three days before Castro henchmen took over what remained of Cuba's free press, Prohias fled to N.Y. stone broke. Once here, he came directly to MAD. Among the things he showed us was this captivating cartoon-sequence of friendly rivalry called

Parents work so they can give their children a better life than they had — and then complain about how easy they've got it.
—Alfred E. Neuman

44

A MAD SAMPLER

ESPECIALLY EMBROIDERED FOR MAD MAGAZINE BY MARGARET SZEP

SUITABLE FOR FRAMING

THE YELLOWED KIDS DEPT.

Everybody gets old! Everybody, that is, except most comic strip characters! These jokers have the uncanny ability to remain the same dull age year after year, getting into the same dull situations. So MAD's gonna break the monotony . . . bearing in mind that if these comic strip characters were to age, one good aspect would be that they'd soon die off and we wouldn't have to suffer through them any more. Anyway, let's take away their fountains of youth, and see what the future would be like . . .

SUPERMAN

DICK TRACY

IF

COMIC STRIP CHARACTERS WERE AS OLD AS THEIR STRIPS

ARTIST: WALLACE WOOD   WRITER: EARLE DOUD

POPEYE

"... Don't Put All Your Yeggs In One Casker"—Brotherhood of Underworld Funeral Directors

"Money can't buy happiness — but it can rent it repeatedly!"

LI'L ABNER

HENRY

MANDRAKE THE MAGICIAN

DENNIS THE MENACE

"As Chief U.S. Delegate to the United Nations, I would like to report that I have, through protracted discussion and extended mediation, accomplished the following: I have solved the Vietnam crisis . . . I have straightened out the Berlin situation . . . I have come up with a mutually acceptable disarmament plan . . . and I've put chewing gum on all your seats!"

TARZAN

Several years ago, a Magazine Editor (who was probably separated from his wife) coined the word, "togetherness." And it took the country by storm. We were bombarded with messages of "togetherness" by magazines, newspapers, skywriting, and even deodorant commercials. Now, thanks to television, the ultimate in "togetherness" has been achieved . . . The Family Western. Gone are the gunfights and the killing and the brutality. Instead, we're getting love and romance and even compatible color—in . . .

BANANAZ
The "Family Togetherness" Western

ARTIST: MORT DRUCKER

WRITERS: EARLE DOUD WITH LOU SILVERSTONE

** LOUIS ARMSTRONG was born in SATCH, MO.

#73 SEP '62

MAD is often asked why it doesn't have expensive full-color three-page fold-outs the way other high-class magazines like "Life" and "Play-boy" have. There are two reasons for this! One: MAD is against ostentatious, snobbish, status-seeking gimmicks, and Two: MAD is cheap! So here instead is our economy-minded black-and-white one-page

MAD FOLD-IN

ARTIST & WRITER:
AL JAFFEE

FOLD PAGE OVER LIKE THIS

FOLD THIS SECTION OVER TO LEFT   FOLD THIS SECTION BACK TO RIGHT

Elizabeth Taylor, looking radiantly beautiful at the premiere of her latest film, is positively enchanted by | escort Richard Burton, who glows in the knowledge that he is the only one in her heart, and that she is his. | Meanwhile, people push and shove for autographs while police try to keep them in check! Hey! Take a look at | the handsome young stranger in the crowd moving in for his chance. Obviously, he's destined to be next in line.

MAD is often asked v
fold-outs the way of
boy'' have. There are
tatious, snobbish, st
So here instead is

MAD

ARTIST & WRITER:
AL JAFFEE

FOLD PAGE OVER LIKE THIS

FOLD THIS SECTION BACK TO RIGHT

Elizabeth Taylor, looking radiantly beautiful at the premiere of her latest film, is positively enchanted by | the handsome young stranger in the crowd moving in for his chance. Obviously, he's destined to be next in line.

IND MAD

No. 91   Dec. '64   25¢ CHEAP

OUR PRICE
25¢
CHEAP

IF YOU THINK OUR

LAST ISSUE

WAS BAD, WAIT'LL YOU READ THIS ONE!

We at MAD feel that the designs of today's Christmas toys reflect our warped adult sense of values. We at MAD also feel that the success of today's Christmas toys exposes our basic insecurity as parents trying to buy the love of our children with material things. But mainly, we at MAD feel too cheap to spend that money on our kids! So here is our idea: Instead of nuclear physicists designing complicated costly toys, why not let kids design them? Children's drawings show simple, beautiful, joyous viewpoints that no grown-up can hope to capture. Here, then, is what we would be seeing . . .

IF KIDS DESIGNED THEIR OWN XMAS TOYS

STORY AND MODELS BY AL JAFFEE   PHOTOS BY LESTER KRAUSS

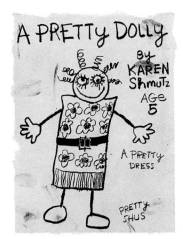

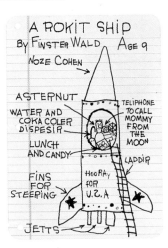

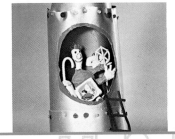

Dolls have become so complicated and realistic today, they're almost human. But little girls don't want human dolls. If you don't believe it, watch how little girls torture baby brothers or sisters. We interrupted little Karen Shmutz while she was sticking her finger down her baby brother's throat, and asked her to design this doll.

Nine year old Finster Wald's design for a rocket ship seems far more interesting to us than the realistic ones turned out by areo-space scientists working for toy companies. And it probably works as well as the ones these guys designed for the U.S. space effort before they left to go to work for the toy companies.

#76 JAN '63

Many long-time smokers end up having a coffin fit!

—Alfred E. Neuman

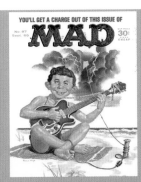

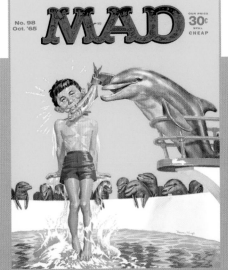

Those who don't learn from history are doomed to repeat it.
And the same is true for all your other classes.

—Alfred E. Neuman

U.N., THE NIGHT, AND THE MUSIC DEPT.

Practically everybody has seen "West Side Story"—which is about a couple of tough gangs on New York's West Side. Well, we think the producers of this show really missed the boat. Like, they went to the wrong side. If they thought the gangs on the West Side were tough, they should have taken a look at those two rival gangs on the East Side — mainly those two rival gangs at the U.N.! Because if they had, they might have come up with a musical called:

EAST SIDE STORY

ARTIST: MORT DRUCKER
WRITER: FRANK JACOBS

#18 APR '63

BERG'S-EYE VIEW DEPT.

Here we go with the 2nd of a three-part series on "Parties." Last issue we looked at "Adult Parties." Next issue we will cover "Kids' Parties." But this time, it's—

THE LIGHTER SIDE OF TEENAGE PARTIES

ARTIST & WRITER: DAVE BERG

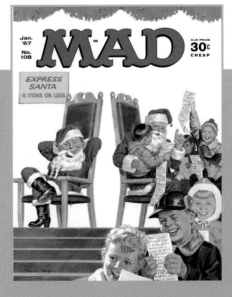
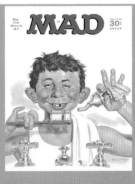

The problem with instant gratification is that it often takes too long.

INHALE-SAFE DEPT.

Smoking has been linked with so many horrible sicknesses, you'd imagine that everybody would be giving it up. Not so! Most smokers simply cannot! And so—they are now doubly-plagued! Not only are they deteriorating physically from smoking, but mentally, too—from worrying about it. In order to help all these poor trapped souls, we now offer . . .

SOME MAD DEVICES FOR
SAFER SMOKING

ARTIST & WRITER: AL JAFFEE

A SMOKER'S MENTAL PICTURE OF WHAT'S HAPPENING INSIDE HIM

Cigarette smoking is largely a nervous habit in which the act of "lighting up" and "taking a deep drag" is more important than the actual smoke!—so say leading psychologists. With this in mind, MAD has designed—and now offers—these devices which retain the main actions of smoking while eliminating the smoke itself . . .

DISPOSABLE LUNG-LINER TIPS

"Lung-Liner Tips" come in boxes of 20 to accommodate regular pack of cigarettes.

X-Ray view of Tip reveals folded plastic bag inside.

Liner Tip attaches to the cigarette, and looks just like a regular filter tip.

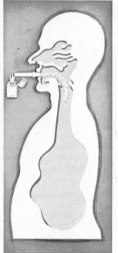

As smoker inhales, folded plastic liner is drawn down throat into lungs. Plastic is extremely thin, clings like Saran Wrap to insides.

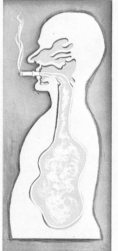

Thus, "Lung-Liner" transmits 90% of smoking's sensation with 100% safety. After use, liner is easily withdrawn for convenient disposal.

PORTABLE FILTRATION UNITS

"Filtration Unit" is small, but efficient version of a Military Gas Mask canister.

Close up of cross-section shows pinch-proof construction of tubes "A" and "B".

Filtration Units can be fitted into any number of portable containers, such as attache case, lunch box, handbag, etc.

In use, when smoker inhales, harmful smoke travels down from cigarette thru tube "A" to Filtration Unit, returns as pure fresh air thru tube "B" to healthy satisfied smoker.

#91 DEC '64

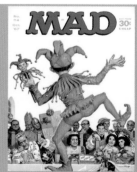

54

Make Beautiful Hair

B L E C C H

THERE ARE THREE BLECCH SHAMPOOS FOR THREE DIFFERENT HAIR CONDITIONS

Are you a teenage boy with Beautiful Hair? Well no wonder the girls hardly notice you. Today, you've got to be a teenage boy with Blecch hair. Then the girls will scream with delight, roll on the floor and kick their feet when they see you. So why waste another minute? Shampoo your hair with Blecch tonight. Blecch comes in three special formulas:

● For dry hair—a special formula that takes neat crew-cut type hair and lays it down over your ears. ● For oily hair —loosens up that slick-combing stuff so it spills down over your eyes. ● For normal hair—gives it proper body so it mushrooms all over your head. Get the shampoo that's right for you, and make your hair "Blecch"! Yeah! Yeah! Yeah!

#90 OCT '64

Are you plagued by clods who ask stupid questions? We mean the kind of questions to which the answers are painfully obvious. Doesn't it drive you nuts to have to give such answers? Don't you wish you could come up with snappy answers that would put these dolts down, like the comics on TV always do? Well, you can! All you need is a sense of humor, a little practice, and a mean, rotten disposition. You also need to convince yourself that there is

MAD'S SNAPPY ANSWERS

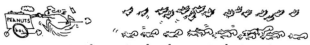

nothing worse than stupid clods who ask pointless unnecessary questions. Is that clear? Do you undertand what we mean? Are we getting the point of this article across to you? Isn't this the perfect time to come up with one of them snappy answers? Okay! Study the typical situations on these pages and practice giving the snappy answers we've printed. Then start making up your own. Before long you'll see how gratifying it is to humiliate people with . . . .

TO STUPID QUESTIONS

ARTIST & WRITER: AL JAFFEE

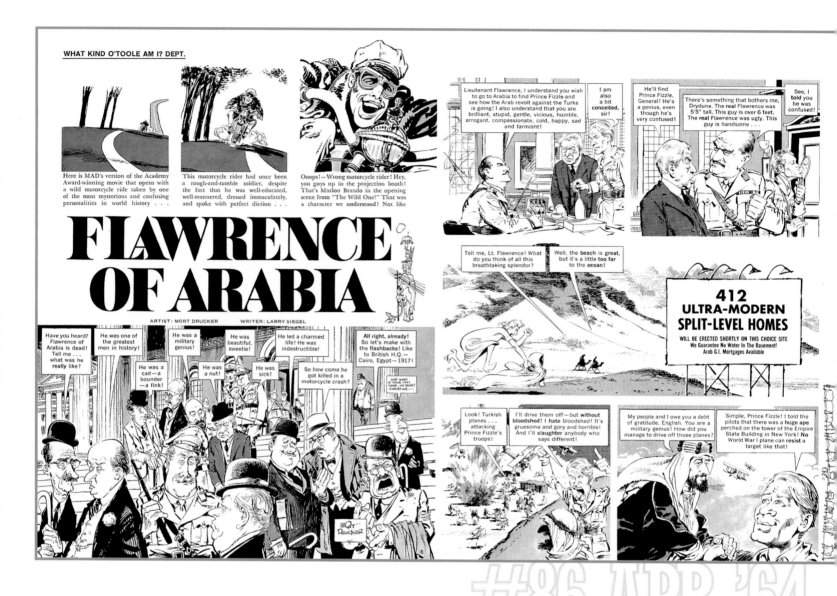

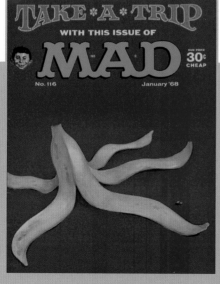

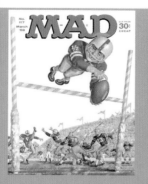

SELF-PORTRAIT

WRITER & ARTIST: AL JAFFEE

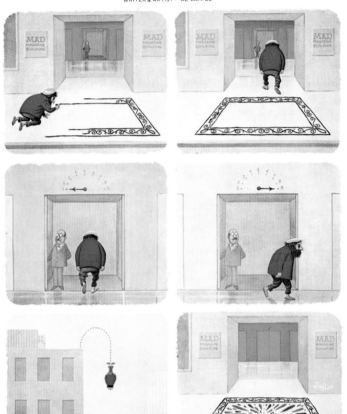

IN THE DELICATESSEN

ARTIST: DON MARTIN

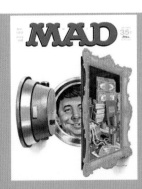

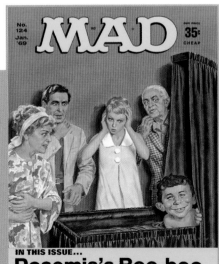

Rosemia's Boo-boo

Talk is cheap. But say the wrong thing to your parents and it will cost you!

HORROR Movie Scenes We'd Like To See

ARTIST: JACK DAVIS   WRITER: DON EDWING

#99 DEC '65

For years, the nation's educators have been howling about the evils inherent in such big time college sports as football and basketball. They contend that there's too much professionalism, that not enough boys have a chance to participate, etc. But no one really lifted a finger to correct the situation until MAD's Athletic Council went to work—and he's come up with a brand new sport that promises to provide good, clean amateur fun for all. Here, then, are the rules for this great new national pastime of the future. Digest them carefully and be the last person in your neighborhood to play . . . as . . .

MAD MAGAZINE
introduces
43-MAN SQUAMISH

ARTIST: GEORGE WOODBRIDGE   WRITER: TOM KOCH

A Squamish team consists of 43 players: the left & right Inside Grouches, the left & right Outside Grouches, four Deep Brooders, four Shallow Brooders, five Wicket Men, three Offensive Niblings, four Quarter-Frummerts, two Half-Frummerts, one Full-Frummert, two Overblats, two Under-blats, nine Back-Up Finks, two Leapers and a Dummy.

Each player is equipped with a long hooked stick known as a Frullip. The Frullip is used to halt opposing players attempting to cross your goal line with the Pritz (ball). The Official Pritz is 3¾ inches in diameter and is made of untreated Ibex hide stuffed with Blue Jay feathers.

Play begins with the Probate Judge flipping a new Spanish peseta. If the Visiting Captain calls the toss correctly, the game is immediately cancelled. If he fails to call it correctly, then the Home Team Captain is given his choice of either carrying the Pritz . . . or defending against it.

#95 JUN '65

The game of Squamish is played on a 5-sided field known as a Flutney. The two teams line up at opposite sides of the Flutney and play seven Ogres of fifteen minutes each — unless it rains, in which case they play eight Ogres.

The defending right Outside Grouch signifies that he is ready to hurl the Pritz by shouting, "Mi Tio es infermo, pero la carretera es verde!"—a wise old Chilean proverb that means, "My Uncle is sick, but the highway is green!"

The offensive team, upon receiving the Pritz, has five Snivels in which to advance to the enemy goal. If they do it on the ground, it's a Woomik and counts 17 points. If they hit it across with their Frullips, it's a Durmish which only counts 11 points. Only the offensive Niblings and Overblats are allowed to score in the first 6 Ogres.

Special rules, applicable only during the seventh Ogre, turn the game into something very akin to Buck Euchre. During this final Ogre (and the eighth, if it rains), the four Quarter-Frummerts are permitted to either kick or throw the Pritz, and the nine Finks are allowed to heckle the opposition by doing imitations of Barry Goldwater.

A typical seventh Ogre play is shown below. Team "A"— trailing 516—209, is in possession of the Pritz with fourth Snivel and half the Flutney to go. Suddenly, the left Underblat, going for the big one, sends two Shallow Brooders and the Full-Frummert downfield. Obviously, he is going to try for a Woomik when the opposition expects a Durmish. A daring play of this type invariably brings the crowd rising to its feet and heading for the exits.

A variety of penalties keep play from getting out of hand. Walling the Pritz, Frullip-gouging, icing on fifth Snivel, running with the mob and raunching are all minor infractions subject to a ten-yard penalty. Major infractions (sending the Dummy home early, interfering with Wicket Men, rushing the season, bowing to the inevitable and inability to face facts) are punishable by loss of half the Flutney, except when the Yellow Caution Flag is out.

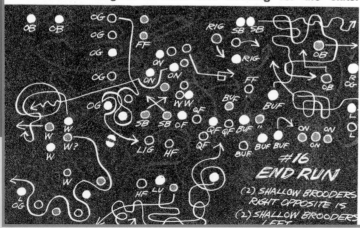

Squamish rules provide for 4 officials: a Probate Judge, a Field Representative, a Head Cockswain and a Baggage Smasher. None has any authority after play has begun. In the event of a disagreement between the officials, a final decision is left up to the spectator who left his car in the parking lot with the lights on and the motor running.

In the event of a tie score, the teams play a sudden-death overtime. The exception to this rule occurs when opposing Left Overblats are both out of the game on personal fouls. When such is the case, the two teams line up on opposite sides of the Flutney and settle the tie by shouting dirty limericks at each other until one team breaks up laughing.

Amateur Squamish players are strictly forbidden to accept subsidies, endorse products, make collect phone calls or eat garlic. Otherwise, they lose their amateur standing. A player may turn Pro, however, merely by throwing a game.

Schools with small enrollments which preclude participation in 43-Man Squamish may play a simplified version of the game: 2-Man Squamish. The rules are identical, except that in 2-Man Squamish, the object of the game is to lose.

The original charter calls for an annual meeting of the National Squamish Rules Committee. At its inaugural meeting, the committee approved a re-wording of Article XVI, Paragraph 77, Section J of the rules. This section, which formerly read: "The offensive left Underblat, in all even-numbered Ogres, must touch down his Frullip at the edge of the Flutney and signal to the Head Cockswain that he is ready for play to continue," has now been simplified

to read: "The offensive left Underblat, in all even-numbered ogres, must touch down his Frullip at the edge of the Flutney and signal to either the Head Cockswain, or to any other official to whom the Head Cockswain may have delegated this authority in writing and in the presence of two witnesses, both of whom shall have been approved and found to be of high moral character by the Office of the Commissioner, that he is ready for play to continue."

A BOY
and his
CHEMISTRY
SET

ARTIST: DON MARTIN

Junior!? What are you *doing*??

Gad! It's my **Mother!**

Nothing, Mom...just playing with my chemistry set!

THE REPLACEMENT

ARTIST: BOB CLARKE   WRITER: DON EDWING

#103 JUN '66

#100 JAN '66

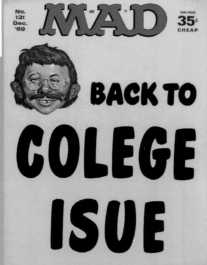

BACK TO COLEGE ISUE

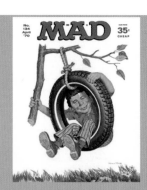

WASTE OF SPACE DEPT.

STAR BLECCH

ARTIST: MORT DRUCKER   WRITER: DICK DE BARTOLO

"THESE ARE THE VOYAGES OF THE STAR-SHIP 'BOOBY-PRIZE'! ITS MISSION, TO EXPLORE STRANGE NEW WORLDS, TO SEEK OUT NEW LIFE, AND TO BOLDLY GO WHERE NO MAN HAS EVER GONE BEFORE!"

Vegetarians who go back to meat have
to start with eating crow!

—Alfred E. Neuman

IN THIS ISSUE:
SLEAZY RIDERS

IN THIS ISSUE:
BOTCH CASUALLY AND
THE SOMEDUNCE KID

IN THIS ISSUE
BOOB & CARNAL & TAD & ALAS & ALFRED

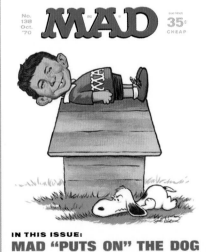

IN THIS ISSUE:
MAD "PUTS ON" THE DOG
(AND THE REST OF THE "PEANUTS" GANG)

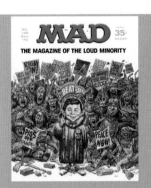

THE MAGAZINE OF THE LOUD MINORITY

HERE WE GO WITH ANOTHER "MAD" VERSION OF THE CONTENTS OF...
A CELEBRITY'S WALLET

WRITER:
ARNIE KOGEN

My darling Timmy,

What's happening to my son?

You used to be such a nice sensible boy--a college professor at Harvard--I was so proud of you. But now you've changed. I don't understand you any more. What's gotten into you?

I write you a civil letter asking how you are--and all I get back is a package of sugar cubes and a note filled with nonsense about "freak outs" and "vibrations" and "visions" and "voyages" and "expanding spiritual horizons". I'll expand your spiritual horizons for you-- right over your head! You keep this up and I'll come to Millbrook and give you such vibrations, you'll see visions for two weeks from my vibrations.

So you'd better shape up and be a good boy. And remember, no matter what kind of trouble you're in, I still love you. I know that basically you never meant any harm.

Mother

P.S. I just had my tea--and I used your sugar cubes! *Whoooopie!!*

Copake Church Supply Co.
Peekskill, New York

Dr. Timothy Leary
Minister
League for Spiritual Discovery
Millbrook, N.Y.

Dear Dr. Leary:

Thank you for your recent order. We supply church equipment for all major religious denominations and, although we have not previously heard of your "League for Spiritual Discovery", we will make every effort to meet your specifications. Shipment should be completed within 3-4 weeks.

However, there is one unusual item that disturbs us. Perhaps you will be good enough to satisfy our curiosity. We don't know what kind of services you conduct, but would you please explain why you ordered pews with <u>seat belts</u>?

Sincerely yours,
Millard Traymor
Millard Traymor
Sales Director

J. Walter Doyle & Dane Bernbach Thompson
ADVERTISING AGENCY
666 MADISON AVENUE   NEW YORK CITY

Mr. Timothy Leary
Millbrook, N.Y.

Dear Mr. Leary

Thank you for your letter outlining methods for bringing the United Fruit Company's advertising campaign up to date.

We are sorry to inform you that a cigar company is already using the slogan you suggested, and therefore it would be inappropriate for "Chiquita Banana" to say:

"<u>Why don't you pick me up and smoke me some time?</u>"

As for your other suggestion, although you may be quite right in asserting that LSD is colorless, odorless, non-addictive and most beneficial, we do not see what can be gained by conducting a "challenge race" between LSD and Bufferin to see which gets into the bloodstream fastest.

However, thank you for thinking of us.

Sincerely yours,
Alan Goldman
Alan Goldman
Account Executive

CITY OF MILLBROOK, NEW YORK
DEPARTMENT OF TRAFFIC

Name: TIMOTHY LEARY Date: 11/2/67

Nature of Traffic Violation: EXCEEDING SPEED LIMIT DOWN MAIN ST. SMASHING INTO FIRE HYDRANT, CAREENING 6 FEET IN THE AIR, PLOWING THROUGH CROWD OF PEDESTRIANS AND CRASHING THROUGH A DEPARTMENT STORE WINDOW.

Arresting Officer: B. Smoot

Shield No. 784

Comments by Arresting Officer: SUBJECT WAS NOT DRIVING A CAR AT THE TIME!

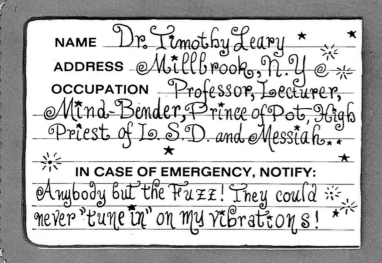

NAME Dr. Timothy Leary

ADDRESS Millbrook, N.Y.

OCCUPATION Professor, Lecturer, Mind-Bender, Prince of Pot, High Priest of L.S.D. and Messiah.

IN CASE OF EMERGENCY, NOTIFY:
Anybody but the FUZZ! They could never "tune in" on my vibrations!

To Tim with love! Sandra

Jennie:—
Here is the Menu for tomorrow. Please see to it that all items are included, as I have carefully calculated these meals to meet the minimum daily adult requirements —
T.L.

BREAKFAST
Chilled Morning
Glory Seed Juice

Heroin Hot Cakes
LSD Omelette
Morphine Toast
Tea

LUNCH
Airplane Glue Soup
Hashish Salad
LSD Burger
French Fried Hemp
Poppy Seed Pudding
Tea

DINNER
LSD Cocktail
Sacred Mushroom Soup
Marijuana Marinara
Choice of:
"Pot" Roast
"Pot" Pie
or
"Pot" Cheese
Peyote Popovers
Tea

MIDNIGHT SNACK
LSD Cookies
and Milk

Mutual OF OMAHA

Mr. Timothy Leary
Millbrook, N.Y.

Dear Mr. Leary

We are in receipt of your air mail special delivery letter requesting immediate coverage for you and the 23 members of your group in the amount of $250,000 (the maximum) each.

Before we can underwrite such a policy, we will need some additional information:
(1) Would you please tell us exactly what kind of "Flight Insurance" you had in mind?
(2) Do you plan on flying together as a group, or separately?
(3) Is this Flight Insurance for <u>one</u> round-trip, or do you and your group plan on making <u>more than one trip</u> each year? In which case, would you want to be covered?
(4) How about <u>one-way</u> trips? Will there be any?
Awaiting your prompt reply, I remain

Very truly yours,
Al State
Al State
New Policy Dept.

HARMS MUSIC PUBLISHING, INC.
Brill Building, New York City

Dear Mr. Leary:

In answer to your recent inquiry, the phrase you are referring to is from a Cole Porter song, copyright 1935, entitled "Just One Of Those Things".

As far as we can determine, Mr. Porter had no actual basis in scientific fact for using the phrase, and it is NOT possible to take "a trip to the moon on gossamer wings"!

Thank you for your interest.

Very truly yours,
Norman Blagman
Norman Blagman
Research Dept.

LEAGUE FOR SPIRITUAL DISCOVERY
Sanctuary For Psychedelic Scholars, Millbrook, New York

MEMO TO: Dr. Timothy Leary
FROM: Carmine Flippo, Student

Last night, I took my first "LSD trip". You promised me that I would experience breathtaking beauty, divine energy, a spiritual awakening, a sensual unfolding and incredible ecstasy. Instead, all I got was like this tremendous pain in my head. Should I take an aspirin?
CF

Don't be a fool, Carmine! We still don't know exactly how aspirin works, and whether it can be harmful if taken indiscriminately.
Dr. L.

MAD's Great Moments In Politics

#116 JAN '68

Early One Morning In The Jungle

ARTIST: FRANK FRAZETTA   WRITER: DON EDWING

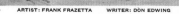

#106 OCT '66

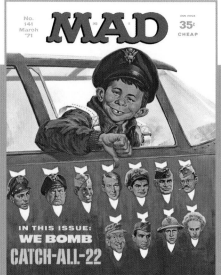

The further she is ... the closer you should look!*

Much has been written about hallucinogenic drugs like LSD, and the glories (or dangers) of taking psychedelic "trips". Some unsavory magazines have even featured this topic on their covers in order to sell copies. (See MAD #116.) And so, because MAD is interested

A PSYCHED

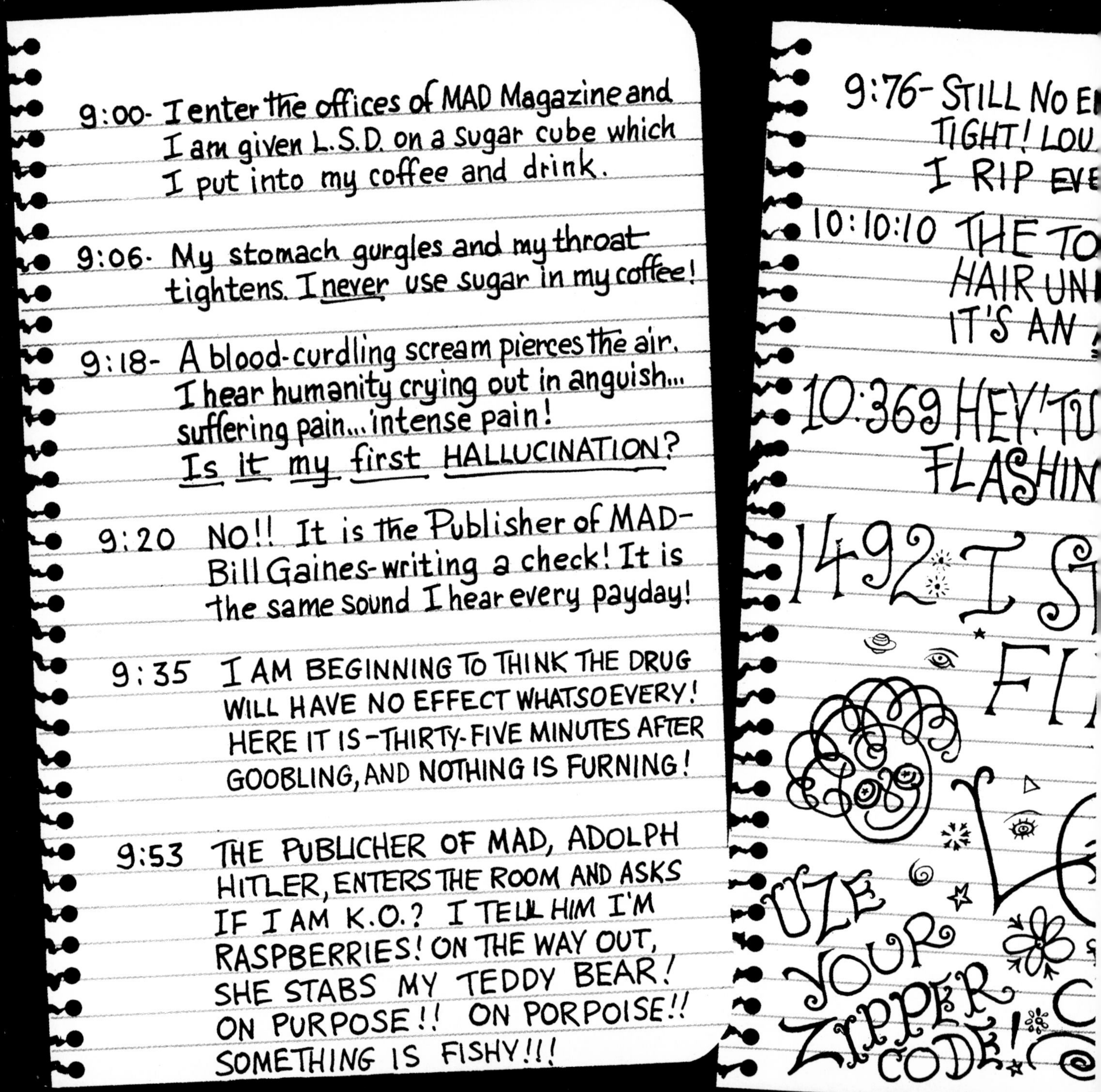

9:00- I enter the offices of MAD Magazine and I am given L.S.D. on a sugar cube which I put into my coffee and drink.

9:06- My stomach gurgles and my throat tightens. I never use sugar in my coffee!

9:18- A blood-curdling scream pierces the air. I hear humanity crying out in anguish... suffering pain... intense pain! Is it my first HALLUCINATION?

9:20 NO!! It is the Publisher of MAD— Bill Gaines-writing a check! It is the same sound I hear every payday!

9:35 I AM BEGINNING TO THINK THE DRUG WILL HAVE NO EFFECT WHATSOEVERY! HERE IT IS —THIRTY-FIVE MINUTES AFTER GOOBLING, AND NOTHING IS FURNING!

9:53 THE PUBLICHER OF MAD, ADOLPH HITLER, ENTERS THE ROOM AND ASKS IF I AM K.O.? I TELL HIM I'M RASPBERRIES! ON THE WAY OUT, SHE STABS MY TEDDY BEAR! ON PURPOSE!! ON PORPOISE!! SOMETHING IS FISHY!!!

9:76- STILL NO E
TIGHT! LOU
I RIP EVE

10:10:10 THE TO
HAIR UN
IT'S AN

10:369 HEY! TU
FLASHIN

1492 I S
FI

UZE
YOUR
ZIPPER
CODE!

in truth, because MAD desired to find out once and for all what taking an LSD "trip" was like, and mainly because MAD wanted to feature this topic once again in order to sell copies, we talked one of our writers into taking LSD, and describing his experiences in

ELIC DIARY

WRITER: DICK DEBARTOLO

FECK! MY SKIN IS ON TOO
SY TAILOR! LOUSY BURTON!
RYTHING OFF!!

RTOISE IS RACING THE
DER MY ARMS!
ARMS RACE!!!

RN OFF THOSE
'G BRIGHT LICE!!

ILL FEEL
NE

URB YOUR
CAR

12:30 THE PLUBISHER OF MUD, HUGH HEFFER, TAPS ME ON THE BROCCOLI—

90:76 I MAKE OUT SHAPES IN THE ROOM A DESK - A LAMP - A STAGECOACH - A PHUNG

1:15 - PEOPLE ARE STAIRING AT ME! I'M A STAIR-CASE! I TRY TO EXPLAIN THAT SOME FUNNY THINGS HAVE HAPPENED TO MY. BUT IT'S NO.

1:30 - EVERYTHING IS BECOMING EXTREMELY CLEAR! BUT IS IT REALITY? DO I REALLY LIVE? OR DO I JUST EXIST IN A CHINGE OF MY BLUK?

1:45 - WHAT IS NOT? AND WHY, IF WE, DO WE? OF COURSE!

2:00 A blood-curdling scream pierces the air. I hear humanity crying out in anguish... suffering pain...intense pain! IS IT AN HALLUCINATION AT LAST ??

2:03 NO!! It is the Publisher of MAD— Bill Gaines - writing another check!

2:05 - Everything is back to norbal.

WHAT INDUSTRY CONTRIBUTES MORE TO AIR POLLUTION THAN ANY OTHER?

HERE WE GO WITH ANOTHER RIDICULOUS
MAD FOLD-IN

More and more concern is being expressed over the problem of Air Pollution. And yet, year after year, one industry consistently pollutes the air while the vast majority of Americans quietly accept it. To find out who this villain is, fold page in as shown.

ARTIST & WRITER:
AL JAFFEE

A▶   FOLD THIS SECTION OVER LEFT   ◀B FOLD BACK SO "A" MEETS "B"

FOLD PAGE OVER LIKE THIS!

WHAT INDUSTRY CONTRIBUTES MORE TO AIR POLLUTION THAN ANY OTHER?

FOLD PAGE OVER LIKE THIS!

ARTIST & WRITER:
AL JAFFEE

A ▶◀ B   FOLD BACK SO "A" MEETS "B"

SPECIAL INFLATION ISSUE

MAD

IN THIS ISSUE WE DEFLATE "FIVE EASY PIECES" AND "THE OWL AND THE PUSSY CAT"

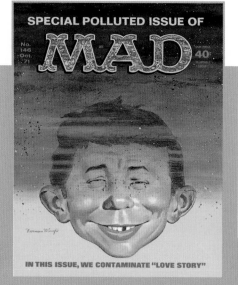

SPECIAL POLLUTED ISSUE OF

MAD

No. 146 Oct. '71   40¢

IN THIS ISSUE, WE CONTAMINATE "LOVE STORY"

No. 147 Dec. '71   MAD   40¢ CHEAP

NO!

REMEMBER, MAD DAD IT FIRST!

No. 149 March '72   MAD   40¢ CHEAP!

IN THIS ISSUE WE TEAR APART "WILLARD"

JOKE AND DAGGER DEPT.

THE BEAT GENERATION

ARTIST & WRITER: SERGIO ARAGONES

WACK!

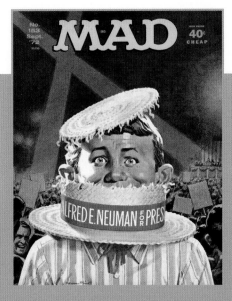

If you've seen it, you'll know exactly what we're talking about! And
If you haven't seen it, rest assured that we've just saved you from

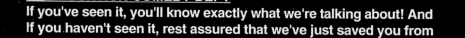

201 :MIN. :OF: A SPA

THE DAWN OF MAN

Excuse me— Are you **Maurice Evans?**

. . . Nope!

. . . Nope!

. . . Nope!

Then you must be **Roddy McDowell?**

Don't tell me you're **Kim Hunter!**

Isn't this **"PLANET OF THE APES"?**

No, this is **"201 MIN. OF A SPACE IDIOCY"!**

But why not work here with **us** and **then** go over and work on **"PLANET OF THE APES"?**

Oh, boy! **Two** jobs in **one** year! That's enough to drive me **Man!** What do I do?

Act bored!

That's a snap! And with **this** script, it's **not** even an **act!**

And keep your eye out for a **mysterious big black thing** that will **excite us** and make us want to do **intelligent things!**

ARTIST: MORT DRUCKER

You may not **believe** this—but I'll **swear** someone just threw a **bone** at our spaceship!

It's probably some ape from **another airline!** We could only accept **"plug money"** from **one!** Would you like some more food, Doctor?

No, thanks! I've eaten so much food **already,** I may throw up!

You **can't** throw **UP!** We're in **zero gravity!**

Well— how about **throw OUT?**

Not unless you mind **staring** at it in **mid-air** for another 19 hours!

CE IDIOCY

Look at that! What is it—a Prehistoric Handball Court!

Who ever heard of a Handball Court that plays music?

Maybe it's a giant-size Prehistoric Transistor Radio?

Or a Dawn of Man Tape Deck?!

You're ALL wrong! It's the mysterious big black thing that's supposed to excite us and make us want to do intelligent things!

Y'know, you're right! I FEEL like doing an intelligent thing . . . !

I feel like QUITTING this stupid movie—RIGHT NOW!!

WRITER: DICK DE BARTOLO

Never mind! I'll keep my hand over my mouth!

You'll get used to the little problems . . . like sneezing the same sneeze in and out ten times!

Is that our space station?

I sure hope so! Last month, our Captain tried to land us in the giant Ferris Wheel at Coney Island!

Did you have a pleasant 250,000 mile Express Flight up from Earth, Dr. Haywire?

Yes! We had "In-Flight Movies" . . . They showed us "Doctor Dolittle", "Ben Hur", "Dr. Zhivago", "The Ten Commandments", "War & Peace", "Gone With The Wind", "Camelot"—

You're lucky! On the Local Flights, they show slides of "Sap-Gathering In Maine"!

HOWARD JOHNSON'S EARTHLIGHT ROOM

VANILLA MOON FIZZ
PLUTO BANANA
JUMBO JUPITE
OUT OF THIS WORL
CHOCALATE
CHERRY SATI
STRAWBERR

PRUN
ALMO
WALN
NE
ZO
NASA
VANI

#125 MAR '69

Has MAD Ever Been Sued? By Frank Jacobs

During Bill Gaines' reign as publisher, MAD was probably the only publication that included "Lawsuits" on its masthead along with the name of its chief attorney. This was a service offered to offended readers so they would know whom to contact when they sued.

An example was the complaint of one Cynthia Piltch, then a freshman at Brookline High School in Massachusetts. The cause of her displeasure was an item in "Protest Magazine," a 1966 MAD piece spoofing the protest movement. Writer Larry Siegel had included this item:

Bowing to psychopathic pressure from prudish school authorities in Brookline, Mass., Yetta (Get Mt. Rushmore Out Of South Dakota) Piltch (ABOVE) has finally agreed to go to school in tight slacks. For the past three months, Yetta has been attending classes naked. They may have won the battle, Yetta, but they haven't won the war!

Cynthia Piltch and her parents felt the similarity in names was too close for coincidence and sued MAD for $250,000. Cynthia had been "injured in her reputation and health" and had "suffered damage to her feelings, mental anxiety and annoyance." It was a coincidence, of course, but a pesky one. MAD's attorney Jack Albert suggested that Gaines settle the case out of court. Gaines refused. To him it was cut and dried. MAD was a magazine of satire and was not obliged to check out every made-up name it used in its articles. If anything, the piece had raised Cynthia Piltch to a position of some fame in her school. Furthermore, another Piltch, namely Annabelle Piltch, of Flushing, NY, was delighted to see her family name in the magazine. Wrote Annabelle:

"The success of your satires, I feel, is due to your imaginative choice of fictitious names. The most hilarious name thus far...is Yetta Piltch. I trust that all your readers have as fine a sense of humor as we do."

Gaines pondered it all. It seemed that one Piltch's meat was another Piltch's poison. He reconsidered and decided that perhaps MAD had hurt the Brookline Piltches. If this were so, MAD should make amends, and so MAD did, settling out of court for what may be described as a modest sum.

Almost all the lawsuits involving MAD would wind up no more than footnotes in law journals. One case, however, changed the face of American pop culture.

Part of MAD's business model was to publish "annuals." These issues contained previously published articles but were sweetened with an item that no true MAD fan could pass up. Sometimes it was a small-size recording featuring an original song, or a thingamajig mobile such as the MAD Zeppelin. For one of the annuals in 1961 the choice was "Sing Along With MAD," an inserted mini-magazine containing parodies of popular songs.

Larry Siegel, myself, and the editors collaborated on 57 parodies. The lyrics were almost completely distorted as were most of the song titles. For example, this offering by Siegel from "Songs of Education":

ON THE SEAT WHERE I SIT

ON THE SEAT WHERE I SIT

A tribute to the crowded conditions in our schools.
Sung to the tune of: "On The Street Where You Live"

I have often sat in this seat before,
But I never shared it with Joe, Jim, and
    Pete before,
Oh how sad am I, four kids occupy
This old desk and the seat where I sit.

I can hardly move, books are poking me,
There are now 12 arms and legs here that are
    choking me.
And to seal my doom, I can't "leave the room,"
Things are tough in this seat where I sit.

And oh that horrible feeling
When I know that lunch-time is near.
That very terrible feeling
That any second I may lose a nose or ear.

Taking spelling tests is no fun for me,
By the time I reach my pen, we are on history.
The best seat in school is the Dunce's Stool,
I'll go there from this seat where I sit.

Or this parody I wrote for "Doctors and Medicine":

YOU'RE THE TOP

A doctor expresses love in the only way he knows. Sung to the tune of "You're the Top":

You're the top!
You're a steady itching!
You're the top!
You're a muscle twitching!
You're the painful point
On an elbow joint that locks!
You're an inflammation!
You're heat prostration!
You're chicken pox!...(etc.)

The cover of MAD's 1961 57-song mini magazine insert.

"Easter Parade" became "Beauty Parade," a spoof of beauty pageants. "Cheek to Cheek" was turned into "Sheik to Sheik," a commentary on oil-rich desert potentates. Song after song became parodies to reflect "the idiotic world we live in today."

The songbook was well received by MAD's readers. It was not, however, well received by the Music Publishers Protective Association, which felt that 12 of its member publishers had suffered copyright infringement. MAD, the association charged, had marketed versions of songs, without any authorization, which "caused substantial and irreparable damage" to the publishers and the composers and lyricists of the songs.

The plaintiffs were not small-fry. Among them were such giant corporations as Irving Berlin, Chappell, T.B. Harms, and Leo Feist. Twenty-five of their songs had been parodied – songs by such greats as Jerome Kern, Cole Porter, Richard Rodgers, Lorenz Hart, Oscar Hammerstein II, and, of course, Irving Berlin.

The association was playing hardball, suing Gaines and everyone connected with writing, illustrating, editing, and distributing the songbook for one dollar per song per each copy the magazine sold. More than one million copies had been sold, which meant that Gaines and his codefendants were being sued to the tune of $25 million.

During the three years it took to decide the case, Gaines went about his normal business. He knew that losing the suit would create some thorny financial problems. He was also aware that losing the case would close off a fertile field of parody and satire. If he was shaken by the lawsuit, he covered it up, not wishing to be an alarmist. Years later, he told me that he truly was unconcerned, if for no other reason than he was convinced he had done nothing wrong.

The case came to trial in the United States District Court in 1963. The publishers association complained that the MAD parodies had the same meter as the original songs and were "counterparts," because readers were informed that the parodies could be "sung to the tune of" the originals. MAD, it was further charged, "substantially copied" the original lyrics.

MAD's attorneys countered that MAD was not a music magazine and that neither the original lyrics nor the music were printed in "Sing Along With MAD." The parodies were not copies; only the titles of the original songs were printed. There was no "sinister or insidious intent," as was charged in the complaint. If anything, the mention of the original titles glorified the popularity of the original songs.

Confidently both sides submitted examples of the two sets of lyrics — the originals and the parodies. Each side believed that a hard look at the differences, or similarities, would prove its argument.

Judge Charles M. Metzner handed down his decision in June, 1963. *Variety* headlined it:

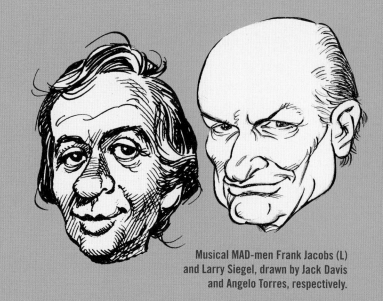

Musical MAD-men Frank Jacobs (L) and Larry Siegel, drawn by Jack Davis and Angelo Torres, respectively.

PUBS LOSE PIRACY SUIT VS. 'MAD' MAG

MAD had won the first round. Judge Metzner ruled that the subject matter of the MAD lyrics was "completely different" from that of the originals. As an example, he noted that "to the tune of 'A Pretty Girl is Like a Melody,' the defendants have written 'Louella Schwartz Describes Her Malady.' "

The judge viewed the battle with a fresh eye. He ruled that the MAD lyrics were not parodies but satires "in original words and thought" of "several aspects of modern life." He said that the new lyrics had "little in common" with those of the music publishers, then tossed a bouquet MAD's way by describing the new lyrics as "original" and "ingenious."

However, Judge Metzner ruled against MAD on two of the 25 songs, both by Berlin. One was "Always," sung to the tune of "Always," which I turned from a love ballad into an anthem for a psychiatrist. The judge felt that both lyrics allowed the word "always" to constitute the theme of the song. The other nixed number was "There's No Business Like No Business," sung to the tune of "There's No Business Like Show Business," which I wrote as a "ballad for small businessmen during recessions." Judge Metzner deemed the titles too similar, remarking that both lyrics revolved around the word "business."

The music publishers, apparently after all or nothing, did not

Judge Kaufman commented "our individual tastes may prefer a more subtle brand of humor."

give up. They appealed the case, and a year later it reached the U.S. Court of Appeals. There three judges took another look. Shouted Variety:

'MAD' MAG'S PARODY WIN NO LAUGHING MATTER TO PUBLISHERS; THEY'LL APPEAL

The Appeals Court upheld the verdict. Writing the court's opinion, Judge Irving R. Kaufman said the satirical take-offs deserve "substantial freedom both as entertainment and as a form of social and literary criticism." He added that the magazine used only the meter of the original lyrics and thrust them into "a totally incongruous setting. "We doubt," he wrote, "that even so eminent a composer as Irving Berlin should be permitted to claim a property interest in iambic pentameter."

Judge Kaufman was not bowled over by the quality of the MAD lyrics, commenting that "our individual tastes may prefer a more subtle brand of humor." But subtle or not, MAD had won again.

The music publishers fought on, and the case eventually reached the highest tribunal, the United States Supreme Court, which declined to hear the case, thereby upholding the decision of the lower court.

MAD had won. It was a landmark case, and lawyers Martin Scheiman and Jack Albert had good reason to feel proud. The right to publish parody lyrics or satirical lyrics or whatever one wished to call them had become the law of the land.

A 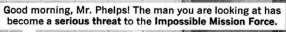 TV SCENE WE'D LIKE TO SEE

Good morning, Mr. Phelps! The man you are looking at has become a **serious threat** to the Impossible Mission Force.

He has squandered **millions of dollars of government funds** on such useless and extravagant contrivances as laser-beam fountain pens, radar wrist watches, closed-circuit mini-TV cameras embedded in belt buckles, and invisible sneakers . . .

In addition, he has created an unusual **high-risk factor** by ordering his co-workers to perform **needlessly complex** and **dangerous tasks** in order to carry out assignments that could have been accomplished relatively safely and simply.

In other words, Mr. Phelps . . . **YOU'RE FIRED!!**

Good luck in your next TV series, Jim . . .

This sink will self-destruct in five seconds . . .

ARTIST: JOHN CULLEN MURPHY   WRITER: CHEVY CHASE

#134 APR '70

ONE DAY IN A CRASH-PAD

ARTIST: DON MARTIN

Introducing A New MAD Feature Which Takes A Humorous Look At The War Between

HAWKS & DOVES

MAJOR HAWKS PRIVATE DOVES

ARTIST & WRITER: AL JAFFEE

#139 DEC '70

#137 SEP '70

AUTO-SUGGESTION DEPT.

SPORTS CARS WE'D LIKE TO SEE

WRITER & ARTIST: BASIL WOLVERTON

THE DRAGGING DRAGSTER

To most sports car enthusiasts, no beast is worth driving unless it is extremely low slung. Here is one design that is tops at hitting bottom. Flexible chassis slithers over ground on small rollers, causing onlookers to wonder just how low a driver can get. Not recommended for rocky roads.

THE TERRIFIC TIRE TOTER

This design should be a sheer delight to those sports car enthusiasts who think mostly in terms of tires—big, wide, whirring tires. There are no distracting bumpers, fenders, etc. to hide these tires from full sight. Even the spare is in good view, because there's no room for it elsewhere.

THE BASHED-IN BOLTER

Comes direct from the factory looking like a wreck to give the impression that the driver is a hot-headed daredevil who better not be crossed. Just the thing for the timid sports car lover who wants to feel dangerous and powerful.

THE STANLEY SCREAMER

Tire manufacturers will adore this innovation in design which produces, even in slow moving traffic, the shrieks and squeals that otherwise come from gunning and skidding sports cars at high speeds. Special pedal pushes back and front wheels together so they rub against each other. Odor of burning rubber, smoke, and ear-splitting screeches are thus produced, even while car is going ten miles an hour.

THE X-1 EXHAUSTER

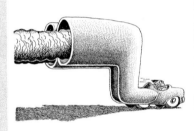

This model is designed to appeal to sports car buffs who feel that the size of the exhaust pipes together with the smoke and sounds that come from them should be emphasized. Smoke bombs and firecrackers from a special year's supply are automatically ignited every time the car is started.

THE CLASSY CLATTERER

Since big sound and fury is necessary to many sports car buffs, here is the ultimate for them, based on the simple "spoke-clackers" that kids attach to the forks of their bicycles. In this model, two sheets of steel clang against heavy metal bars extending from the oversized rear wheels.

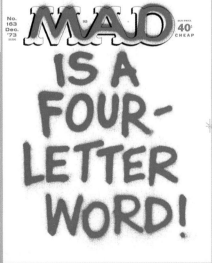

ALTAR EGO

ARTIST: WALLACE WOOD   WRITER: MARYLYN IPPOLITO

I found the entrance **too small**, and had it **re-designed**! The architect's plans called for **12 marble columns**, so I imported them from **Italy**! They were **expensive**, but they're **beautiful**!

I commissioned **Guglielmo Negron**, the famous **Spanish sculptor**, to do these **four statues**! You wouldn't believe the **prices** he charges for his work!

I have these **fresh flowers** flown in daily from all parts of the country! That **really** eats up the budget!

The **new air conditioner** makes quite a big **difference**! Even though it cost a **fortune**, it was **well worth it**!

And this is my pride and joy . . . my **new organ**! Every part is **hand-made in Switzerland** by craftsmen, crated **separately**, and **re-assembled** here by an **expert**! It took over **six months**!

I'm also having **new pews** and a **new bell carillon** installed!

Everything is certainly **very beautiful**! But it's all so **expensive**! How are you going to manage to **pay** for it all?

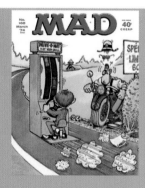

LITTLE BIGOT MAN DEPT.

Ever since Television began, situation comedies have been, more or less, the same. Now, all of a sudden, a new situation comedy has come along . . . and it's entirely different from the old-fashioned family fare. It doesn't deal with the same old stupid subjects involving idiotic, unbelievable characters. Instead, it concerns itself with relevant "now" subjects, involving even more idiotic unbelievable characters! Here, then, is MAD's version of . . .

GALL IN THE FAMILY FARE

This Week's Episode: "A Visit From A World War II Buddy"

ARTIST: ANGELO TORRES   WRITER: LARRY SIEGEL

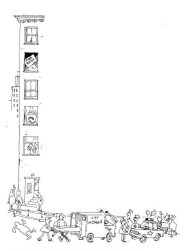

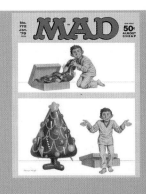

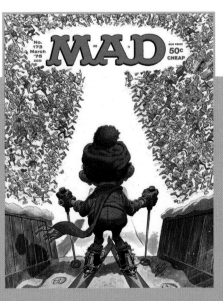

No one can fault the success of teaching children basic things in entertaining ways, and the television series "Sesame Street" does it better than most. Unfortunately, it helps little Johnny to read—but not between the lines! What we need is a television show that will prepare our youth for what <u>really</u> lies ahead, a program like

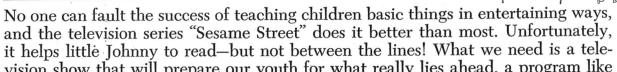

ARTIST: JACK DAVIS   WRITER: DICK DE BARTOLO

MAD'S REALITY STREET

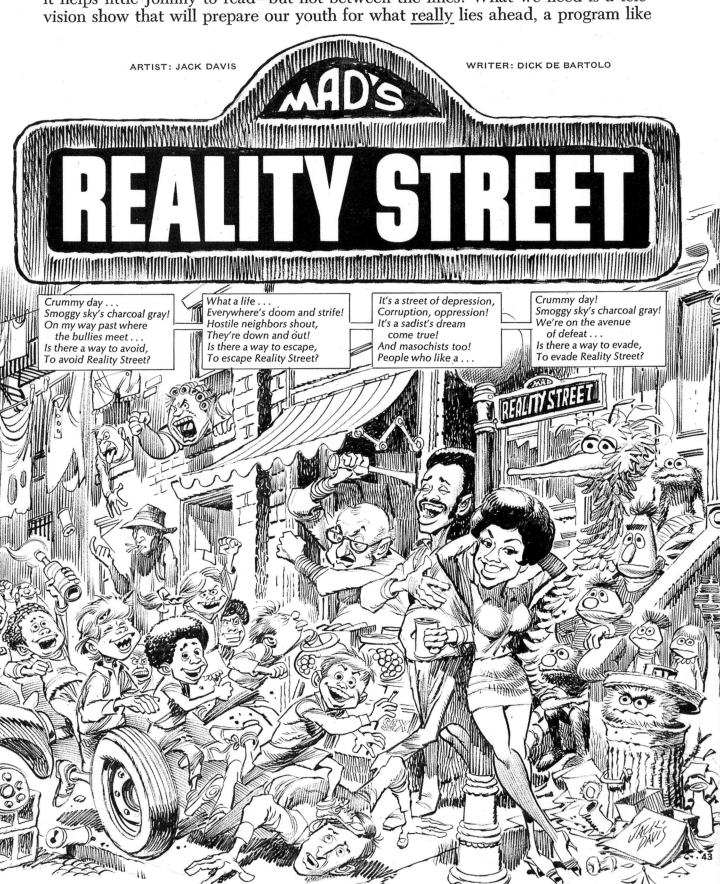

Crummy day . . .
Smoggy sky's charcoal gray!
On my way past where
    the bullies meet . . .
Is there a way to avoid,
To avoid Reality Street?

What a life . . .
Everywhere's doom and strife!
Hostile neighbors shout,
They're down and out!
Is there a way to escape,
To escape Reality Street?

It's a street of depression,
Corruption, oppression!
It's a sadist's dream
    come true!
And masochists too!
People who like a . . .

Crummy day!
Smoggy sky's charcoal gray!
We're on the avenue
    of defeat . . .
Is there a way to evade,
To evade Reality Street?

Hi, cats! My name is Gorgon, and this portion of **Reality Street** is brought to you by the letter **P** . . .

Now, the letter **P** stands for:
Please
Pardon
Polite . . .
Words that are all just about Passé!

Pusher

Puff

Psychedelic

Physician

Peaceful

Poacher

BANG!

Pelts

LEOPARD SORRY EXTINCT!

Pity

Prolific

Population

Peril

PILL

Pill

Now that last one, **Pill**, can be replaced by **Pope** if there's any objection! But before we go over to Curt and Ornery, let's take a **Pregnant Pause** . . .

Hey, Ornery, you said you would teach me how to **tell time** today! And not that "big hand on the 12, little hand on the 7" stuff, either!

Okay! We'll start with some **easy** ones! What time does a 9:00 o'clock plane leave the airport?

That's simple! **9:00 o'clock!**

You're simple! A 9:00 o'clock plane will leave at 11:00, if you're **lucky!**

What time does a train scheduled to arrive at 9:00 **actually** arrive?

11:00 o'clock?

A.M. or **P.M.?**

Gee, this is **tougher** than I thought!

#146 OCT '71

BACK IN THE OPERATING ROOM WITH DON MARTIN
DURING A HEART TRANSPLANT

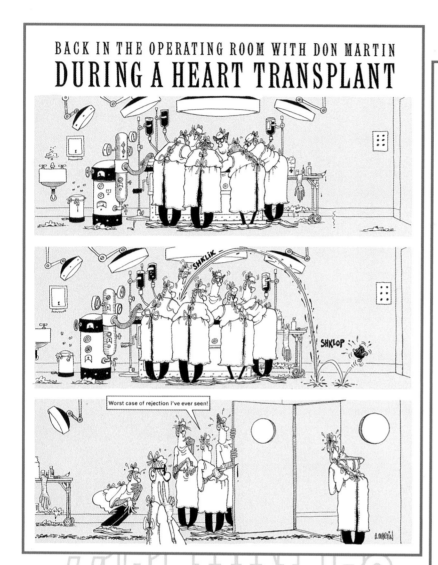

Worst case of rejection I've ever seen!

#151 JUN '72

A MOVING JUNGLE TALE

WRITER: DON EDWING   ARTIST: JACK DAVIS

FOR SALE

#158 APR '73

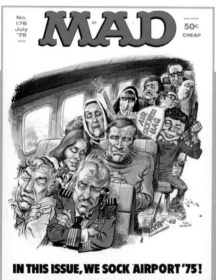

IN THIS ISSUE, WE SOCK AIRPORT '75!

IN THE IRE OF THE BEHOLDER DEPT.

Ever meet a "Bigot"? Ever try to talk sense to him? If you have, then you know it's a losing proposition. Because no matter what you say, he has an answer that supports his warped point of view. If you don't believe it, then try reading the following examples which clearly demonstrate exactly why...

YOU NEVER CAN WIN WITH A BIGOT!

ARTIST: PAUL COKER, JR.   WRITER: FRANK JACOBS

"Two out and the bases are loaded! A hit now would tie the game!" / "Ferget it! A Nigger's comin' t' bat! They always choke up in a tight spot!"

"He hit a home run!" / "Whaddya expect! All them Coons are strong as apes! Comes from all those years in the jungles!"

"That big party at my table is leaving!" / "Lousy penny-pinching Jews! I'll bet they stiff you on the tip!"

"They left me $20!" / "Why shouldn't they?! They got all the money in the world!"

"I wonder what the mechanic's going to charge us for fixing the car?" / "PLENTY! Those Italians will cheat you any chance they get!"

"The whole job only cost us seven dollars—including labor!" / "That don't surprise me! Them Wops are too dumb to figure out a bill right!"

"Ben Muncrief is 75 years old today!" / "We oughta get rid of all them old people! They're a drain on Society!"

"Do you know he still puts in an eight-hour day at the store?!" / "Them old crumbs should be forced to retire so the young men coming up can have their jobs!"

"That car ahead is slowing up!" / "Lousy women drivers! They're always screwing up traffic!"

"She's got a flat! She's pulling off the road to fix it!" / "Lousy women drivers! They're always screwing up tires!"

"Have you met that family of German refugees that moved in down the block?" / "Le'me tell you, I get sick from all those deadbeat foreigners coming over here and living off Welfare!"

"I understand he has a big job as an Electrical Engineer!" / "Those smart-ass Krauts, comin' here an' takin' all the good jobs away from us Americans!"

"I think we're lost! I'd better ask directions in Kelly's Store over there!" / "You're gonna ask a dumb Mick? They're so stupid, they couldn't give you the right time!"

"He gave me very precise, complete directions on how to get back to the main road!" / "I knew he would! Give an Irishman a chance to talk and you'll never get him to stop!"

"Did you hear about Bill? He was named Vice-President of his firm!" / "Big deal! His family's been in this country for 300 years! You can bet he got it through knowing the right people!"

"Yes, but he quit to become a Teacher!" / "That's par for the course! Them WASPs don't have the stomach for business!"

"Look at those students demonstrating!" / "Long-haired creeps! They'll wreck this country with their screaming and riots!"

"But they're demonstrating to get out the vote on Election Day!" / "Dumb kids! As if anybody's gonna listen to a lot of harebrained idiots!"

16

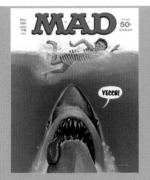

Hey, Gang! Tired of all the garbage they're showing on motion picture screens lately? Well, here's a "Family" film for a change! And now, meet the "Family":

This is Don Vino Minestrone. Not too long ago, he was just a poor immigrant from Sicily. Now he's a leading racketeer, extortionist and killer. How did Don Vino get where he is today? By putting his faith in The American Way of Life.

Here's Mama Minestrone, a typical lovable Sicilian housewife. It seems like only yesterday at another wedding that Mama herself said, "I do!" Come to think of it, that was the last time she opened her mouth.

This is Don Vino's daught Canny, and her bridegroo Carly. Such a nice coup Everyone is saying that D Vino is not really losing daughter. No, actually, this kind of Family, h probably lose a Son-in-la

And so, with such a strange family and such weird children

THE ODD

This is some swell wedding!

It's THE Social event of 1945!

Everybody who is anybody in organized crime is here!

Look! Here comes the Odd Father!

They say he's the biggest Mafia leader in the country!

Hey, you! I'm with the Italian Anti-Defamation League! Don't you know you're not supposed to use the word "MAFIA" in this picture!?!

Sorry! Er—they say he's th biggest Italian racketeer a murderer in the country!

That's much better!

This is Sinny Minestrone, the Don's eldest son. He's next in line, and it's only a matter of time before he gets the Family business. That is, of course, unless a rival Family decides to give him the business first.

This is the Don's second son, Freako. He's a sad, gentle soul. He cries at weddings and all kinds of Family crises. But he can also be a barrel of laughs. Just catch him at a funeral some time.

This is Tim Haven, the Don's adopted son. He's shrewd and smart. All his life, he dreamed of being a criminal lawyer. But he only finished half of his education —the "criminal" part.

And this is Micrin, the Don's youngest son. He's a college graduate, a veteran war hero, an honest law-abiding citizen —and a disgrace to the entire Family.

it's easy to see why Don Vino Minestrone is known as...

FATHER

ARTIST: MORT DRUCKER
WRITER: LARRY SIEGEL

What a fantastic make-up job they've done on Marlin Brandow! How did they ever get him to look so OLD?

Very simple! They made him watch his last four movies, and he aged 20 years!

I still can't believe it's Marlin Brandow!

Mumble mumble mumble mumble

It's Marlin Brandow, all right!!

...IT IS YOUR HONOR TO INVITE ME TO YOUR DAUGHTER'S BRISS...

Papa, I'm so happy on my Wedding Day! Why aren't you happy too? Why do you look so pained?!?

You think it's easy to see your little girl grow up? You think it's easy to give her away to another man? You think it's easy to talk with eight pounds of cotton in your cheeks?

But you talk like that WITHOUT cotton in your cheeks!

#155 DEC '72

Most people still believe in a hard day's work — but they also think it should be spread out over the course of a week or two.

—Alfred E. Neuman

OUR AMERICAN HERITAGE

ARTIST: BOB CLARKE   WRITER: MAX BRANDEL

#143 JUN '71

DON MARTIN DEPT. PART II

ONE WEDNESDAY EVENING IN A RESTAURANT MEN'S ROOM

#193 SEP '77

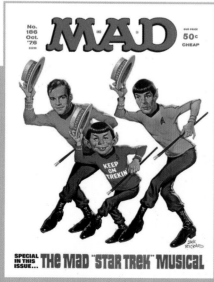

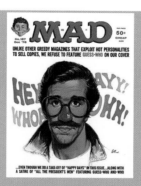

DEATH BY ELOCUTION DEPT.

MAD'S GUARANTEED EFFECTIVE ALL-OCCASION NON-SLANDEROUS POLITICAL SMEAR SPEECH

ARTIST: GEORGE WOODBRIDGE   WRITER: BILL GARVIN

My fellow citizens, it is an honor and a pleasure to be here today. My opponent has openly admitted he feels an affinity toward your city, but I happen to *like* this area. It might be a salubrious place to him, but to me it is one of the nation's most delightful garden spots.

When I embarked upon this political campaign I hoped that it could be conducted on a high level and that my opponent would be willing to stick to the issues. Unfortunately, he has decided to be tractable instead—to indulge in unequivocal language, to eschew the use of outright lies in his speeches, and even to make repeated veracious statements about me.

At first I tried to ignore these scrupulous, unvarnished fidelities. Now I will do so no longer. *If my opponent wants a fight, he's going to get one!*

It might be instructive to start with his background. My friends, have you ever accidentally dislodged a rock on the ground and seen what was underneath? Well, exploring my opponent's background is dissimilar. All the slime and filth and corruption you can possibly imagine, even in your wildest dreams, are glaringly nonexistent in this man's life. And even during his childhood!

Let us take a very quick look at that childhood: It is a known fact that, on a number of occasions, he emulated older boys at a certain playground. It is also known that his parents not only permitted him to masticate excessively in their presence, but even urged him to do so. Most explicable of all, this man who poses as a paragon of virtue exacerbated his own sister when they were both teen-agers!

I ask you, my fellow Americans: is this the kind of person we want in public office to set an example for our youth?

Of course, it's not surprising that he should have such a typically pristine background—no, not when you consider the other members of his family:

His female relatives put on a constant pose of purity and innocence, and claim they are inscrutable, yet every one of them has taken part in hortatory activities.

The men in the family are likewise completely amenable to moral suasion.

My opponent's second cousin is a Mormon.

His uncle was a flagrant heterosexual.

His sister, who has always been obsessed by sects, once worked as a proselyte outside a church.

His father was secretly chagrined at least a dozen times by matters of a pecuniary nature.

His youngest brother wrote an essay extolling the virtues of being a homo sapiens.

His great-aunt expired from a degenerative disease.

His nephew subscribes to a phonographic magazine.

His wife was a thespian before their marriage and even performed the act in front of paying customers.

And his own mother had to resign from a woman's organization in her later years because she was an admitted sexagenarian.

Now what shall we say of the man himself?

I can tell you in solemn truth that he is the very antithesis of political radicalism, economic irre-

sponsibility and personal depravity. His own record *proves* that he has frequently discountenanced treasonable, un-American philosophies and has perpetrated many overt acts as well.

He perambulated his infant son on the street.

He practiced nepotism with his uncle and first cousin.

He attempted to interest a 13-year-old girl in philately.

He participated in a seance at a private residence where, among other odd goings-on, there was incense.

He has declared himself in favor of more homogeneity on college campuses.

He has advocated social intercourse in mixed company—and has taken part in such gatherings himself.

He has been deliberately averse to crime in our city streets.

He has urged our Protestant and Jewish citizens to develop more catholic tastes.

Last summer he committed a piscatorial act on a boat that was flying the American flag.

Finally, at a time when we must be on our guard against all foreign isms, he has coolly announced his belief in altruism—and his fervent hope that some day this entire nation will be altruistic!

I beg you, my friends, to oppose this man whose life and work and ideas are so openly and avowedly compatible with our American way of life. A vote for him would be a vote for the perpetuation of everything we hold dear.

The facts are clear; the record speaks for itself. Do your duty.

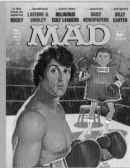

Men who will only eat their mother's cooking have an edible complex.

WE GOT YOUR PENUMBRA DEPT.

Who Knows What Evils Lurk In The Hearts Of Men?

THE SHADOW KNOWS

WRITER & ARTIST: SERGIO ARAGONES

#159 JUN '73

MAD

PSSST!

KEEP THIS ISSUE OUT OF THE HANDS OF YOUR PARENTS!

(MAKE 'EM BUY THEIR OWN COPY)

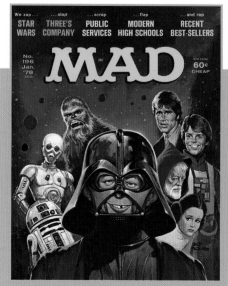

We zap... ...slap ...scrap ...flap ...and rap
STAR WARS THREE'S COMPANY PUBLIC SERVICES MODERN HIGH SCHOOLS RECENT BEST-SELLERS

No. 196 Jan. '78 MAD 60¢ CHEAP

We're ring ...sing ...sing ...sing ...and sing
STAR WARS LITTLE HOUSE ON THE PRAIRIE "IN SEARCH OF..." MOVIES PHYSICAL FITNESS THE CARTER FOLLIES

No. 197 March '78 MAD 60¢ CHEAP

MAD

HOPES THIS ISSUE JAMS EVERY COMPUTER IN THE COUNTRY...

70989 33230

...FOR FORCING US TO DEFACE OUR COVERS WITH THIS YECCHY UPC SYMBOL FROM NOW ON

We gazz... ...scare ...explore ...deplore ...and ignore
THE SPY WHO LOVED ME PUNK ROCK WHAT'S HAPPENING? TELEVISION COMMERCIALS DONNY & MARIE

MAD

EXCLUSIVE: FBI RELEASES BIONIC MAN'S FINGERPRINTS

94

Ms. LIBERTY

WOMEN'S
LIB
MDCCXLXXV

ARTIST: MUTZ   IDEA: AL JAFFEE

ANOTHER
MAD
MINI-
POSTER

Scenes We'd Like To See

ARTIST: JACK RICKARD   WRITER: DON EDWING

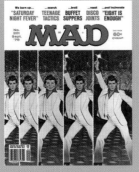

WHAT SIMPLE PASTIME IS FAST BECOMING A LUXURY THAT MANY AMERICANS CAN NO LONGER AFFORD?

A▶

HERE WE GO WITH ANOTHER RIDICULOUS
MAD FOLD-IN

The United States is one of the most beautiful and bountiful nations on earth. And yet, the way the cost of living is climbing, there are a lot of simple pleasures that many Americans will have to start doing without. To discover one popular pastime that is quickly becoming impossibly expensive, fold in page as shown.

FOLD THIS SECTION OVER LEFT **◄B** FOLD BACK SO "A" MEETS "B"

FOLD PAGE OVER LIKE THIS!

AMERICA AFFORDS MANY DIVERSE PLEASURES TO EACH CITIZEN. BUT INCREASING COSTS ARE STARTING TO MAKE SOME LUXURIES IMPOSSIBLE TO ENJOY

ARTIST & WRITER: AL JAFFEE

A▶　　　　**◄B**

WHAT SIMPLE PASTIME IS FAST BECOMING A LUXURY THAT MANY AMERICANS CAN NO LONGER AFFORD?

FOLD PAGE OVER LIKE THIS!

A▶ ◄B FOLD BACK SO "A" MEETS "B"

EATING

ARTIST & WRITER: AL JAFFEE

A▶ ◄B

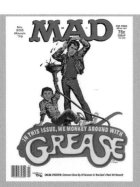

THE LIGHTER SIDE OF... THE ENERGY CRISIS

BERG'S-EYE VIEW DEPT.

ARTIST & WRITER: DAVE BERG

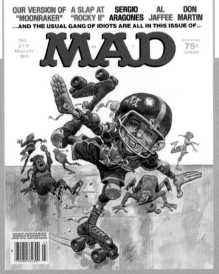

PLAYING IT FOR SHARK VALUE DEPT.

There's a sick new trend in movies! It started with "Airport", continued with "Towering Inferno", sunk to a low with "Earthquake" and has now reached the depths with the movie that's REALLY packing 'em in, the one about a giant shark that terrorizes a summer community! Yep, it's obvious that people get their kicks out of seeing other people die . . . in every horrible way possible, which includes being . . .

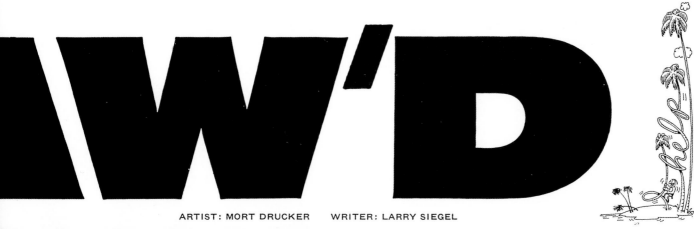

AW'D

ARTIST: MORT DRUCKER WRITER: LARRY SIEGEL

My ankle! He's got me by the ankle!

Man, that Freddie is really somethin' else!

Wow! Ankle-biting! What a wild, crazy turn-on!

Frankly, I'm **worried** about Brenda . . . all the way out there with Freddie . . .

YOU'RE worried! I'm **FREDDIE**!!

What do we know about this reported missing person . . . ?

Is it **a boy** or a **girl**?

Look! **Nowadays** that description is **no proof one way or the other!**

I got **NEWS** for you! Nowadays, **THAT's** no proof either!

The description I got, Chief, was that it's a **teenager** . . . shoulder-length hair, wearing earrings . . .

Aw — **c'mon** now, Chief!

We **KNOW** it's a girl, Chief! When she was last seen, she was **NAKED!**

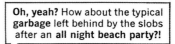

What do you think could have **happened** to her, Chief?

I hate to **say** it, but if you've been around here as long as I have, you've **seen** those **hideous, ugly** monsters . . . **attacking** everything in sight . . .

And then again, if we're **lucky**, maybe it was only a **SHARK!**

I know! I've **been** in the **halls** of the High School!

I . . . *choke* . . . I **found** something . . . Chief!!

Is it—what—you **thought** it was??

Ugh . . . ecch . . . it's what I **thought** it was . . . all right!!

Listen to me! Get **hold** of yourself! You're a **Police Officer!** You can stand up to **any-thing,** even the remains of a **body** after a **shark** gets through with it!

Oh, yeah? How about the typical **garbage** left behind by the slobs after an **all night beach party?!**

Oh, God! **Anything** but that!

#180 JAN '76

Parents are the ones who are there when you want to be alone with a date and nowhere to be found when you need five bucks.
—Alfred E. Neuman

STATUS QUOTES DEPT.

WHEN YOU'RE POOR…AND…WHEN YOU'RE RICH

ARTIST: JACK DAVIS   WRITER: FRANK JACOBS

WHEN YOU'RE POOR…

…you're a glutton.

WHEN YOU'RE RICH…

…you're a gourmet.

WHEN YOU'RE POOR…

…you breed kids like rabbits.

WHEN YOU'RE RICH…

…you're blessed with a large family.

WHEN YOU'RE POOR…

…you gossip.

WHEN YOU'RE RICH…

…you bring each other up to date.

WHEN YOU'RE POOR…

…you throw your money away on booze.

WHEN YOU'RE RICH…

…you have a well-stocked bar.

WHEN YOU'RE POOR…

…you're the town weirdo.

WHEN YOU'RE RICH…

…you're the local eccentric.

WHEN YOU'RE POOR…

…you own a mutt.

WHEN YOU'RE RICH…
…you possess a mixed breed.

WHEN YOU'RE POOR…

…you vomit.

WHEN YOU'RE RICH…

…you succumb to a sudden attack of nausea.

WHEN YOU'RE POOR…

…you gamble away your salary at the track.

WHEN YOU'RE RICH…

…you have a bad day, handicapping.

WHEN YOU'RE POOR…

…you're a punk who's a menace on the highway, and should be locked up.

WHEN YOU'RE RICH…
…you're sowing wild oats and getting some devilishness out of your system.

#190 APR '77

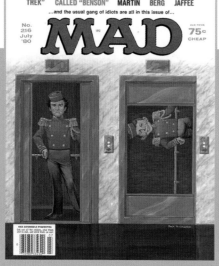

100

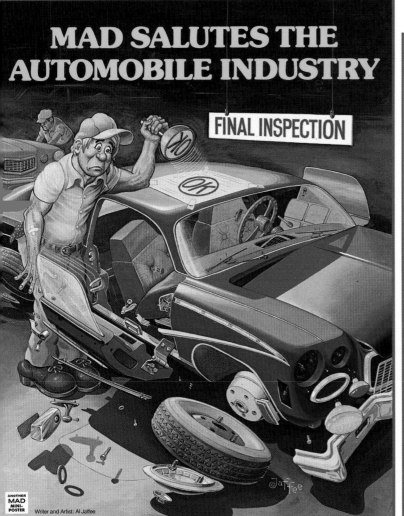

MAD SALUTES THE AUTOMOBILE INDUSTRY

FINAL INSPECTION

Writer and Artist: Al Jaffee

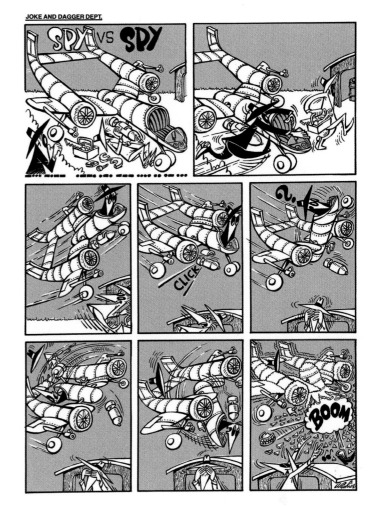

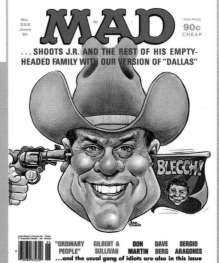

For years, Hollywood made movies about the Fight Game that were loaded with clichés. Recently, however, instead of bringing back another one of those "Joe Palooka" pictures, they made a brand new type movie about the Fight Game . . . loaded with brand new clichés. You'll see what we mean in this version of

ROC

KHEAD

ARTIST:
MORT DRUCKER

WRITER:
STAN HART

Hey, Rockhead! You're out of **shape!** You gotta give up **smoking!**

Aw, do I **have** to?!

Well, at **least** while you're in the **ring!!**

Y'know, you **goldfish** are my **only** friends . . .

. . . but I'm afraid **YOU'RE** out of shape, **too** . . .

. . . 'cause every time I take you out for a **walk**, you **pass out** before we're halfway down the **block!**

Gee, I'm lonely! . . . I had **visitors** walkin' in an' outta here **all the time!** But the place got so **filthy**, they don' **come** no more! They got **too much self-respect!**

Can you **imagine . . .?!** Bein' **snubbed** by **ROACHES?!**

Hey . . . whaddya say we **talk**, huh?

I'd . . . I'd **rather not!** I'm **too shy!**

Is that why you got your **head** in the **birdcage?**

Yeah! And at the **same time**, I'm havin' my **HAIR frosted!**

#194 OCT '77

Combine a dynamic young TV star with the soundtrack of a hot, exploitable singing group and some "R"-rated dialogue, insure it with some sub-plots from other hit films like "Rocky," "American Graffiti," "West Side Story," "Mean Streets," and "Beach Blanket Bingo"...and you've got the formula for one of the biggest blockbuster movies of the year, right? Wrong! Because the best "hustle" may not be the one they're dancing up on the screen, but the one foisted on us by the producers—for making millions on a film that does have spectacular choreography...but not much else! Yep, as far as we at MAD are concerned, you wasted your money on...

SATURDAY NIGHT FEEBLE

Uh—I seen this groovy **shirt** in a window, an' **tonight's Saturday** . . . so—*uh*—can I have an **advance**, Mr. Fungo?

No! Payday is **Monday!**

Okay! **Forget** it! I gotta hurry home!

But you **HATE** your home life!

I know! But **each new scene** that we do gives 'em a chance to change the background music! You dig?!?

Hey, you **can't** go throwin' away your **money!** You gotta think of the **future**, Tony! And you got a future right here in my **paint store!**

Screw the future! **Tonight's** the future! All **I'm** interested in is **dancing** and **pop music!**

It's **no use!** I'm trying to teach the jerk about **SHERWIN-WILLIAMS** . . . an' all he cares about is **PAUL WILLIAMS!**

ARTIST: MORT DRUCKER   WRITER: ARNIE KOGEN

Okay . . . they've cued in a **new background song** so they can **exploit the soundtrack**, and they've put me in **bikini briefs** so they can **exploit my body!** Now I go through the **painstaking ritual** of **primping** for a big night at the **disco!**

What I'm trying to **achieve** here is a **total macho-disco-stud look!** First, I **blow-dry** my **hair** for four hours . . . then I put on **chains**, pick out a **body shirt** . . . select platform shoes and **tight pants** and—

Dinner's onna table! Y'Mudder made **spaghetti, linguini, vermicelli,** and **drippy manicotti!**

Somehow, this is **not** quite the total macho-disco-stud look I was **going** for . . . **unless,** of course, I'm doing the **Tango Hustle** at a **Ku Klux Klan** meeting!

Okay, let's all settle down to a **nice, typical Italian family meal!** We'll pass it around the table starting from left to right . . .

Who Was Bill Gaines? Part Two

□ By Frank Jacobs

Without a doubt, Bill Gaines will be best remembered as founder and publisher of MAD. But that describes only one part of the man. In a nutshell, which is an inadequate container, he was, to distort the Boy Scout Oath, appreciative, compulsive, exasperating, unkempt, earthy, loyal, stubborn, godless, hairy, gluttonous, generous, and insatiable. He garnered wealth and achieved a measure of fame — an updated Horatio Alger hero nurtured on expensive wines, rich food, a love of zeppelins, and a lifelong reverence for King Kong and the Marx Brothers.

As MAD prospered, Gaines increasingly revealed his inner nonconformist self. In and out of the office he was almost always attired in a faded sport shirt and rumpled slacks. Most of his bespectacled face was buried beneath a hopelessly untrimmed beard. The rest of his head was enshrouded in a puzzle of hanging hair, styled only by the force of gravity. In his closet hung slacks for seven different weights, each pair numbered on a sliding scale from 1 (smallest) to 7 (largest). The overall effect was what fashion experts might regard as the Laundry Look. MAD writer Larry Siegel once described Gaines as "the ten worst-dressed men in the world."

Half gourmet, half glutton, Gaines courted food as a gigolo stalks wealthy widows. Eating was his life schtick. He belonged to six wine and food societies and could, if he wished, attend three dinners or wine tastings a week.

One evening I was invited for dinner at Gaines' apartment. His soon-to-be third wife Annie prepared a sumptuous meal, which was not unexpected. What did surprise me were the eight empty wine glasses beside each place setting. As the banquet progressed, a bottle would appear and a glass would be filled with a pricey wine, each deemed appropriate for a particular course. Included was a well-aged Clos Vougeot, which Gaines, tapping his remarkable memory bank, knew was my favorite Burgundy. To say I was touched is an understatement.

MAD writer Arnie Kogen was especially impressed by the total hospitality extended by Gaines to his visitors. After one banquet,

Kogen looked out the window and saw a fire raging through a building several blocks away. Kogen turned to his wife, Sue, and said, "Bill will do anything to entertain his guests."

In restaurants, Gaines was an accepting patron who rarely caused a scene. There were exceptions. One evening he and his second wife, Nancy, dined at the Asti, a restaurant that features opera singers. Gaines had just begun his main course when a tenor and a soprano took up a full-voiced duet. Gaines couldn't stand opera, much less when he was eating. He rose from the table, left Nancy, and carried his plate to the kitchen, where he finished his meal in relative quiet.

Gaines with his beloved wine collection. According to John Ficarra, Gaines knew everything about wine. "He could tell you the name of the guy that picked the grape."

Food being Gaines' passion, it was unfortunate that he was compelled to deal with a weight problem, his poundage ranging from a low of 185 to a high of 285. Every year or so, he steeled himself and went on a diet. He tried a dozen or so, but the only one that proved effective was Metrecal, a then-popular diet shake.

"Each time I hit the Metrecal trail," he said, "it means giving up any kind of social life for months. My social life is food. I can't go anywhere, I can't do anything, because the only thing I know how to do is eat."

He wrapped up his first Metrecal diet at 185, a weight he remained at for one day, after which he rewarded himself with a 10-day eating tour of France.

> Half gourmet, half glutton, Gaines courted food as a gigolo stalks wealthy widows.

Gaines carried memories of his favorite restaurants in his taste buds. His list of memorable eateries included one New York establishment that will not be found in any guidebook.

"For getting sick, I like Doctors Hospital. Though it may not have the medical repute of, say, New York Hospital, it is the most enjoyable hospital to be sick in, if for nothing else than its food, which is excellent for a hospital. They even have room service, so you can order up a snack for a visiting guest."

One night he and I were strolling to a restaurant.

"Frank, please," he objected.

"What's wrong?" I asked.

"You mustn't walk so fast. We are going one degree uphill."

Gaines had special routes for getting about Manhattan and was known to walk three blocks out of his way to avoid a short stretch of uphill climbing. Of course, these were one-way routes. When he left the MAD office to lunch at a place, say, five blocks downhill, he returned in a taxi.

Gaines ran MAD on his own terms and would have preferred running the rest of his life the same way. Shortly after the magazine moved into its offices at 485 MADison Avenue, he toddled down for a chat with the manager of the building's restaurant, Morgen's East.

"I'm going to be in this building for at least 10 years and I'm going to eat in this restaurant, sometimes with guests, at least four times a week, 40 to 50 weeks a year," Gaines said. "The only thing I wish is to not wear a tie. If you insist on my wearing a tie, you will lose a lot of business."

"I'm sorry," the manager said, "but we can't let anyone eat here without a tie."

"Okay," Gaines said, and left, crossing the place off his list.

Food for one. Would Gaines fly commercial today, given airlines' current meal policies?

Gaines' largest pajamas could accomodate MAD staffers Marla Wyche (L) and Amy Vozeolas.

Several years later, the restaurant lifted its ban and allowed guests to dine tieless. But if Morgen's East thought that Gaines would now become a patron, it was mistaken. He never set foot there again.

This was, in some ways, a pity, because Gaines liked comfort and convenience in his life, and the restaurant offered both. But to him, there were some things that couldn't be forgiven.

If Gaines had had his way, the outdoors would have been air-conditioned in the summer and heated in the winter, and all stairs would have been replaced by escalators. But, alas, he had to deal with a world not of his making.

1970, Japan. A MAD meal with (L-R) Al Jaffee, George Woodbridge, Gaines, Dick DeBartolo and Don Martin. The bibs are probably a good idea.

Back in the 1930's, kids loved those Saturday matinee "Movie Serials" in which the hero battled against incredible odds and miraculously survived one threat to his life after another—and always just in the nick of time. There was an art to making those marvelous old "Chapters" . . . and it was only a matter of time before someone would revive the "cliff-hanger" gimmick in a modern full-length feature. That's why we call the Producers of this recent box-office-smash-hit thriller . . .

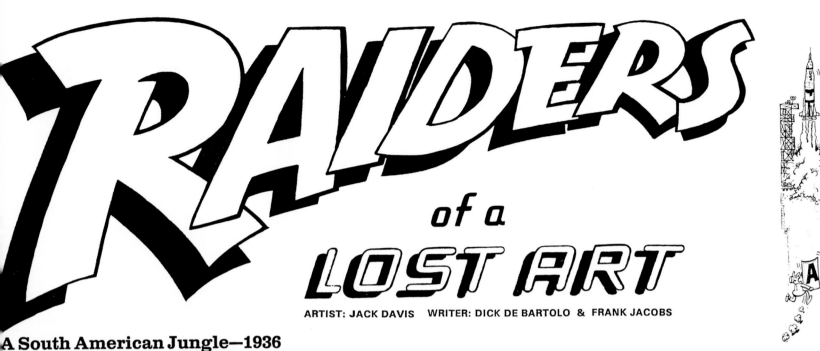

RAIDERS of a LOST ART

ARTIST: JACK DAVIS   WRITER: DICK DE BARTOLO & FRANK JACOBS

A South American Jungle—1936

This **lost Inca** temple is really **incredible**, isn't it? The **floors** sink under your **feet**, and the **walls move** . . . !

Construction Contractors weren't much better **3000 years ago** than they are today!

There it is . . . the **Golden Idol of the Incas** . . . exactly where all those tales we heard **said** it would be!

Then it **wasn't** just **IDOL GOSSIP!**

Listen, **this** is a mission to find prim-itive **ART** . . . not primitive **HUMOR!!**

My **traitorous** guide is **dead**, this huge **boulder** is crashing down on me, Pres-ident Roosevelt can't get his new law passed in **Congress** and Joe DiMaggio went **0 for 4** against the **Tigers!** Boy, talk about your **rough days** in 1936!!

I'll take that idol, Inbanana . . . !

Darn it, Bollix! I nearly get trap-ped in the temple, my guide tries to kill me, I escape poison darts and **booby traps** of all kinds . . . and you take the idol . . . just like that!

What do you **mean**, ''just like that!''? Do you know how **long** I've been standing out here in the **hot sun**, waiting for you?!

A North American Jungle—1937

I'm sorry to inter-rupt your **flirting**, Professor Jones . . . but some **important people** are here to **see** you! Excuse **yourself** from **class** for a few months!

Jones, we're from **Army Intelligence!**

Gee, I **didn't** think those two words **went together!**

We've heard a **great deal** about you, Jones! You're a **top Archeolo-gist**, an **expert** on the **occult**, an **obtainer** of **rare artifacts**, and . . . judging by your **last remark** . . . a **wise-ass!!**

#228 JAN '82

ARTIST & WRITER: JOHN CALDWELL

ARTIST: DON MARTIN   WRITER: DON EDWING

110

GAMES FEEBLE PLAY DEPT.

MAD PASTIMES FOR THE BEDRIDDEN

ARTIST AND WRITER PAUL PETER PORGES

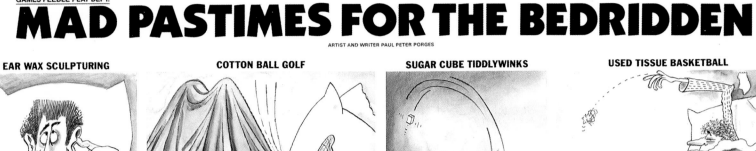

EAR WAX SCULPTURING

COTTON BALL GOLF

SUGAR CUBE TIDDLYWINKS

USED TISSUE BASKETBALL

MEDICATION SOCCER

MERCURY "SPACE SHOTS"

TOE MUPPETS

UNDER-THE-BED LINT SAILING REGATTAS

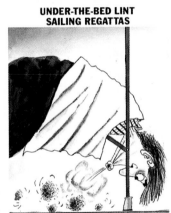

BREAKFAST TRAY LIMBO

CHICKEN SOUP BLIND MAN'S BLUFF

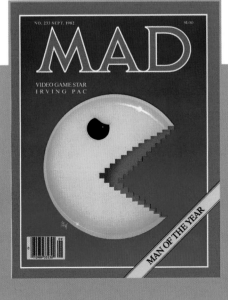

So you really think that just because Ronald Reagan became President, he gave up acting?! Well, shows how much you know!! Because once an actor, always an actor! It's kinda like herpes! And now that he IS President, instead of waiting around

NOW STARRING

...as "Hamlet"...

GESUNDHEIT!

To **tax**...? Or **not** to tax? **That** is the question!

Whether 'tis better to **relieve** the **poor man's** suffering...

Or to take action against **outrageous fortunes**, and by **taxing friends,** offend them?

Does the President **usually** spend a lot of time **asking** himself questions?

Yeah! That's why he gets so many goofy answers!

Well, at least he's **thoughtful!**

He's **not** thoughtful! He's **SENILE!!**

for a great role like "Bonzo's Pal" to come along, Ronnie can play any role that he wants. In fact, we here at MAD have detected him playing many famous, sought-after parts since he took office. Here are just few we've observed...with...

AT THE WHITE HOUSE

ARTIST: MORT DRUCKER   WRITER: STAN HART

...as Ron Corlione...in "The Godfather"...

Hey, **Cappo!** You're gonna go over to **Europe,** an' you're gonna make those **Heads of State** an **offer** they **can't refuse!** We're putting **more missiles** into their countries... **or else!!**

But, supposing one of them **refuses** to **go along** with us?

Then **you** give 'im **"The Kiss Of Death"!**

In **that** case, I'm **quitting!**

How come...?

It's a lot **easier** to **resign my post** than to kiss Margaret **Thatcher** on the **lips!**

...as Ron Quixote...in "Man Of La Mancha"...

Fear not! The Communist dragon will **never** take over and destroy your **cherished Salvadorian way of life!**

I would **love** to take that crazy man's **horse** home with me! It would make my **children** so **happy!**

To **ride** it?

No, to **eat** it!!

A SNAPPY ANSWERS TO STUPID QUESTIONS "MOTHER GOOSE" FOLD-IN

HERE WE GO WITH ANOTHER RIDICULOUS **MAD FOLD-IN**

Humpty Dumpty fends off some pretty stupid questions in this Mother Goose scene . . . but to get the FINAL SNAPPY ANSWER, you've got to fold in the page as shown at right!

ARTIST & WRITER: AL JAFFEE

A◀ FOLD THIS SECTION OVER LEFT ▶B FOLD BACK SO "A" MEETS "B"

FOLD PAGE OVER LIKE THIS!

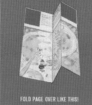

DID YOU GET SCRATCHED AND HURT WHEN YOU FELL OFF THE WALL?

NO, I AM FULLY ASSEMBLED WHEN CRACKED IN TWO!

WILL YOUR EGO SUFFER FROM THIS AWFUL EXPERIENCE?

NO, A COUPLE OF BUSTED LEGS MAKE MY SPIRITS SOAR!

WOULD YOU LIKE TO BE PUT BACK TOGETHER AGAIN?

NO, I'M HAPPIER WHEN I'M SPREAD ALL OVER THE PLACE

GOODY! I JUST LOVE...

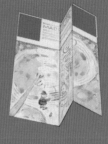

A SNAPPY ANSWERS TO STUPID QUESTIONS "MOTHER GOOSE" FOLD-IN

FOLD PAGE OVER LIKE THIS!

ARTIST & WRITER: AL JAFFEE

A▶B FOLD BACK SO "A" MEETS "B"

SCRAMBLED

EGGS

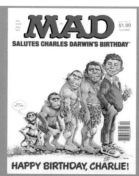

JOKE AND DAGGER DEPT.

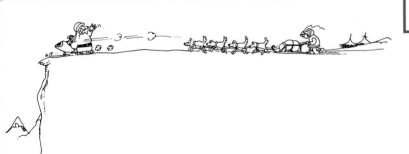

ANOTHER SCENES WE'D LIKE TO SEE (THE FROG PRINCE)

ARTIST: DON MARTIN

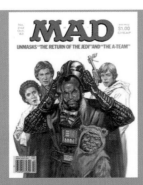

"SUPERMAN III" IN THIS ISSUE

Have you ever noticed what happens to a TV situation comedy that's lucky enough to stay on the air beyond its opening season? The network "experts" immediately begin to tinker with its characters, its setting and even its basic premise in an effort to make sure the program has "something for everyone." In no time at all, the show becomes a total mish-mosh that includes "nothing for anyone." If you can remember the good old days when Archie Bunker still had a wife and a daughter and worked on a loading dock, or when Laverne and Shirley were brewery employees living in Milwaukee, then you're already familiar with the winding path that must be followed in this ridiculous article that studiously charts:

THE EVOLUTION OF A TV SITUATION COMEDY

ARTIST: HARRY NORTH

WRITER: TOM KOCH

THE FIRST SEASON

THE SECOND SEASON

To the surprise of the network and the horror of many viewers, "Idle Hours" makes a successful debut. It is a nostalgic comedy about three high school chums (Nipsy, Conrad and The Horse) growing up in Kokomo, Indiana in 1946. Their idle hours are spent working as klutzy pin boys at a bowling alley which is owned by a retired clarinet player named Elsa. Also featured are the boy's gym teacher, Mr. Faunce, and Conrad's little sister, Buffy Lu. Buffy Lu is a typically American 14-year-old sexpot, whose smutty one-liners provide endless mirth.

To avoid critics' charges that the show is too sugary, the network adds "social significance" by introducing The Horse's cousin, Mangler, as a new member of the cast. Mangler is a certified psychopath (but a funny one) who has chosen to hide in Kokomo following his escape from a southern chain gang. The leading characters try to rehabilitate him to a life of unending dullness by convincing him that he should enroll as an apprentice mortician at Kokomo's funeral home, which is operated by another new series regular, Mr. Ferndipper.

PHOTOGRAPHER: IRVING SCHILD   WRITER: BILLY DOHERTY

TRUTH

You found out!

The Truth. That even smoking the one enjoyable ultra low tar cigarette doesn't make it any less deadly.

Warning: The Surgeon General Has Determined That ALL Cigarette Smoking Is Dangerous To Your Health.

Family reunions are when relatives gather from all over to be reminded why they scattered in the first place.

—Alfred E. Neuman

Hey, gang! After ten years, it's time once again for MAD's nutty "Cliché Monster" game! Here's how it works: Take any familiar phrase or colloquial expression, give it an eerie gothic setting so you create a new type monster, and you're playing at

HORRIFYING CLICHÉS

ARTIST: PAUL COKER   WRITER: FRANK JACOBS

Going Out With A BANG

Coming To A SCREECHING HALT

Driving A HARD BARGAIN

Hanging On To The BITTER END

Losing One's VIRTUE

Bottling Up One's EMOTIONS

Ducking An ISSUE

Weighing The ALTERNATIVES

Throwing A TANTRUM

Opening An OLD WOUND

#248 JUL '84

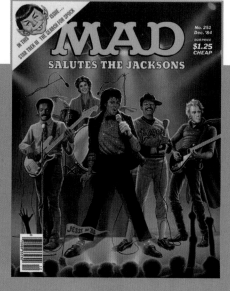

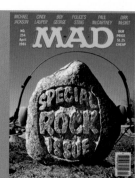

GEORGE SLAVE-OWNER

PRISSY

KHO MANIAC

DEAD MEESE

HOT AIR HELMS

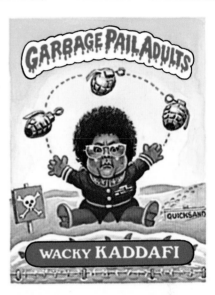

WACKY KADDAFI

BULLY BOTHA

YUCKY ARAFAT

MOUTHY McENROE

Artists: Will Elder and Harvey Kurtzman

#265 SEP '86

If you've ever flown, you know that every airline passenger is provided with reading material to help while away the time and make you forget how boring and uncomfortable the trip really is. This reading material usually consists of three items: (1) A magazine that extols the virtues of the airline you're flying, (2) A mail order catalogue of products that are sold by the airline you're flying, and (3) A safety information guide that makes you wish you'd never heard of the airline you're flying. With this idiotic article, we take

A MAD LOOK AT AIRLINE SAFETY INSTRUCTIONS

Airline emergency procedures look great...on paper!

SAFETY INFORMATION
INFORMATION DE SEGURIDAD
RENSIGNEMENTS POUR VOTRE SÉCURITÉ
ROTSA RUCK

BOING FATBELLY
727 FEET (AROUND THE MIDDLE)

HOW TO LOCATE THIS CARD

WRITER AND ARTIST: AL JAFFEE

FORCED LANDING AT SEA PROCEDURE

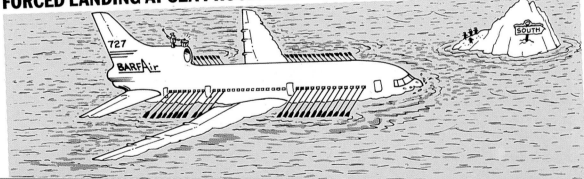

#251 DEC '84

122

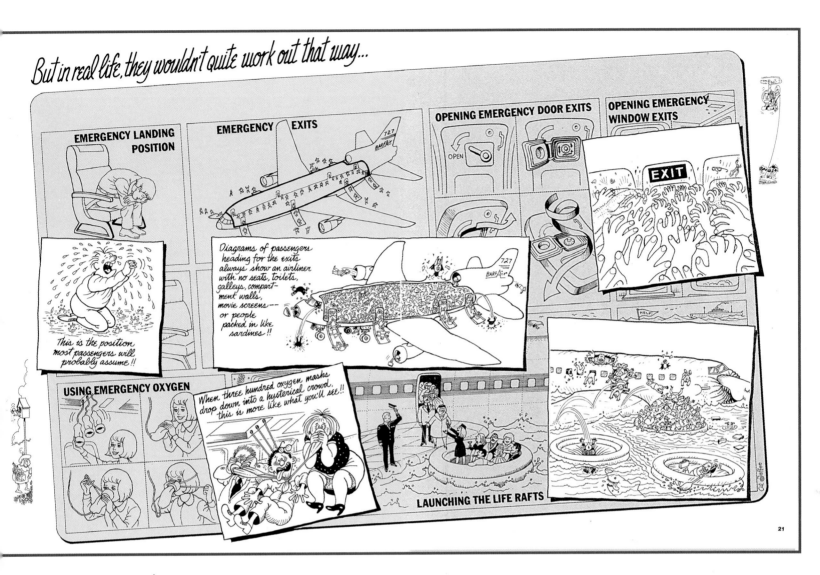

But in real life, they wouldn't quite work out that way...

EMERGENCY LANDING POSITION

This is the position most passengers will probably assume!!

EMERGENCY EXITS

Diagrams of passengers heading for the exits always show an airliner with no seats, toilets, galleys, compartment walls, movie screens — or people packed in like sardines!!

OPENING EMERGENCY DOOR EXITS

OPENING EMERGENCY WINDOW EXITS

EXIT

USING EMERGENCY OXYGEN

When three hundred oxygen masks drop down into a hysterical crowd, this is more like what you'll see!!

LAUNCHING THE LIFE RAFTS

21

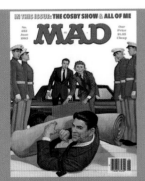

Parents are the ones who never listen to a word you say — until you mutter something under your breath.

—Alfred E. Neuman

ARTIST: ANGELO TORRES   WRITER: ARNIE KOGEN

#249 SEP '84

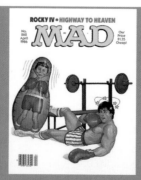

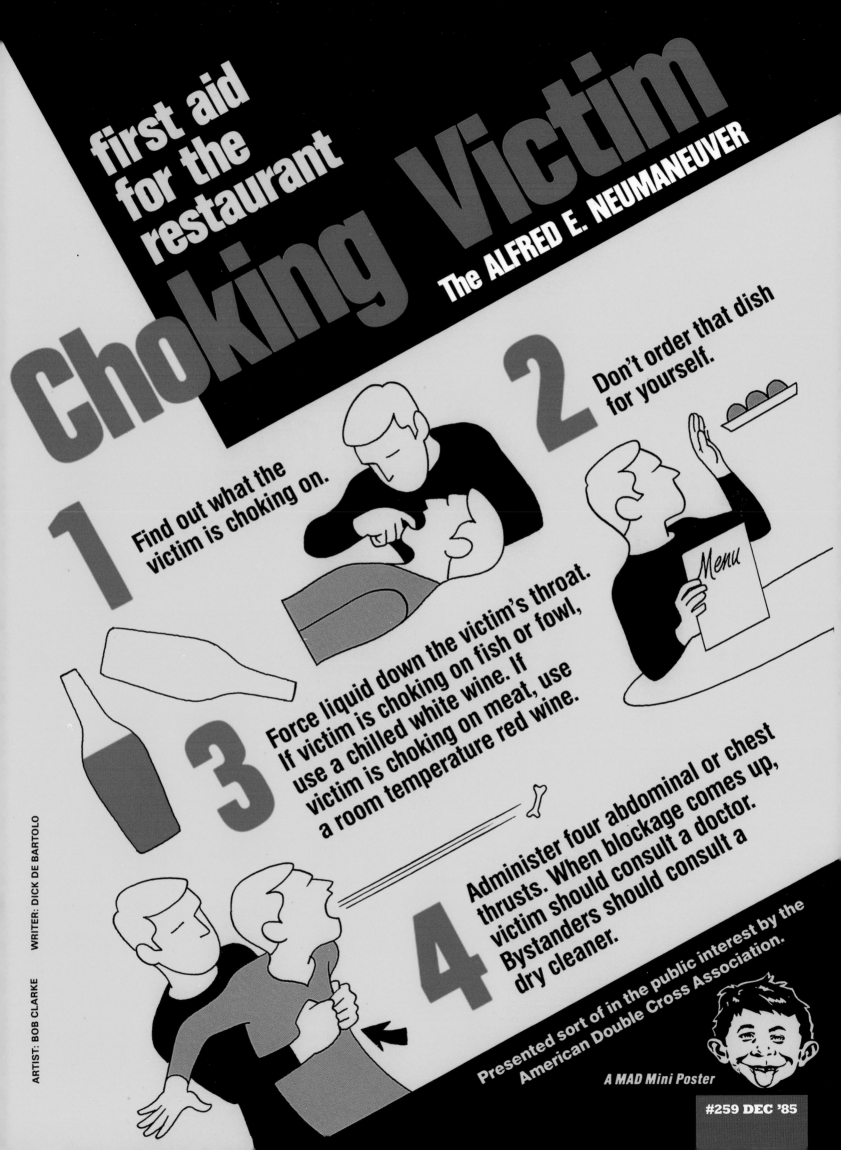

MR. CAFFEINE

"Keeping America Awake For 3 Generations"

Sale Price $39.95
Manufacturer's Rebate... −$10.00
YOUR COST
AFTER REBATE $29.95

For the benefit of those who have been on planet Mars since the decade's latest sales gimmick was born, the ad to the left is <u>not</u> trying to sell you a coffee maker for less than 30 bucks. Rather, it's trying to sell you a coffee maker for considerably more, and then telling you how to get part of your money refunded. Now you may ask why manufacturers just don't lower prices by the amount they seem anxious to give back anyway. The answer? That would <u>really</u> cost them money! But manufacturers figure that by making you go through a time consuming and complex (not to mention annoying!) rigamarole, the odds favor something going awry and they will never have to give any of your money back. Confused? Unconvinced? Then see for yourself as we now expose...

WHY 999 SHOPPERS OUT OF 1,000
NEVER COLLECT THOSE MANUFACTURERS' REBATES

Among 1,000 shoppers chosen at random...

...183 will never get the product at all because they don't realize they have to take enough cash to the store to pay full price, and then engage in a major hassle to try to get some of it back.

Of the remaining 817...

...151 will attempt to get the rebate coupon and will be told that the store has just run out of them—but will not return the purchase price of the item, which has already been paid for.

Of the remaining 666...

... 46 will succeed in getting the coupon, only to find the model they just bought is not the one qualifying for the rebate.

Of the remaining 620...

...12 will be mugged in an alley next to the store and robbed of the product, the rebate coupon, the sales slip and maybe, their shoes.

ARTIST: PAUL COKER   WRITER: TOM KOCH

#264 JUL '86

Of the remaining 608...

...32 will buy more than one product offering a rebate, thus setting the stage for total failure when the coupons get mixed together and are ultimately all mailed to the wrong manufacturers.

Of the remaining 576...

...67 will never know if the date is printed on the register receipt because the lettering is a little too faint for them to read and a lot too faint for the manufacturer to accept.

Of the remaining 239...

...27 will thoughtlessly transpose the manufacturer's post office box number and zip code, resulting in delivery to someone thousands of miles away who has no idea what all those papers are.

Of the remaining 212...

...54 will do an acceptable job in getting all of the correct documents into a properly addressed envelope and then will forget to put a stamp on it before they drop it in a mailbox.

Of the remaining 509...

...40 will permanently install their purchase with its serial number facing the wall before they read that it must be copied onto the rebate application.

Of the remaining 469...

...72 will put the empty box out with the trash, forgetting that the "Proof Of Purchase" label printed on the side of it must also be mailed to the manufacturer.

Of the remaining 158...

...11 will remember to put a stamp on the envelope but then carelessly leave it in their coat pocket when they take the garment to the dry cleaners.

Of the remaining 147...

...9 will prove to be the owners of new puppies that love to chew anything made of paper into tiny little bits—especially the outgoing mail.

Of the remaining 397...

...23 will successfully grab the box back from the trash man, and then discover that they don't know what a "Proof Of Purchase" label looks like.

Of the remaining 374...

...18 will give the product to someone as a gift, and then face the embarrassing job of trying to get the box back to obtain that vital "Proof Of Purchase" label.

Of the remaining 138...

...52 will assume they've mailed their rebate application when they thoughtlessly drop the envelope into a laundry chute, bank depository or public trash can.

Of the remaining 86...

...5 will leave their applications for the mailman, not knowing he's a grump who shows anger over making pickups by stuffing them in a storm-drain.

Of the remaining 356...

...52 will buy a defective product, and then learn their warranty isn't any good unless they return the item with the same sales slip and register receipt they planned to use to collect the rebate.

Of the remaining 304...

...65 will successfully manage to assemble the rebate coupon, proof of purchase label, sales slip and register receipt, only to realize they have no idea where they're supposed to send it.

Of the remaining 81...

...15 will have their application returned through the mail and get the cheery news the manufacturer moved and conveniently forgot to leave a forwarding address.

Of the remaining 66...

...65 will have forgotten about the whole thing before their rebate check arrives six months later and will toss out the unopened envelope, thinking it's an ad.

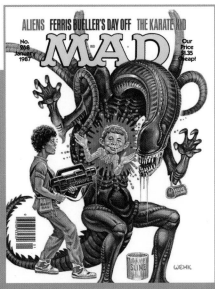

The only time most people are modest is in describing their own faults.

RICH MAN, POE MAN DEPT.

THE REAGAN

(with apologies to Edgar Allan Poe)

ARTIST: GERRY GERSTEN **WRITER: FRANK JACOBS**

Once upon a cold November, back in '80, you'll remember,
Came to pass a great election, with a wondrous change in store;
By a landslide, one was winning, promising a new beginning;
Tall and proud, he stood there, grinning, like so many times before;
Who was he, this cool one, grinning, like so many times before?
'Twas The Reagan, nothing more.

Once he was inaugurated, Reaganomics he created,
Promising a balanced budget, like we had in days of yore;
"Though," he said, "our debt is growing, and a bundle we are owing,
"I'll cut taxes, 'cause I'm knowing this will save us bucks galore;"
"Please explain," a newsman asked, "how this will save us bucks galore?"
Quoth The Reagan, "Less is more."

Pushing for defense, he pleaded, brand-new missiles would be needed:
"That's the only way," he said, "to keep the country out of war;"
"True," he said, "they're not required, and they're not meant to be fired;
"In five years they'll be retired—still we must build hundreds more;"
"Tell us why," a newsman asked, "we must be building hundreds more?"
Quoth The Reagan, " Jobs galore."

Was he real or from a movie? "Make my day" sure sounded groovy,
Standing up to Congress or the rebels in El Salvador;
Flicks like "Rambo" he promoted (sev'ral times, it should be noted);
Once John Wayne he even quoted, when Kaddafi threatened war;
"Does this mean," a newsman asked, "we're heading toward a Mid-East war?"
Quoth The Reagan, "Hit the shore."

During times he wasn't dozing, many plans he was proposing,
Dealing with the deficit, which he no longer could ignore;
"Cuts," he said, "I'm recommending, pending our ascending spending,
"With attending trends suspending, then extending as before."
"Does this mean," a newsman asked, "a balanced budget like before?"
Quoth The Reagan, "Nevermore."

#265 SEP '86

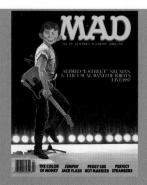

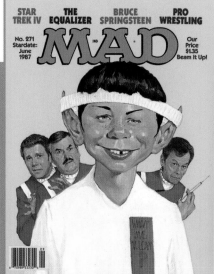

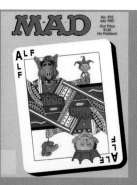

DAILY BREAD DEPT.

A PSALM FOR THE MODERN TELEVISION PREACHER

The Lord is my meal ticket; I shall not starve.

He alloweth me to lie outrageously on TV; He leadeth me beside the rich and powerful.

He restoreth my ratings.

He helpeth me to sell cheap merchandise in His name's sake.

Yea, though I owe a bundle to the I.R.S., I will fear no audit:

For Thy tax shelters and Thy tax exemption, they protect me.

Thou preparest a platform for me to spew bigotry in the presence of mine viewers; Thou swellest my head with ego; my bankbook runneth over.

Surely power and money shall follow me all the days of my life; and I will dwell in my house on Easy Street for ever.

ARTIST: GEORGE WOODBRIDGE   WRITER: BARRY LIEBMANN

TALES FROM THE DUCK SIDE DEPT.

THE DREADED DENTAL DEBACLE

DOCTOR MARROW, JANE CIANCI IS ON THE PHONE AND SHE'S...DOCTOR? DOCTOR MARROW?

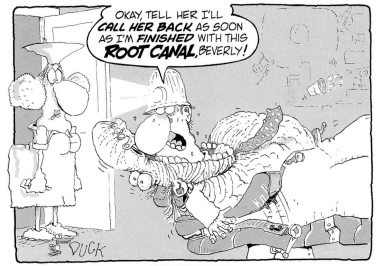

OKAY, TELL HER I'LL CALL HER BACK AS SOON AS I'M FINISHED WITH THIS ROOT CANAL, BEVERLY!

ARTIST AND WRITER: DUCK EDWING

48

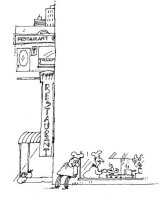

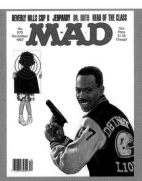

ALFRED E. NEUMAN

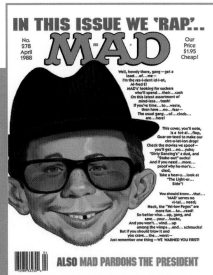

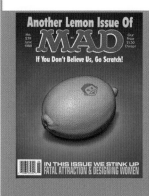

Most storytellers bring a *little* of themselves to the stories they tell. Others bring way to

FAMOUS STORIES AS T

ARTIST: BOB CLARKE

Once upon a time there was an Italian-American named Don Corleone. Mr. Corleone was a successful olive oil importer. He was called Godfather because he was always being asked to be the Godfather of the children of his many friends and employees. The key to Mr. Corleone's success in business was his relationships with his customers. He made them offers they couldn't refuse. When Don Corleone died peacefully in his tomato patch, his son, Michael, inherited the family business.

During the war Michael was a marine and he received many decorations for bravery. But because he was from New York and was of Italian descent, a group of politicians accused this war hero of being involved in something called the "MAFIA." Michael, naturally, was cleared.

He sold the family olive oil business and bought several hotels in Las Vegas. Michael would like his son to go into politics because he wants to prove that any American can be elected to national office, even if his last name ends in a vowel.

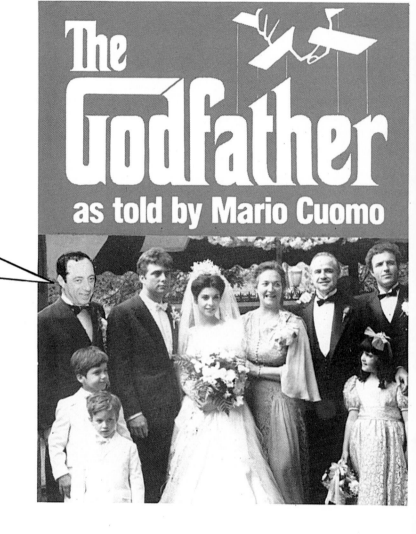

The Godfather
as told by Mario Cuomo

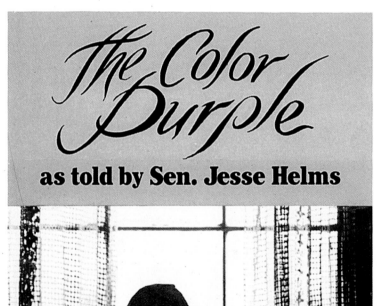

The Color Purple
as told by Sen. Jesse Helms

There was this nigra family livin' in the sovereign state of Georgia. They were your typical colored folks, they was into incest and havin' illegitimate babies and puttin' on airs. For example, the husband, Mister, insisted his wife Celie call him "Mister," when we all know he shoulda been called "Boy."

The nigra women folk used to go to church on Sunday and pray to our white God, which shows you how benevolent He is. Celie's sister, Nettie, went to Africa to be a missionary, which is a fine place for colored folks to go.

Mister treated Celie like a slave, which gets me to thinkin' that maybe the nigras really didn't object to slavery at all. Too bad Lincoln didn't mind his own business. Besides beatin' on his wife, Mister had a few other good points, like he smoked tobacco and we all know that the good Lord gave us tobacco for everybody to enjoy, even blacks!

Celie got into the women's movement thing and of course, she became involved in an unnatural, disgustin' relationship which is what women's lib is all about.

Mister summed it all up by tellin' Celie, "You black, you poor, you ugly and you a woman." Shoot, I couldn't have put it better myself.

much of themselves to the stories they tell. You'll know what we mean after reading these...

OLD BY FAMOUS PEOPLE

WRITER: LOU SILVERSTONE

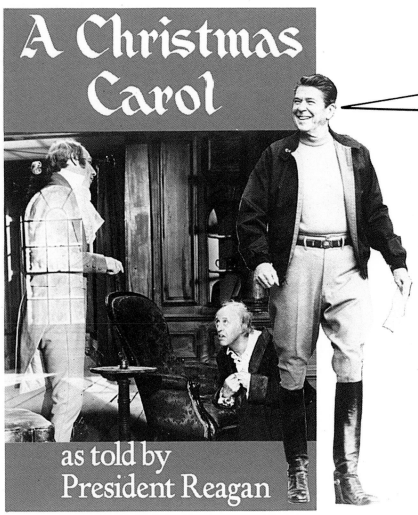

A Christmas Carol
as told by President Reagan

Ebenezer Scrooge was a hard working businessman. He employed Bob Cratchit as a clerk. Cratchit complained constantly. He wanted "more holidays," and "more money." He was always whining about the office being "too cold," and other such nonsense. It never occurred to Cratchit to roll up his sleeves and do an honest day's work or go to night school and pull himself up by his bootstraps. No, it was easier to complain.

When Christmas time came around the Cratchit family blamed Mr. Scrooge because they couldn't afford an elaborate dinner or expensive presents for their children.

On Christmas Eve, Mr. Scrooge had a terrible nightmare. He dreamt he was visited by his dead partner, Marley, and three ghosts. These ghosts, using Marxist-Lenin propaganda techniques, made Mr. Scrooge feel guilty because he was a success and Cratchit was a failure.

Mr. Scrooge allowed his own good fortune to trickle down by buying expensive gifts for the Cratchit children. He treated them to a fancy Christmas dinner and he paid their medical bills. Even though Cratchit received a fair salary, Mr. Scrooge gave him a raise, which only added to the inflationary spiral. I know this sounds familiar, because it's the same principle as our own welfare system—something for nothing—and it just doesn't work.

Well, we can only pray that next Christmas, Mr. Scrooge will be visited by three Conservative ghosts who will show him the error of his ways.

Yankee pride comes right from the top, the team owner. Naturally, Lou Gehrig was a ball player who knew the meaning of Yankee pride. Whether he was hurt or not, Lou played every day. He hit for average, he drove in plenty of runs and hit the long ball. Best of all, Lou's salary was less than I pay my groundskeepers today. Lou never asked to be traded or went crying to the press to complain about the owner. He was my kind of guy.

In many ways, Lou reminds me of myself. Yes, "the Boss" and "the Iron Horse" had a lot in common. Lou Gehrig and George Steinbrenner both had football backgrounds, we both wore our pinstripes with pride, we both knew what loyalty to our fans was all about and we were both proud to be Yankees—New York Yankees. I'm sure if Lou was still with us, he would be proud to be a New Jersey Yankee, if that's the way the ball happens to bounce.

I still get a lump in my throat when I think of Lou Gehrig Day. Yankee Stadium was packed and the owner didn't have to give away free bats or helmets. Now that's what I really call "Pride of the Yankees"!

The Pride Of The Yankees
as told by George Steinbrenner

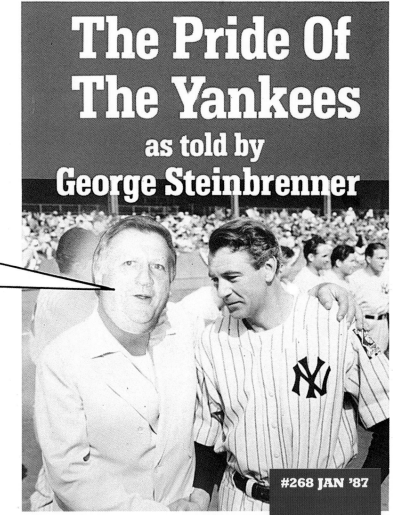

The stupid person says, "It's impossible." The smart person says, "It's possible if we can get enough stupid people to do it.

—Alfred E. Neuman

If you live to 80, you're doing fine. If you live to 90, you've really beaten the odds. However, there are some among us who believe they'll live forever. We're referring to Mr. Clean, Cap'n Crunch and the rest of that copyrighted gang. Well, we've got some news for them! Eventually *everyone* dies, them included! So, to show them what's in store, we've prepared these…

OBITUARIES
For Merchandising Characters

FRED WHIPPLE DIES AT 54

Fred Whipple died today of suffocation after being squeezed to death under a truckload of toilet tissues. He was 54.

Whipple began his career at the Charmin Company as a sheet counter, and later became chief roll inspector and scent supervisor.

"We shall miss him greatly," said a Charmin spokesman. "After all, we have lost our Number Two man."

In accordance with Whipple's last request, his body will be wrapped in 5,000 squeezably soft sheets and placed on permanent display at a local supermarket.

Campbell Kids Die

Boris and Doris Campbell, famed for decades as the Campbell Soup Kids, died today within hours of each other.

Doctors at the scene believe both succumbed to the Smurf Disease, otherwise known as "acute cuteness."

Mr. Clean Dies at 33; Victim of Pollution

Mr. Clean died today after losing a fight with lung cancer. He was 33.

He was a battler to the last," said his son-in-law, Brawny, "but the filthy air and polluted environment were too much for him."

During his final months, the once-muscular Mr. Clean wasted away to a shadow of his robust size. Despite his terminal illness, he poured himself into his work, continuing to attack his sworn enemies, grease, dirt and soot.

"We tried to keep him alive with ammonia transfusions," said a hospital spokesman, "but by then it was hopeless. Still, he fought to the last drop before throwing in the sponge."

In his will, Mr. Clean left his entire estate to the EPA, except for his earring, which he bequeathed to Miss Clairol.

ARTIST: BOB CLARKE
WRITER: FRANK JACOBS

PILLSBURY DOUGHBOY AN APPARENT SUICIDE

Poppin' Fresh, the Pillsbury Doughboy, is dead at 36, a probable suicide. His body was discovered early today in an unattended oven heated to 450° F.

According to a neighbor, Betty Crocker, who identified the body, Fresh had been suffering from depression. "He'd become very silent and withdrawn," Crocker said. "Nobody could get a rise out of him."

It is believed that the Doughboy first became depressed when he realized he hadn't grown an inch in more than 30 years. His outward cheerfulness apparently concealed a deep inferiority complex, which worsened with age.

"He was always so pitifully pale," said Crocker. "Now at least there's some color to him."

Funeral services will be held tomorrow at the Duncan Hines Funeral Home. Mourners may view the body, once it has been frosted.

Ronald McDonald Dies

Ronald McDonald is dead at 19. According to a distant relative, Herb, death was due to over-exposure.

Mr. Goodwrench Dies in Garage Accident

Mr. George Melvin (G.M.) Goodwrench, an auto mechanic, was crushed to death today when an '82 Buick Regal toppled from a faulty hydraulic lift.

According to a garage co-worker, Mr. Goodwrench had a history of being "accident-prone." In 1985, he was hospitalized after his head became entangled in a moving fan-belt. A year earlier, he narrowly survived after being sucked under in a grease pit.

At last report, Mr. Goodwrench's body remained trapped beneath the Buick Regal.

"We're jammed up just now," said a garage spokesman. "We'll get to him just as soon as there's someone available."

Morris the Cat Dies for the Ninth Time

Morris the cat is dead at 23. The famed finicky feline died of starvation following a 38-day, "Liver-or-else!" hunger strike.

According to his veterinarian, Morris had apparently suffered eight previous deaths, but had "miraculously" survived each time. "The ninth was one too many," the doctor said.

A loner to the end, Morris had no close friends. There are several distant cousins—Heathcliff, Garfield, Felix, Tom, Sylvester and Bill, none of whom care to get involved.

#274 OCT '87

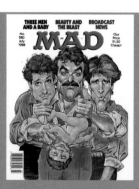
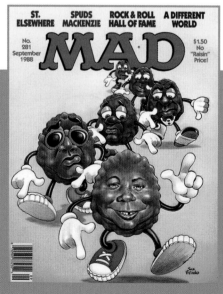

SERGE-IN GENERAL DEPT.

A MAD LOOK AT DISNEY CLASSICS

ARTIST & WRITER: SERGIO ARAGONES

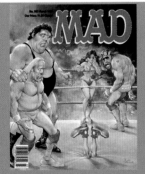

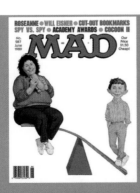

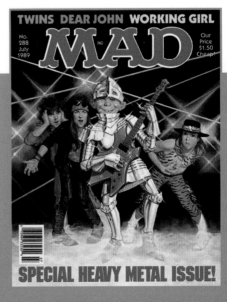

SPECIAL HEAVY METAL ISSUE!

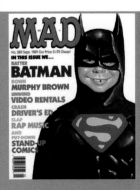

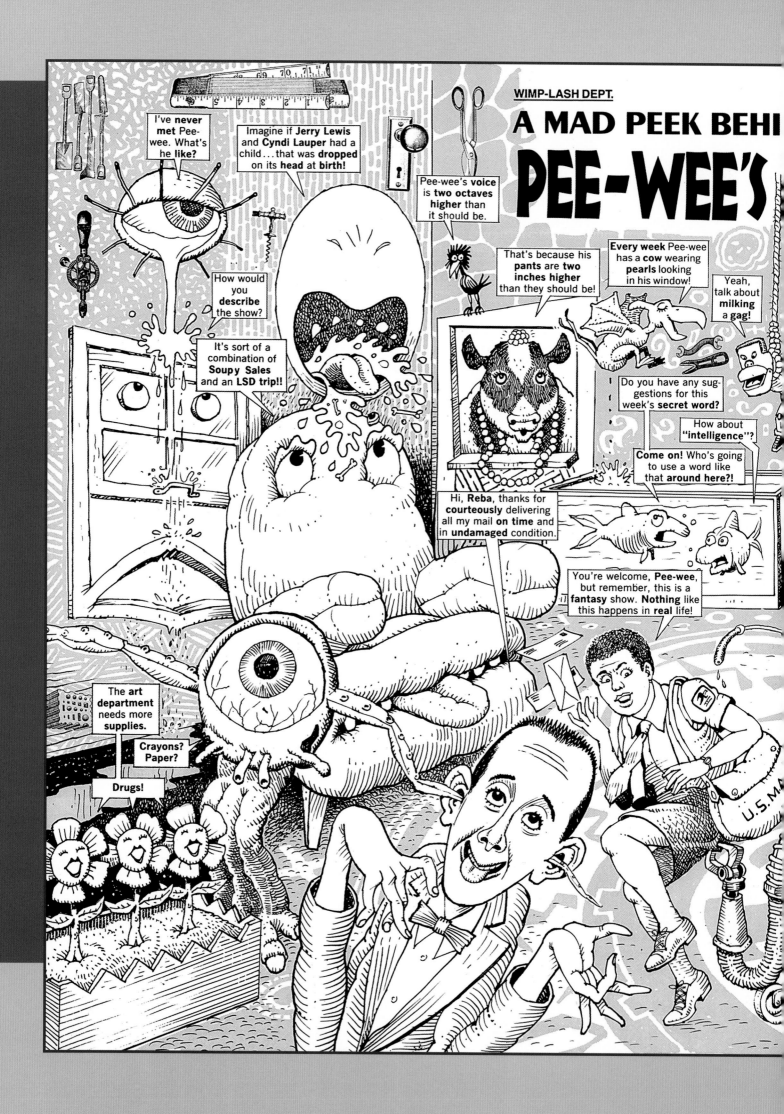

To be a member of the upper crust you need a lot of dough!

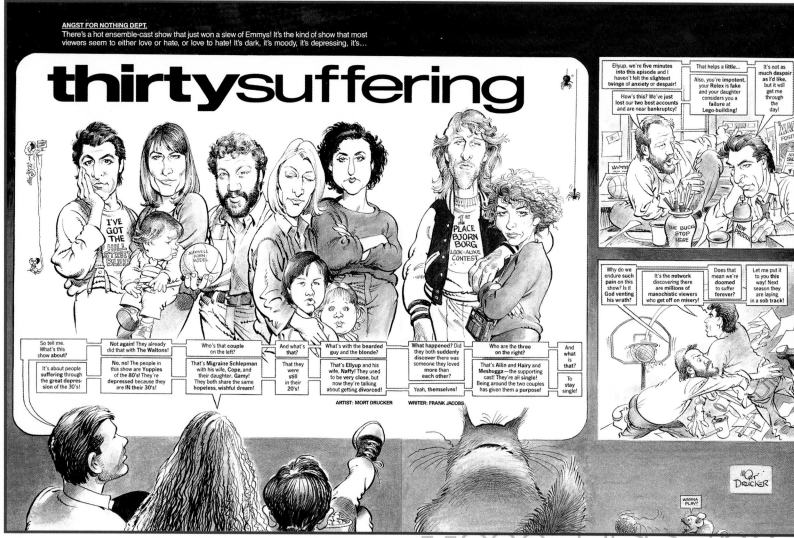

There's a hot ensemble-cast show that just won a slew of Emmys! It's the kind of show that most viewers seem to either love or hate, or love to hate! It's dark, it's moody, it's depressing, it's...

thirtysuffering

So tell me. What's this show about?

It's about people suffering through the great depression of the 30's!

Not again! They already did that with The Waltons!

No, no! The people in this show are Yuppies of the 80's! They're depressed because they are IN their 30's!

Who's that couple on the left?

That's Migraine Schleman with his wife, Cope, and their daughter, Gamy! They both share the same hopeless, wishful dream!

And what's that?

That they were still in their 20's!

What's with the bearded guy and the blonde?

That's Ellyup and his wife, Naffy! They used to be very close, but now they're talking about getting divorced!

What happened? Did they both suddenly discover there was someone they loved more than each other?

Yeah, themselves!

Who are the three on the right?

That's Ailin and Hairy and Meshugga—the supporting cast! They're all single! Being around the two couples has given them a purpose!

And what is that?

To stay single!

ARTIST: MORT DRUCKER   WRITER: FRANK JACOBS

Ellyup, we're five minutes into this episode and I haven't felt the slightest twinge of anxiety or despair!

How's this? We've just lost our two best accounts and are near bankruptcy!

That helps a little...

Also, you're impotent, your Rolex is fake and your daughter considers you a failure at Lego-building!

It's not as much despair as I'd like, but it will get me through the day!

Why do we endure such pain on this show? Is it God venting his wrath?

It's the network discovering there are millions of masochistic viewers who get off on misery!

Does that mean we're doomed to suffer forever?

Let me put it to you this way! Next season they are laying in a sob track!

WANNA PLAY?

#286 APR '89

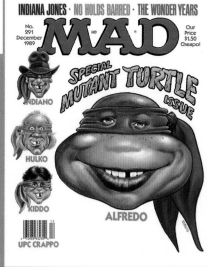

No. 291 December 1989

MAD

Our Price $1.50 Cheapo!

SPECIAL MUTANT TURTLE ISSUE

INDIANO
HULKO
KIDDO
ALFREDO
UPC CRAPPO

No. 290 October 1989

MAD

Our Price: $1.50 Cheap!

IN THIS ISSUE WE SLIME GHOSTBUSTERS II

IN THIS ISSUE WE SMASH... NINTENDO VIDEO GAMES | HONEY I SHRUNK THE KIDS | MARRIED WITH CHILDREN

No. 292 January 1990

MAD

Our Price $1.50 Cheapo!

No. 293 March 1990

MAD

Our Price $1.75 Chilling!

No. 294 April 1990

MAD

Our Price $1.75 Trashy!

In This Issue We Shovel... DOOGIE HOWSER & EMPTY NEST

A SCENE WE'D LIKE TO SEE

EXXON

ANOTHER MAD MINI-POSTER

CHAIRMAN OF THE BOARD
EXXON CORPORATION

PHOTO BY IRVING SCHILD

#290 OCT '89

Whoever said fighting never solves anything obviously never won a fight.

—Alfred E. Neuman

ALONG THE SNIDE LINES DEPT.

Over the years, we here at MAD have discovered that nastiness is actually therapeutic. There's just something about hurling insults at self-satisfied celebrities and foolish fads that soothes the heart and cleanses the soul. No wonder we gleefully look forward to this dangerous moment when we relieve ourselves (mentally, that is) by spewing out...

the MAD NASTY FILE
VOLUME III

ARTIST: GERRY GERSTEN   WRITER: TOM KOCH

HULK HOGAN

...enables us to show the Iranians that our country can produce raving lunatics, too.

...markets a Hulk Hogan Doll that's an exact replica of himself—except it's smarter.

...made wrestling his career because he was afraid to take his chances in a competitive sport.

DAVID LETTERMAN

...avoids putting viewers to sleep by coming on the air after they're already asleep.

...may be the funniest man to come from Indianapolis since John Dillinger.

...smokes big, smelly cigars, but relies chiefly on his personality to drive people away.

#282 OCT '88

GOLD MEDDLING DEPT.

Ever since the first modern Olympics were held in Athens in 1896,* politics has intruded into what is supposed to be a celebration of individual athletic achievement. What do we at MAD think can be done about this travesty? NOTHING! C'mon, Olympic Organizing Committee, get off your high horse! It's time to admit there's not a thing you can do to keep politics out of the Games! You might as well welcome it in with open arms by introducing these...

POLITICALLY INSPIRED OLYMPIC EVENTS

ARTIST: BOB JONES   WRITER: MIKE SNIDER

OLYMPIC BOYCOTTING

Since "not showing up" has become such a popular feature of the Games (The U.S. in '80, the Soviets in '84)—why not turn it into an event? Judges will award points for: Best-sounding excuse for staying away; number of other countries the boycotting nation pressures into staying away; and most effective silencing of whiny athletes who think sports and politics don't mix. A money-saving event, since none of the winners will be present to get their medals!

PERSIAN GULF MINE-DODGING

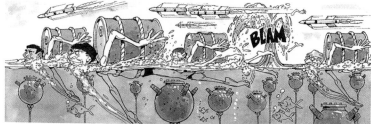

In this event, competing teams of international swimmers strap 50-gallon oil drums to their backs and swim through the mine-infested waters of the Straight of Hormuz. Points are awarded for speed, style and total number of Silkworm missiles avoided.

*See? Who says MAD isn't educational!

#283 DEC '88

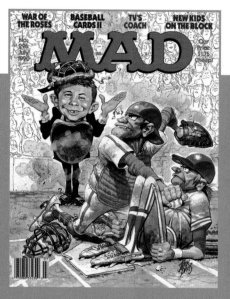

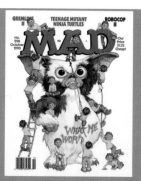

140

GAG REFLECTS DEPT.

Used to be a joke had two parts: the set-up and the punchline. Not with today's comedians! To see what we mean, just imagine...

IF DIFFERENT COMEDIANS TOLD THE SAME JOKE

(There's a fly in my soup...)

ARTIST: MORT DRUCKER   WRITER: RUSS COOPER

ROBIN WILLIAMS

What's this fly doing in my soup? Wow! Fly in my soup? What a concept! (*Peter Lorre voice*) Oooh myyy! Tere's a flyyy een my sooop, massster! (*Herve Villechaize voice*) Ze fly, Boss! Ze fly! (*Elmer Fudd voice*) Kill du fwy...Kill duh fwwwy... (*Regular voice*) Fly in my soup! I want to DIE! (*High-pitched voice, as in the movie "The Fly"*) Help me! Help meee! (*Liz Taylor voice*) There's a what in my soup..? A fly? Only one? (*Panicky voice*) BEEP BEEP! MAYDAY! MAYDAY! (*Unintelligible*) I mean...it's crazy... fly in my soup... I mean, it's like Nancy Reagan on steroids! Just say NO! (*Incoherent babbling*)

DAVID LETTERMAN

But you know...Ye-ah! What's next? What are we doin'? Oh, a joke? Do we have time for this, Paul? Hey, Paul...are you paying attention, Paul? Should we do this one or not? It's up to you, Paul. (*Audience groans, annoyed*) Okay... Uh oh! (*Goes bug-eyed*) I been hyp-mo-tized!! Don't know why I said that, I just like saying the word "hyp-mo-tized." Ye-ah! But you know... (*silence*) Did you hear that, Paul? Silence. Sort of a "comedy lull"...We're just coasting, right Paul? A little breather between jokes. Just saving our energy for the...you know, Paul, I went to a restaurant the other day, don't want to name the restaurant, but it was (*NBC lawyers bleep out name*), and I don't want to say anything, just...don't order the soup, okay? That's all I'm saying. So here he is, you know him, you love him...

RODNEY DANGERFIELD

Hoo...heh...I'm tellin' ya...Went to a restaurant. Tough place, really tough...the black-eyed peas had real black eyes! (*Tugs on tie, rolls eyes, starts to perspire*) I asked the waiter what was on the menu. He said he thought it was tomato sauce...Like I tell ya, I get no respect. (*Thunderous applause*) I asked for the chicken soup. Big mistake. There was a fly in it. (*Yanks tie, eyes bulge, sweats heavily*) I asked the waiter why there was a fly in my soup. He said it wasn't a fly, it was a very small chicken... No respect, no respect at all. (*Wrenches tie, eyes spin wildly, sweat sprays onto audience*)

SAM KINISON

Yeah...I went to this restaurant the other day...ordered some soup...there was a fly in it. Waiter asks me what's wrong. I say, "Oooooh, nothing. Just that there's this FLY IN MY SOUP! I CAN'T BELIEVE IT! A FLY IN MY SOUP!!! AAARRGHGHGH! I'm sorry if I seem a little upset, but excuse me if I'd rather not be served a meal with LIVE MEMBERS OF THE ANIMAL KINGDOM SWIMMING AROUND IN IT! AARRRRGHGHGH! Call me crazy, but if I wanted to consume insects as part of my daily diet I'D GET MARRIED AGAIN! I WAS IN 'NAM! I WAS MARRIED FOR TWO YEARS! I WAS A HOSTAGE IN HELL FOR TWENTY-FOUR MONTHS! AAARRRGHGHGH-GHGHGH!" Thank you. You've been great.

GEORGE CARLIN

Went to a restaurant...weird, man. Got a fly in my soup. Why do they call flies "flies," man? Ever wonder? I mean birds fly too, right? The weird thing is that flies don't fly that much. The flies I see, they crawl all the time. (*New York voice*) "Gee, Martha, dere's a crawl in my soup." Why do they call fleas "fleas"? What are they running from? Are they fleeing the soup? Then don't order scary soup, man...After all, what is soup but just a bowl of wet food...right? I don't trust soup anyway. Soup is food right before you throw it away... Soup is food's last chance to get eaten...I figure, if it ain't been eaten by now, let the flies have it, man! (*Makes a real goofy face, then leaves stage*)

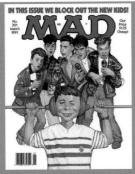

Remember the movie "Saturday Night Fever" starring **What's-his-name?** It was about **dancing!** No? Hmm…

How about "**Flashdance**," that movie about **dancing** starring that girl who wasn't a good dancer so they had to use a **stand-in** for her? You remember **that**, don't you?

Ah hah! A glimmer of recognition flickers in your otherwise dull, uncomprehending eyes! Well, you can bet your twine collection the people who made **this** movie remember!

It's so nice to go to a place where they serve you **three meals a day!**

Not if they're served at the same time!

Our socially conscious daughter thinks we should send this food to **starving Asians!**

We'd also have to send the **Marines** to **make them eat it!**

I think the folks **baby** you too much!

Yeah! But it's getting **better!** Last week I was finally taken off **breast feeding!**

What do you get with the **breakfast special?**

Gas!

This is such a corny, **1940-ish** type picture!

ARTIST: MORT DRUCKER

What are **you** doing here? Guests aren't allowed at **staff parties!** Get lost!

Just who do you think you're talking to?

Judging by your **profile**, I'd say **Barbra Streisand's daughter!**

CLICHÉ!: Rich girl meets boy from the wrong side of the tracks…

Bubbie, you have to concentrate on the **music!** That's all that matters! You have to **feel** the **music** and **nothing else!**

Not even your **hand** on my **tush?**

Not if you want to **lose** your **inhibitions!**

I think I'm going to lose **more** than my **inhibitions** before **this** dance is over!

CLICHÉ!: Repressed virgin discovers her sexuality…

So much so that they took **every lousy cliché** from **those two** and **every other dancing film ever made** and stitched them together to make **this** forgettable fiasco!

In fact, there are so many clichés here that we had to use a **special computer** to keep track of them!

Well, folks, that does it for my **opening monologue**! In the actual movie, my voice-over begins the film, then **leaves** and **never returns**! If the **audience** was **smart**, it would do the **same thing**! Mad readers have the same option—keep reading or pass right by...

Dancing

That's why it's back in the 60's! That way the picture is only **20 years** out of date! If it was in the 1980's it would've been **40 years** out of date!

The waiters here are all **college men**! That one is studying to be a **lawyer** and that one is studying to be an **engineer**...

You need a fork? **Call my service**! I don't make **table calls**!

Hmmm, it's **obvious** what this one's **studying to be**!

It's your job to fool the guests into believing they're having a **good time**! Dance with their ugly wives and daughters, or else you're **fired**!

Gee, Max makes me **feel good**!

Really? Are you an **employee**?

No—an **anti-semite**!

WRITER: STAN HART

Johnny, what am I going to do? I'm **pregnant**!

Don't worry, Pinhead! I wouldn't let **anything bad** happen to you!

I think you're a **little late** with **that promise**!

CLICHÉ!: The kindness of the less fortunate working class towards one another...

Bubbie, if I go for an **abortion**, I won't be able to dance with Johnny in the big **dance exhibition** next Saturday!

I can **take your place**!

No, I think I'd better go for the abortion **myself**!

I mean the **dance exhibition**, dummy!

Oh, yeah!

CLICHÉ!: Amateur steps in to perform for the ailing professional...

What Were the MAD Trips?
□ By Frank Jacobs

By 1960, MAD had become an oddball national institution, and Bill Gaines wanted to keep it that way. His method was to create what came to be the MAD Family, made up of the editorial staff, steady contributors, even the magazine's attorneys and accountant. The glue that held the group together was the annual MAD trip. Many of the writers and artists had never met. What better way for everyone to get to know their brethren than to fly them, all expenses paid, for a week or two in a foreign clime? These vacations, with their anticipations and memories, would knot the family ties even tighter. Especially if the trips were stag.

"I never met two wives who could get along with each other," Gaines said at the time. "Bringing wives on the trips would divide the convivial MAD group into cliques. The wives would spend so much on clothing trying to outdo each other that it would cost the boys a fortune, and I can't see any point to that."

Two of the magazine's mainstays, editor Al Feldstein and illustrator Mort Drucker, passed up the trips because of the all-male edict. The other MADmen accepted readily, eager to get a break from the typewriter and drawing-board. Skeptics might point out that Gaines, divorced at the time, was not burdened with the problem of leaving a wife at home. It would take 20 years before the stag rule was relaxed.

The first trip took the travelers to Haiti, one of Gaines' favorite watering holes. The tone was set the first day. Discovering that the magazine had one subscriber in Port-au-Prince, Gaines piled his charges into five Jeeps, drove to the lad's home, and presented him with a renewal card.

The next four trips were to the Caribbean, but Gaines was not happy. The West Indies bored him — especially Puerto Rico, where he spent most of his days reading and napping in his room or ordering a snack on the shaded terrace. Occasionally, in a neighborly gesture, he would tread cautiously across the beach to where the rest of the MADmen were sunning. After a few pleasantries, he would shuffle back to the hotel, relieved to be away from the sun and surf and the picture of grown men actually enjoying the stuff — sometimes, even, exercising in it.

> Gaines took the group to every continent save Australia and Antarctica, 27 trips in all.

There were better places to go with better things to see and better food to eat, and in the fall of 1966 Gaines loosened his belt and took the group to Paris, and then to Surinam, Italy, Kenya, Athens, Japan, London, Copenhagen, and the Soviet Union — to every continent save Australia and Antarctica, 27 trips in all.

The tone was set early on. In Florence, the vacationers were grouped on the steps of the Duomo Cathedral when a shouting parade of striking local laborers stampeded by. In the middle of the marchers, carrying an appropriated picket sign with his clenched fist raised high, was Sergio Aragonés.

In Venice, Nick Meglin scrutinized his admission ticket to the Palace of the Doges. "What does it say?" he was asked. "It says," answered Meglin, "you may have already won this palace." At the Vatican, Dick DeBartolo looked at the opulence and remarked, "God isn't dead. He just can't afford the rent."

In Moscow, Gaines was continually stared at by the local populace. At first it was thought that this was because of his beard and massive mop of hair. It was later learned, however,

MAD's "Usual Gang of Idiots" on vacation in Tahiti, 1974.

that to Muscovite eyes, at least, Gaines resembled Karl Marx. The abundance of beards in the travelers prompted one observer to remark that the MAD gang looked like a road company of Benjamin Harrison's cabinet.

Gaines himself climbed — yes, climbed — to the top of the Leaning Tower of Pisa and there placed an "Alfred E. Neuman for President" poster. It was rumored, but not confirmed, that the tower leaned an inch or two more after that.

After landing in Leningrad, a customs inspector searched for any type of pornography. Staffer Jerry De Fuccio, who was carrying no pornography, expected no complications.

"What are those?" the inspector asked.

"15 copies of MAD magazine," De Fuccio answered.

The inspector leafed through a copy, then summoned another inspector. They scrutinized the magazine. They did not laugh. They did not smile. They confiscated all 15 copies.

Gaines chatted with the editors of the Soviet humor magazine Krokodil and told them that he had occasionally been labeled a Communist.

"But of course I'm not a Communist," Gaines said.

"With your circulation, I wouldn't think you would be," one of the Krokodil editors said.

The most gregarious of the MADmen was Aragonés, whose curiosity and spirit of adventure seldom flagged. In Kenya, he mastered in a day or two enough Swahili to be able to converse, albeit in halting phrases, with the drivers in their native tongue. In Italy, he took over the microphone from the guide on the bus and gave an impromptu, thoroughly inaccurate description

of Ravenna. In Tokyo, he infiltrated tours of Asians who were posing in group photos. As a result, the beaming face of Aragonés remains a towering presence in the vacation scrapbooks of several hundred puzzled Asiatics.

In a French village, the travelers were lunching with local residents. Writer-cartoonist Duck Edwing stood up and made a startling announcement regarding MAD's Dave Berg.

"Seated here," declared Edwing, "is former sergeant Dave Berg, who saved this village when he single-handedly wiped out a nest of Nazi machine guns."

The villagers cheered and applauded, drowning out the laughter of the MADmen, who knew that Edwing's speech was a total fabrication. Berg himself was nonplussed and bewildered and remained silent. He actually had served in World War II as an infantryman — in the Pacific.

Gaines was addicted to the films of the Marx Brothers. On the only MAD trip that took place on a cruise ship, Edwing and DeBartolo sought to replicate, at Gaines' expense, the crowded cabin scene from *A Night at the Opera*.

The prank required considerable planning. Gaines, thanks to his wife Annie, in on the ruse, was relaxing in his underwear. Then entered, one after another, assorted MADmen (and by now, women), maintenance engineers, waiters bearing trays of food and drink, cleaning ladies, ship's officers, in all about 30 people. As the cabin filled up, Gaines soon caught on. It may have been his favorite moment of all the MAD trips.

It was also his last. After his death in 1992, a final trip took place a year later. Some looked on it as a memorial, but it was little more than that. Something was missing, and everyone knew what it was.

Gaines, visible here before his cruise ship stateroom filled to overflowing, Marx Brothers-style.

I'm Will the Thrill,..the Strat-ford..ace,
So better lis-ten..up good, 'cause I'm in..your..face;
The play's..the..thing, but they tell me, a-las,
That you clods fall asleep reading mine..in..class;
Well, I just..found..out what the world..en-joys,
So I've borrowed..this..beat from the Beast-ie Boys;
Is this..a..rap-per..that..you..see?
Gadzooks! Sure is, because the rap's..on..me!
I'm the noblest show-man..of..them..all,
And I've given..my..gigs an o-ver-haul;
Yea, the game's a-foot, and all the world's..a..stage
For the sound and the fury of this hot..new..rage;
A bard should be made of..stern-er..stuff,
So get up..to..date and Rap On,..Mac-Duff!
As…

Mad Raps Up Shakespeare

ARTIST: GEORGE WOODBRIDGE   **WRITER: FRANK JACOBS**

#300 JAN '91

146

The SOLILOQUY RAP from "HAMLET"

So what do I do when life's..a..bitch?
Should I be or not be—I don't..know..which!
Now you may..be..thinkin' I've gone..insane,
But you're lookin' at one mel-an-chol-y..Dane;
If I packed..it..in, I'd get lots..of..Z's;
And I wouldn't have to..worry what this cas-tle..cost;
Or 'bout losin'..my..teeth because I nev-er flossed;
There's just..one..hang-up that bugs..me,..bub—
I could wind up dreamin', and there's..the..rub;
Bein' dead..or alive—either way..I'm..screwed;
As you plainly can..see, I'm one mixed-up..dude!

The BATTLEFIELD RAP from "RICHARD III"

A horse! A horse! I need..one..bad!
And I know it's too late to place..an..ad;
A horse! A horse! That's all..I..need;
I'd swap..my..throne for a slightly used..steed,
Or a broken-down nag that pulls..a..plow;
I'd even con-sid-er a juiced-up..cow,
Or, fail-ing..that, a sheep..will..do;
I'd even look kindly on a kang-a-roo,
Or an ox or a camel or a slimmed-down..yak
Or a very large woman with a good..strong..back;
If I've nothing..to..ride, you have..my..word
You can say..good-bye to Richard..the Third!

The BALCONY RAP from "ROMEO AND JULIET"

Juliet baby, you're chill,..you're..rad!
If we got to-geth-er, we could make..it..bad!

Romeo honey, you've a real..smooth..line;
So what's the story—your place..or..mine?

Not so fast there, sweetie—let's..not..forget
I'm a Mon-ta-gue,..you're a Cap-u-let;

You're the Number One stud in this wack-wack..town!
Let's get..it..on before our bods..cool..down!

Both families hate the oth-er's..guts;
If we tied..the..knot, they'd all..go..nuts!

If it busts..their..chops, they all..can..choke!
So hear..me..good—I ain't blow-in'..smoke!

You know that we'll wind..up..dead,..of..course;

Well, dying's..no..kick,..but it beats..di-vorce!

MARC ANTONY'S FUNERAL RAP from "JULIUS CAESAR"

Hey, friends and Romans, Big Julie's been..hit,
So clean out..your..ears while I do..my..bit;
He was one..tough..dude—the town's..top..gun,
And for years in the charts was Num-ber..One;
But Brutus and his gang..said, "We'll wax..the..schmuck,"
So they took..a..stab and Big Julie..got..stuck;
Now I wantcha..to..know that they're sweet-ie..pies,
Even though some peo-ple think oth-er-wise;
Sure they did..Big Julie, a-gain and a-gain,
But we know..the..swine are honor'ble men;
No, they're not..the..kind that we should..con-demn,
Though you wouldn't want your sis-ters to mar-ry..them;
And I'm not sug-gest-ing that you wax..them,..too,
Even though it might..seem like the thing..to..do;
But if..you..should, and the rats..all..die,
If you need a new boss, then I'm..your..guy!

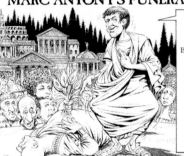

All right boys and girls, settle down now, it's time for your lesson! Biff, stop talking! Ann, take the gum out of your mouth! Tommy, put your .44 caliber pistol away! It's time to learn the ABCs, that is...

The ABC's of ROCK

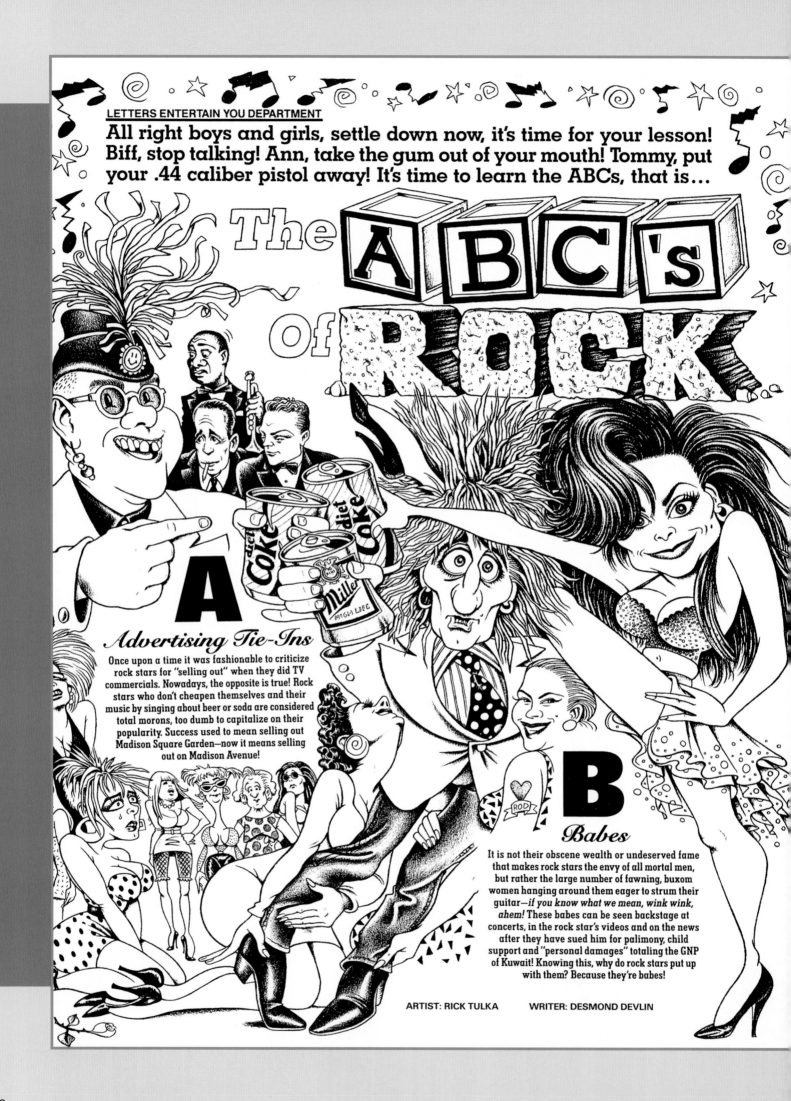

A
Advertising Tie-Ins

Once upon a time it was fashionable to criticize rock stars for "selling out" when they did TV commercials. Nowadays, the opposite is true! Rock stars who don't cheapen themselves and their music by singing about beer or soda are considered total morons, too dumb to capitalize on their popularity. Success used to mean selling out Madison Square Garden—now it means selling out on Madison Avenue!

B
Babes

It is not their obscene wealth or undeserved fame that makes rock stars the envy of all mortal men, but rather the large number of fawning, buxom women hanging around them eager to strum their guitar—*if you know what we mean, wink wink, ahem!* These babes can be seen backstage at concerts, in the rock star's videos and on the news after they have sued him for palimony, child support and "personal damages" totaling the GNP of Kuwait! Knowing this, why do rock stars put up with them? Because they're babes!

ARTIST: RICK TULKA   WRITER: DESMOND DEVLIN

C

Charity Projects

Rock stars are quick to align themselves with worthy causes. Is it because they are deeply concerned about the happiness of others? No! If they were, they wouldn't torture us with barf-inducing, sappy anthems like "We Are The World"! Rockers do it for the press! No critic would dare blast such a "noble song"—and let's face it, it can't hurt sales of their next CD either!

D

Double Albums

Releasing a double album tells the world a rock star's truly got something to say, like, "I want to charge $22.95 for a CD!" True, by throwing in every unfinished demo and six minute drum solo they have they can't promise high quality—but hey, high **quantity** is the next best thing! Loyal fans will call them "prolific geniuses," while their bankers will call them "sir"! (For more information, see "Extra CD Tracks")

E

Extra CD Tracks

Rock stars love CDs! This innovative modern technology allows them to force fans to forgo the lower-priced cassette and pay more! They justify this by slapping one or two extra songs on the CD that are so crummy they've been too embarrassed to release them. Now, of course, they call 'em "bonus tracks"—but you don't have to be Stephen Hawking to figure out who's getting the bonus!

F

Farewell Tours

Used to be when a rock group's career dried up they'd just disband and go away. Not anymore! Hitting the road for "one last hurrah" is a proven method for awakening feelings of nostalgia in fans, even if the band is reprehensible! Of course, "saying farewell" sets the stage for the band to reunite two weeks after they're "gone" for— you guessed it—a "Comeback Tour"!

G

Going Solo

When the lead singer of a popular group starts believing he or she is a genius, or that their "marginally talented" cronies are keeping them from superstardom, they try making it on their own. With dollar signs in their eyes (and a full time roadie to carry their egos!), they insist they're doing it for their "artistic development." A few succeed; however most discover there's a direct correlation between going solo and going broke!

H

Hidden Messages

After much debate, no one is really sure whether rock music contains dangerous subliminal messages (No one except Charles Manson!) In the '60s these hidden voices were said to be telling listeners to make a pact with the devil or take drugs. If there are voices, these days they would more likely be saying, "Tipper Gore is a ninny!"

On TV, there is a regular gathering of weird-looking, unworldly, strange and misshapen people we should be thankful we never have to meet face to face. But enough about the McLaughlin Group! The weird and misshapen people we're talking about are the crew on…

I'm **Captain Crisco**, Commander of the space station **Deep Space Swine!** My mission is **twofold!** First, to **assist** the Bon Jourans in **rebuilding** their **world!** It was **torn apart** by 50 years of rule by the hostile **Cardigans!** I've already had a **pot luck dinner** in their behalf and I'm holding a **flea market** on Friday, so things are moving along nicely! The **second part** of my mission is even **more important!** To build a network of **intergalactic toll booths** so Starfleece can **charge** other life forms **big bucks** to use the **mole hole** space shortcut!

I'm **Major Nerds**, a Bon Jouran! My race **excels** in **sophisticated communications, advanced navigation** and **universal languages!** As a matter of fact my race excels in **just about** everything **but plastic surgery**, as you can **tell** from my **botched-up nose job!**

I'm **Mules O'Brain**, the engineer on **Deep Space Swine!** This is one of the **oldest** space stations in operation! **How old is it? So old** that we can't even **generate** our own **power!** We're **plugged in** back on **earth!** But **at least** we can **boast** that we have the **world's largest extension cord!**

You know who I **don't see** here? **Constable Odor**, the **alien** who can **alter his shape** and turn himself into **anything he wants!**

I'm **here!** And **loving every minute** of it! I hope she **never gets up!**

I **married** one of the **women** from the **fantasy deck** and I just **found out** today that she's a **machine!**

What **clued you in?**

I just became the **father** of a bouncing **baby blender!**

STAR BLECCH
DEEP SPACE SWINE

ARTIST: MORT DRUCKER   WRITER: DICK DEBARTOLO

I'm **Quirk**, a **Ferengi** kind of guy who runs the bar! People come in here, have a drink of **Druzzle-Up** and tell me their **problems**! I'm a **good listener**, and with **these ears** I can listen to about **15** or **20** customers at a time—and not miss **a word**!

I'm **Doctor Flasher**! Medicine in the **24th Century** has **advanced tremendously**! It's no more "take two aspirins and call me in the morning." Now it's "take two *dymen-hydro-pullziums* and *beep my communicator at 0700!*"

IT'S A RAID!

I'm **Lieutenant Fax**! I have the **body** of a **young woman** and the **brain** of a **200 year-old man**, which creates a **terrible problem**! My **body** has **desires** but my **mind forgets** what to do about them!

I'm **Jerk**, Captain Crisco's son! But you can **forget about me**, just like the **producers** did after the two hour **pilot episode**! Hopefully they're **saving me** for yet **ANOTHER** spin-off!

THE FRUGIES™ ARE COMING!

I HAVE A SON WHO IS SPACED OUT.

Space Cat

This **joint** serves the best **cat stew** in the galaxy!

Of all the **outer space gin joints**, in **all the galaxies**, in **all the universe**, why did they have to **rip off** our bar scene from **Star Bores**?

Of **all the lines**, in **all the movies**, in **all the world**, why did **YOU** have to **rip off** my **best line** from **Casablanca**?

RICK'S

#321 SEP '93

Haste makes waste, but at least it does so quickly.

Tens of thousands of kiddies have grown up reading about Babar, the king of the land of the elephants. Babar lives in a kinder, gentler world where everything turns out for the best for the elephants and their friends. Yet who knows? Maybe one day they'll have to deal with the not-so-kind, not-so-gentle real world, and we'll have to read

BABAR'S
FINAL ADVENTURE

ARTIST: BOB CLARKE   WRITER: FRANK JACOBS

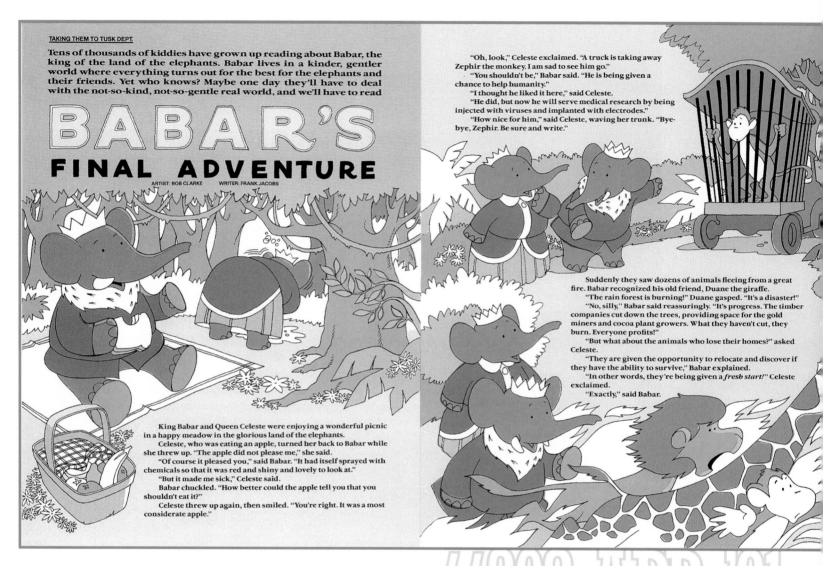

King Babar and Queen Celeste were enjoying a wonderful picnic in a happy meadow in the glorious land of the elephants.

Celeste, who was eating an apple, turned her back to Babar while she threw up. "The apple did not please me," she said.

"Of course it pleased you," said Babar. "It had itself sprayed with chemicals so that it was red and shiny and lovely to look at."

"But it made me sick," Celeste said.

Babar chuckled. "How better could the apple tell you that you shouldn't eat it?"

Celeste threw up again, then smiled. "You're right. It was a most considerate apple."

"Oh, look," Celeste exclaimed. "A truck is taking away Zephir the monkey. I am sad to see him go."

"You shouldn't be," Babar said. "He is being given a chance to help humanity."

"I thought he liked it here," said Celeste.

"He did, but now he will serve medical research by being injected with viruses and implanted with electrodes."

"How nice for him," said Celeste, waving her trunk. "Bye-bye, Zephir. Be sure and write."

Suddenly they saw dozens of animals fleeing from a great fire. Babar recognized his old friend, Duane the giraffe.

"The rain forest is burning!" Duane gasped. "It's a disaster!"

"No, silly," Babar said reassuringly. "It's progress. The timber companies cut down the trees, providing space for the gold miners and cocoa plant growers. What they haven't cut, they burn. Everyone profits!"

"But what about the animals who lose their homes?" asked Celeste.

"They are given the opportunity to relocate and discover if they have the ability to survive," Babar explained.

"In other words, they're being given a *fresh start!*" Celeste exclaimed.

"Exactly," said Babar.

#302 APR '91

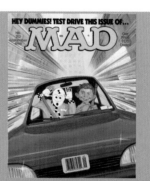

A WOK ON THE WILD SIDE DEPT.

50 lbs. white rice with every order

THE BELCHING DRAGON

Free can soda with orders over $100.00

CHINESE FOOD to EAT IN or TAKE OUT

SOUPS

Dropped Egg Soup 1.75
One Ton Soup 1.75
Hot & Scalding Soup ★ 2.25
Ten Ingredients Water 3.25
Sweet and Salmonella Soup 2.95
Chinese Fire Drill Soup 2.50
Happy Bacteria Cup 2.50

APPETIZERS

Steam-Cleaned Dumplings 3.95
Burn Your Tongue Platter 8.95
Barbecued Bear Ribs 6.30
Scallion Cow Pancakes (for two) 2.95
MSG with Orange Flavor ★ 4.95

NOODLES

Cellophane Noodles with
  Styrofoam Peanuts 5.50
Cold Noodles in Sesame Waste 3.50
Some Glum Noodles 8.25
No Fun Noodles 4.75

PORK

New Shoe Pork 6.75
Roasted Pork in Shriner Hat 6.95
Recently Shampooed Pork 6.95
Andrew Diced Pork 9.75
Roast Pork Puppy Chow ★ 7.25
Porky Pig Cartoonese Style 7.50
Pork And Mindy 6.75

★ **May Not Be Edible**

VEGETABLES

Broccoli in Human Sauce 5.95
Shredded Documents with Peking Sauce ..5.25
Bean Crud with Special Rotting Fungus ..6.25
Snow Shovel with Peas 7.75
Egg Neil Young 4.95
Green Beans with Black Bean Sauce ..4.95
Black Beans with Green Bean Sauce ..5.95
Eggplant Prepared Under
  Mysterious Circumstances.........5.95
Baby Corn with Adoption Papers ★ ..4.95
Vegetables with Tingling Horse Flavor ..5.50

POULTRY

San Diego Chicken with Pine Tar 6.25
Battering Ram Chicken 6.25
Peeking Daffy Duck 7.50
Lemon Pledge Chicken 6.25
Amazing Talking Chicken 8.75
Tongue Licked Duck ★ 7.50
Chicken & Grief 6.25
Duck Edwing Prepared in
  Questionable Taste 6.25
Chicken Escaping With Wings 7.75
Mocked Duck 7.25
General Schwarzkopf Chicken 6.75
Goofy Grinning Chicken 6.75
Innocent Bystander Chicken 6.25
Moo Goo Guy Williams 8.75
Moo Goo Guy Molinari ★ 8.25
Moo Goo Guy Pan & Teller
  In Disappearing Sauce 4.50

BEEF

Air-Dropped Beef 6.85
Double Chin Beef 6.85
Beef with More Beef 7.75
Carnage of Beef 6.85
Sizzling Wanton Beef 6.85
Beef And Dried Pepper
  Spilled on Lap 9.25
Beef with Bad News 8.85
Great Barrier Beef ★ 6.85
What's Your Beef 7.25

SEAFOOD

Squished Eel Delight 8.50
Shrimp with Alibi ★ 8.25
Young Dead Fish 9.25
Crispy Fish with Discarded Needle ...9.95
Prawns in L.L. Bean Sauce 7.50
Aromatic Octopus On Wheels 10.50
Force Fed Shrimp 7.75
Flounder with Water Pistol ★ 8.95

DESSERTS

Unfortunate Cookies 2.50
Sweet Fried Rolaids 3.95
Ice Cream with Garlic Sauce 2.75
Boneless Pudding ★ 3.50
Chicken Almond Ring Ding..........3.95

ARTIST: GEORGE WOODBRIDGE

CHEF'S SPECIALS

 ★
Sesame Street Duck...........11.75
*Choice chunks of undernourished fowl
pelted with waterchestnuts and stir-fried
in a sizzling wok by popular Muppets.*

Overpriced Happy Family..... 14.25
*Scallops, crabmeat and psychotropic
mushrooms sauteed with fresh chef's
thumbs and served on a Sealy
Posturpedic.*

 ★
Tienanmen Square Beef.......17.75
*Oppressed young beef, severely battered,
crushed with bamboo shoots and
brutally smothered as you watch from
your table on a big screen.*

★
**Health Inspector's Seafood
Delight.**...................... FREE!
*Fresh lobster, shrimp and prawns
expertly prepared in the clean Mexican
restaurant down the block, brought in
through our back door and served with a
crisp fifty dollar bill rolled in a napkin.
(Must be ordered in advance.)*

**Cashier will
change shirt
at your request.**

WRITERS: JOE RAIOLA AND CHARLIE KADAU

The legal and ethical arguments surrounding a patient's right to determine his or her own fate are indeed complex and difficult ones. One doctor, Jack Kevorkian, firmly supports a patient's right to die—and has constructed a machine that assists people in doing so. Dr. Kevorkian hopes his point of view becomes the accepted one and that his "suicide machines" become commonplace and available to everyone. Well, Doc, if that happens, your machine will be manufactured by the thousands, sold in retail stores like four-slice toasters or 10-speed blenders and come with one of those dumb instruction manuals just like every other silly household appliance! A manual like...

ARTIST: BOB CLARKE   WRITER: CHARLIE KADAU

The

Panasony

Model No. RIP 2000® Suicide Machine

Owner's Manual/Operating Instructions

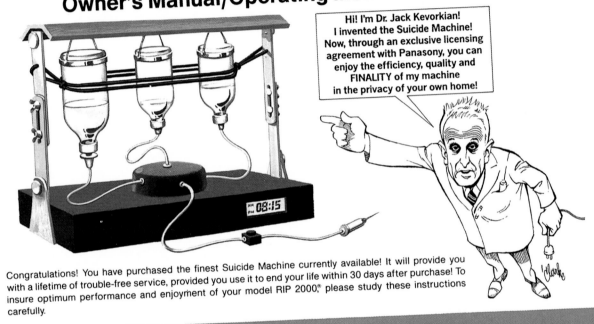

Hi! I'm Dr. Jack Kevorkian! I invented the Suicide Machine! Now, through an exclusive licensing agreement with Panasony, you can enjoy the efficiency, quality and FINALITY of my machine in the privacy of your own home!

Congratulations! You have purchased the finest Suicide Machine currently available! It will provide you with a lifetime of trouble-free service, provided you use it to end your life within 30 days after purchase! To insure optimum performance and enjoyment of your model RIP 2000,® please study these instructions carefully.

GENERAL CARE OF RIP 2000®

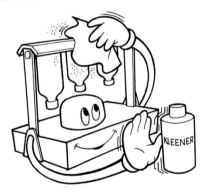

Do not locate your Suicide Machine where it may be exposed to direct sunlight, heat or intense vibration.

Use only a soft dry cloth to clean your Suicide Machine. Water or cleaning solutions may impede the lethal ability of the unit.

Do not expose your Suicide Machine to rain or moisture—fire, electric shock or other personal injury may result!

21

BEFORE USING, BECOME FAMILIAR WITH THE PARTS OF YOUR NEW RIP 2000® SUICIDE MACHINE

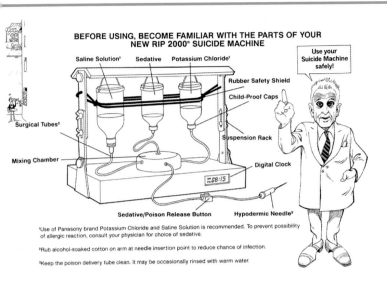

Use your Suicide Machine safely!

- Saline Solution¹
- Sedative
- Potassium Chloride¹
- Rubber Safety Shield
- Child-Proof Caps
- Surgical Tubes³
- Suspension Rack
- Mixing Chamber
- Digital Clock
- Sedative/Poison Release Button
- Hypodermic Needle²

¹Use of Panasony brand Potassium Chloride and Saline Solution is recommended. To prevent possibility of allergic reaction, consult your physician for choice of sedative.

²Rub alcohol-soaked cotton on arm at needle insertion point to reduce chance of infection.

³Keep the poison delivery tube clean. It may be occasionally rinsed with warm water.

OPTIONAL ACCESSORIES ORDER FORM

The perfect complements to your new Suicide Machine!

item	price	qty.	amt.
Suicide Machine Dust Cover	$14.95		$
Mint Scented Poison Solution	$7.95/pint		$
Wireless Remote Control	$12.95		$
6-foot Poison Extension Tube	$17.95		$
Brass Monogram Plate ("this Suicide Machine belongs to")	$9.95 (up to 3 initials)		$
		handling	$3.00
		sales tax	$
	total payment (MUST be received in advance)		$

WARRANTY AND SERVICE INFORMATION

There are no user-serviceable parts inside the Panasony RIP 2000!

The Panasony RIP 2000® Suicide Machine includes a limited 1-year warranty on all parts.

Warranty does not cover:

furniture or other items broken or damaged by slumping lifeless body.

clothing or other fabrics stained by poison solution.

unpaid credit card bills run up by user before killing self.

(Because of state and municipal laws, your survivors or next of kin may have other protections and/or rights not outlined in this manual.)

Should your suicide machine require service, contact the nearest Authorized Factory Service Center:

RIP 2000® SUICIDE MACHINE TROUBLESHOOTING GUIDE

Answers to common problems!

PROBLEM: You are still alive.

TRY: Check connections to Suicide Machine; Is hypodermic needle in vein?

PROBLEM: You black out only temporarily, then wake up slightly nauseous.

TRY: Checking concentration of poison solution; use stronger dosage.

PROBLEM: After using the machine you feel extremely alert and have trouble sleeping.

TRY: 1. Someone has substituted Folger's coffee crystals for the poison solution. Rinse jar, fill with poison and try again. 2. Did you hook yourself up to a Mr. Coffee by mistake?

PROBLEM: After beginning to use the suicide machine your depression ends and you realize you have many good and valid reasons to go on with your life.

TRY: Nothing. It's too late. Try to become depressed with living again.

WARRANTY REGISTRATION CARD

To qualify for warranty coverage, please complete this card and have your funeral director return it to us within 14 days.

Name _____

Address _____

City _____ State _____ Zip _____

Date of Birth: _____ Date of Expiration (Scheduled): _____

Name of next of kin _____

Where did you first hear about the Panasony RIP 2000®?

☐ IRS Audit Bureau Waiting Room
☐ Buffalo Bills Post-Super Bowl party
☐ Court TV coverage of Kevorkian Trial
☐ On radio of car idling in closed garage
☐ Other: _____

What other suicide methods have you tried?

☐ Placing tongue on terminals of 9-volt battery
☐ Repeatedly Listening to Ozzy Osbourne Albums
☐ Driving GM truck
☐ Dining at Jack-In-The-Box restaurants
☐ Other: _____

Your Total Life Insurance Coverage:

☐ Under $10,000 ☐ $10,000–$19,999 ☐ $20,000–$34,999 ☐ $35,000–$49,999 ☐ $50,000 and Over

Panasony occasionally makes the names of its customers available to other companies offering similar products or services. Do you object to receiving future mailings from these companies? (Please check one) YES _____ NO _____

An arrested drunk driver is someone
who got nailed for getting hammered.

—Alfred E. Neuman

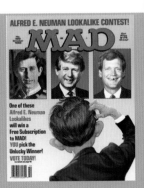

You really shouldn't go the extra mile when you have a specific destination.

EATS MEETS JEST DEPT.

Newspapers and magazines are always filled with reviews of restaurants and other dining spots, but let's face it: these days, how often can you afford to eat out? It's more likely you'll have many more meals at home or at a friend's home...so why not review the food, the atmosphere and the service at those places, right? Reviews kinda like...

MAD'S NEIGHBORHOOD DINING ROUNDUP

(Where our Roving Food Critic surprises different families at meal time)

ARTIST: HARRY NORTH   WRITER: ROBERT BRAMBLE

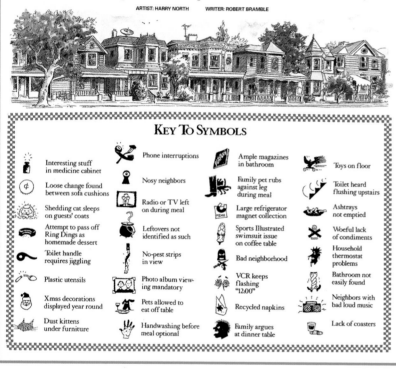

KEY TO SYMBOLS

Interesting stuff in medicine cabinet	Phone interruptions	Ample magazines in bathroom	Toys on floor
Loose change found between sofa cushions	Nosy neighbors	Family pet rubs against leg during meal	Toilet handle flushing upstairs
Shedding cat sleeps on guests' coats	Radio or TV left on during meal	Large refrigerator magnet collection	Ashtrays not emptied
Attempt to pass off Ring Dings as homemade dessert	Leftovers not identified as such	Sports Illustrated swimsuit issue on coffee table	Woeful lack of condiments
Toilet handle requires jiggling	No-pest strips in view	Bad neighborhood	Household thermostat problems
Plastic utensils	Photo album viewing mandatory	VCR keeps flashing "12:00"	Bathroom not easily found
Xmas decorations displayed year round	Pets allowed to eat off table	Recycled napkins	Neighbors with bad loud music
Dust kittens under furniture	Handwashing before meal optional	Family argues at dinner table	Lack of coasters

THE BRONSONS
8 FAIRVIEW LAWN CRESCENT ★★★½

A split-level bungalow and a whiff of charcoal greeted us on a recent weekend afternoon visit. The usual fare (hot dogs, burgers, etc.) is available, but the surprise of the day was "Duck Bronson," a whole duck flung on the sizzling briquettes in the spacious Bronson backyard. This "Charco-duck" was only slightly marred by a few errant feathers and country-western music coming from the yard next to us.

THE COOPERMANS
1329 LOCUST ST. ★★★½

We visited the Coopermans on a Friday, and seafood was the order of the night. Host "Bud" Cooperman insisted on lots of beer to cook the shrimp in while Myrna Cooperman regaled us with juicy stories about the neighbors, especially the "unmarried couple" living two doors down. The shrimp was good, as was the cole slaw; despite Bud's repeated mentions of "shrimp on the barbie" in a strained attempt at an Australian accent.

THE TAYLORS
14 OAKWILLOW COURT ★

Paintings of matadors adorn the walls of the Taylor's paneled living room, where we sipped grape Kool-Aid and awaited Chet Taylor's arrival with extra-crispy chicken bits from the Chicken Bits take-out place. Wife Jennifer explained that it was a hectic day and she had no time to prepare. Despite Chet and Jennifer's enthusiasm (and all the potato chips we could eat), it was still a disappointing dining experience.

#323 DEC '93

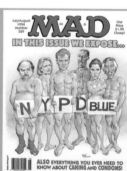

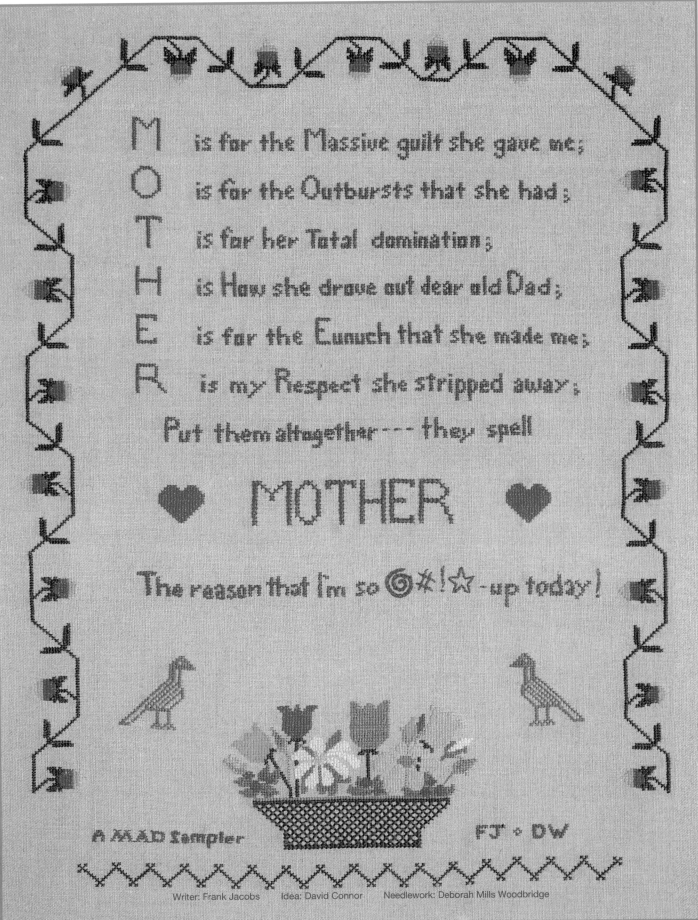

M is for the Massive guilt she gave me;

O is for the Outbursts that she had;

T is for her Total domination;

H is How she drove out dear old Dad;

E is for the Eunuch that she made me;

R is my Respect she stripped away;

Put them altogether--- they spell

♥ MOTHER ♥

The reason that I'm so ⊙*!☆-up today!

A MAD Sampler   FJ • DW

Writer: Frank Jacobs   Idea: David Connor   Needlework: Deborah Mills Woodbridge

#327 MAY '94

GREAT MOMEN

Washington Cross-D

Artist: Richard Williams.

#326 MAR/APR '94

WHAT HAS BEEN MICHAEL JACKSON'S MOST PRIZED ACQUISITION?

HERE WE GO WITH ANOTHER RIDICULOUS
MAD FOLD-IN

Michael Jackson's millions have given him the opportunity to acquire many precious things. But there is one thing he definitely values above all the rest. To find out what this golden thing is simply fold page in as shown.

A ▶   FOLD THIS SECTION OVER LEFT   ◀ B Fold Back So "A" Meets "B"

A VISITOR TO MICHAEL JACKSON'S NEVERLAND IS BOUND TO BE IMPRESSED. THOUGH NOT EVERYBODY'S IDEA OF FUN, MANY UNUSUAL ITEMS, FROM SILLY TO WONDERFUL, ARE FOUND INSIDE ITS FENCE

A ▶   ARTIST AND WRITER: AL JAFFEE   ◀ B

#329 JUL/AUG '94

WHAT HAS BEEN MICHAEL JACKSON'S MOST PRIZED ACQUISITION?

FOLD PAGE OVER LIKE THIS!

A ▶ ◀ B   FOLD BACK SO "A" MEETS "B"

A
BOY'S

SILENCE
A ▶ ◀ B

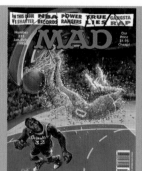

ABUSER FRIENDLY DEPT.

Anyone who's read the comic pages surely has delighted to the happy-go-lucky antics of Billy, Jeffy, Dolly and P.J., who prove that the wonder of childhood is like a precious diamond, with all the sparkle and all the rough edges that make. . .oh, who are we kidding? When does the strip take place, 1953? Dad has the only paycheck in the house, somehow supports five people and three pets, and still has time off for school plays, vacation, and games of catch? The biggest problem this family ever had was when P.J. got scared by the giraffe! It's time we showed these 58-year-old first graders what life is really like in. . .

ARTIST: GEORGE WOODBRIDGE
WRITER: DESMOND DEVLIN

the DYSFUNCTIONAL FAMILY CIRCUS

MONDAY

"See, Jeffy, I told ya-- just like cable!"

TUESDAY

"That was Grandpa. He's in Hell now."

FRIDAY

"If you loved your fish as much as he loved you, maybe he wouldn't have died."

SATURDAY

"Billy will be ready as soon as he's finished changing the bed sheets he wet last night."

WEDNESDAY

"Mommy! Mommy! P.J. found the gun!"

THURSDAY

"You made this card all by yourself? It sucks!"

SUNDAY

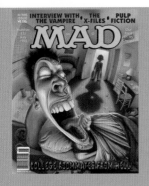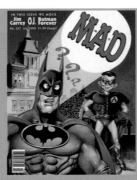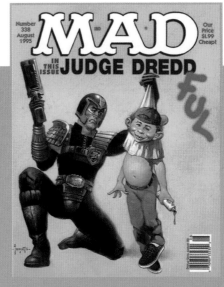

161

In the '60s, TV gave us cute caring doctors like Ben Casey and Dr. Kildare. In the '70s, Marcus Welby M.D., kind and fatherly. And in the '80s, it was the wacky but lovable gang at St. Else- where. But this is the '90s. Health care reform is dead. And no- where is it deader than on NBC's new hospital drama. In this medical zoo, patients check in sick and they leave the place...

★ONE SUNNY MORNING IN L.A.

ARTIST: PAUL COKER   WRITER: DUCK EDWING

Some years back, in issue #155 to be precise, we glorified the great sportscaster Cosell with "Howard At the Mike." Today, _that_ Howard broadcasts from that great sound studio in the sky, but another Howard has emerged, a sex-driven shock-jock now syndicated throughout America. So let us salute Howard Stern and his private parts as we present this new and distinctly different version of...

HOWARD AT THE MIKE

ARTIST: SAM VIVIANO   WRITER: FRANK JACOBS

The programs on talk radio were dullsville years ago,
With hosts as scintillating as a wombat's embryo,
And when Imus proved a stiff and Larry King began to wear,
The public yearned for someone fresh to liven up the air...

#339 SEP '95

When from the Depths there rose a voice, unlike those heard before—
An ego-driven motor-mouth, whom no one could ignore;
Soon scads of sleaze-starved listeners, their dials they would turn
To catch the raunchy ravings of the loud one, Howard Stern.

They signed him up at NBC — 'twas clear they had a prize;
Indeed, with Howard at the mike the ratings reached the skies,
Though sev'ral bigwigs feared he might be coming on too strong
With schticks like Lesbo Dial-A-Date and Virgin Mary Kong.

Soon groupies bared their busty bods to prove they were good sports;
He spanked their bottoms on the air while stripped down to his shorts;
Four-letter words kept spewing out — he couldn't sugarcoat 'em;
Too late the brass discovered Howard's brain was in his scrotum.

They canned him, and throughout the land great discontent was felt;
"An outrage," shouted loyal fans, "a blow below the belt!"
On city streets they mourned as though they'd lost their closest friend;
A few were even heard to ask, "Could this be Howard's end?"

Not yet, for soon a hot new show on K-Rock he would launch;
X-Radio, he called it now, a cavalcade of raunch;
What joy to do the play-by-play of couples having sex,
Away from wimpy prudes, those creepy NBC execs.

Behind his shades he sits on high, his visage long and lean;
Beneath his tumbling locks of hair, five earrings can be seen;
Around him fawn his toadies, as to him their praises sing —
The Prince of Shock, the Earl of Sleaze, the Mouth who would be King.

Each day he holds us spellbound with the spiel that he delivers,
Describing, say, the boob-job of his sidekick, Robin Quivers,
Or telling his disciples of the joys of masturbation
(The cause, some people say, of Joycelyn Elders' Fascination).

To faithful fans, he's like a god who's on a holy mission,
A view not shared by members of the Christian Coalition;
"Clean up your act," they thunder, "or we'll force you off the air!"
"Butt out," he says, "a groupie's here who's shaved her pubic hair."

Though radio has made him rich, at times he's breaking free
To pull in greater megabucks on pay-per-view TV;
And just in case a fan or two might fail to catch him "live,"
They still can buy the video for $19.95.

He wrote a movie, "Fartman," on which all his hopes were pinned—
A superhero powered by the force of his own wind;
The flick was never made — some say the plot was too high-class,
Or else the deal fell through because the script ran out of gas.

He hoped as New York Governor great changes he might bring;
Announcing he would run, he threw his jockstrap in the ring;
He soon dropped out, which filled his many boosters with dismay;
He'd bare his butt for votes, but show his tax returns? No way!

His fans went ape for *Private Parts*, of this there was no doubt;
As Howard, free of censorship, now let it all hang out;
So touching was the tale he told, it's no surprise to learn
His penis size is now a cause of national concern.

With pen in hand, he crossed the land to publicize his book,
As scores of groupies mobbed the stores to get a closer look;
They shed brassieres and thongs for fear they might seem overdressed,
And cheered each time he autographed another naked breast.

Today he lines up top celebs for guest-shots on his shows— Stallone and Richard Simmons, Donald Trump and Axl Rose,

Big stars like Schwarzenegger, politicians like Ed Koch— All come to worship Howard at his temple of the crotch.

Oh, somewhere scuzzballs feed us porn in Hustler and in Screw,
And somewhere lurk the Jerky Boys, who turn the airwaves blue,
And somewhere there's the glitzy sleaze Madonna flings about,
But today they're small potatoes --- raunchy Howard's grossed them out!

HOLIER THAN OW! DEPT.

Body Piercers are a diverse group. Some pierce only their ears from which they hang hoops and diamonds — a statement of taste and fashion. Others pierce their nose and eyelids from which they hang crosses and safety pins — a statement of hipness and rebellion. Still others pierce their nipples and naughty parts from which they hang rings — a statement of sexual kinkiness. We at MAD salute them all! And it is because of our heartfelt concern for these flesh-poking perverts that we descend from our lofty comedic mountaintop to offer up...

THE TEN COMMANDMENTS OF BODY PIERCING

1. Thou shalt not pierce areas of the body in a manner that jeopardizes the function of major organs.

2. Thou shalt exercise caution when connecting one's own piercings to another's.

3. Thou shalt not pierce together parts of the body that are not naturally connected.

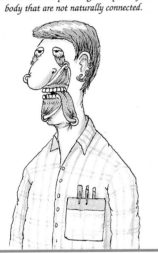

5. Thou shalt not connect excessively long chains between pierced areas of the body.

ARTIST AND WRITER: TOM CHENEY

6. Thou shalt not body-surf while wearing nipple rings.

7. Thou shalt not wear nose pins while suffering from hay fever.

8. Thou shalt not attempt to pronounce the word "Saskatchewan" while wearing tongue pins.

4. Thou shalt not expose thyself to extreme gravitational forces while wearing heavy pieces of jewelry.

9. Thou shalt not French kiss anyone with braces while wearing lip rings.

10. Thou shalt not pierce areas of the body that compromise the structural integrity of a condom.

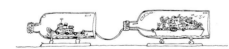

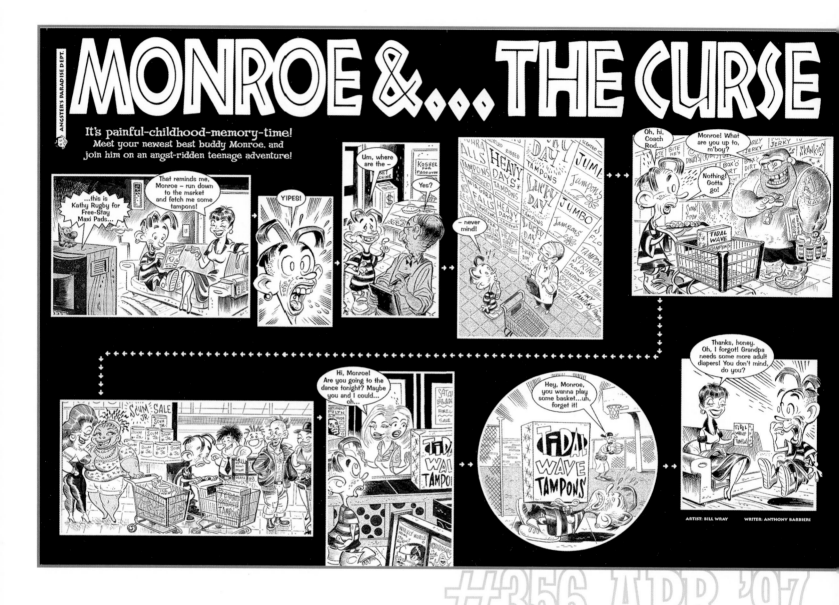

#356 APR '97

THE ZIT

ARTIST: TOM BUNK   WRITER: MICHAEL GALLAGHER

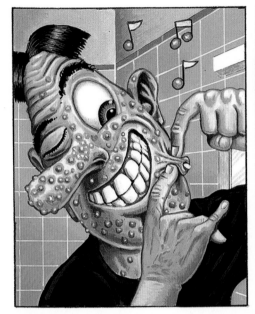

A MAD LOOK AT BODY PIERCING

ARTIST AND WRITER: SERGIO ARAGONES

Consumer Product Factoid: *12% of all Tang is consumed by ex-astronauts who can't admit that they have a real problem.*

#350 OCT '96

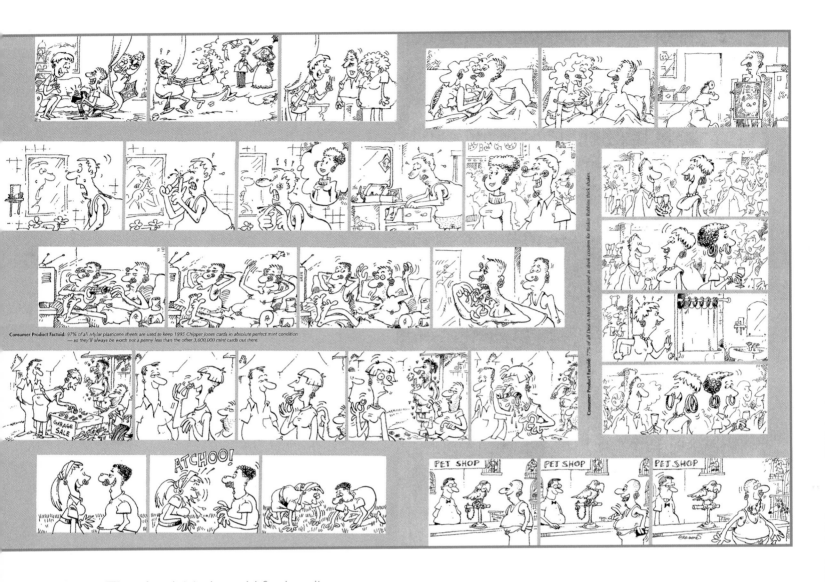

Consumer Product Factoid: 97% of all Mylar plasticene sheets are used to keep 1995 Chipper Jones cards in absolute perfect mint condition — so they'll always be worth not a penny less than the other 3,000,000 mint cards out there.

Consumer Product Factoid: 77% of all Deal-A-Meal cards are used as drink coasters for Baskin-Robbins thick shakes.

> There's a lot to be said for brevity.
> —Alfred E. Neuman

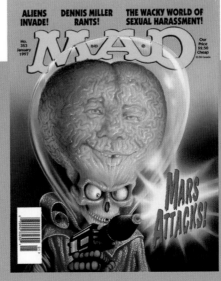

Okay MAD fans, Get out your dictionary and your guide to obscure references, 'cause it's time...

DENNIS MILLER

RANTS

ABOUT

DENNIS MILLER

I don't want to get off on a **rant** here, but **what's the story** with my show? It's on Fridays and rerun on Sundays, when the title *Dennis Miller Live* becomes an **ironic mockery** of itself, though I do get a **kick** out of hearing how many viewers with an **IQ** equal to **Rush Limbaugh's** score on the balance beam compulsories **still** try to call and talk to us when we're just a reel of spinning tape on HBO's big video machine.

You know the drill: I come out, under-dressed and frequently unshaven to the audience's immediate Pavlovian reaction to the **applause sign** – without which, let's face it, our talk shows would be little more than a young **Martin Short** in his attic with a tape recorder. Yeah, the applause sign. If it wasn't here, our performer **egos** would be bruised more than a peach manhandled by **O.J.** in one of his flashback moods. That's something else I do: no matter how **tenuous** the connection, I always mention **The Juice** at least once a show so I can say, "You're a bad, bad man, O.J. A bad, bad, bad, bad man." Why? Because, it kills, which is, in itself, a semi-quasi joke if you really **ratchet up the magnification** on that petri dish I call my sense of humor.

ARTIST: STEVE BRODNER   **WRITER: BUTCH D'AMBROSIO**

ext, I'm arrogant enough to suggest that I can tell you **"who fed it and who ate it."** In reality, I'll be carpet bombing you with payloads of big SAT words like **"zeitgeist"** and a fix of minutiae as **fabulously obscure** as the chick who sings the song on the radio in Pulp Fiction before **Bruce Willis** meets **The Gimp.** Truth be told, by the end of the show you still don't know who fed it and who ate it. I'm just espousing my pragmatic, utilitarian ideas and you're buying them like coke fiends buy tissues. You're running with the **bull#$%*** because between all the big words like "pragmatism" and "utilitarianism," I say stuff like **bull#$%*.** I swear so much because, frankly, I want viewers, and I'm hoping some people might haphazardly channel-surf onto my program and think it's an all-white episode of Def Comedy Jam. Besides, it's in my contract, Babe.

nd what's the deal with my **bottled water?** Seems like I'm sipping it, slugging it, or otherwise chugging it for a full 3 minutes out of every 28-minute show! Am I so busy I can't stop by the water cooler before I go on? Now, I don't want to get off on a diatribe here – you kids thought I was going to say **"rant,"** didn't you? Yeah, I know, a routine is called a "routine" for a reason. Ah hahaha! But the fact is I'm already **in a rant,** and if I started another one, I'd probably be breaking some **obscure metaphysical law** and wind up **dissolving** into myself like **Ron Silver** did near the end of Timecop.

ure, all our bodies have more water in them than a mixed drink at the **Viper Room** – Deppy, baby, it's just a joke – but the fact is bottled water has become the **whiskey flask** of the boomer generation. And, I myself admit that I am one of the greatest practitioners of this self-induced, self-important anti-tap water **paranoia,** this belief that without a plastic bottle of that sparkling mineral mountain stream ménage à trois of Hydrogen and Oxygen known as **l'acqua,** you're nothing in everybody else's eyes. As **Freud** said, "Sometimes a cigar is just a cigar, but eight ounces of Evian is my way of showing you I'm well off enough to plunk down a buck twenty-five for each cool, clear, refreshing swig of put-out-the-fire water I swallow." **Besides,** each sip I take is one less joke we have to write!

fter I finish the **"rant"** portion of the show I stand there, self-conciously shaking my head only slightly less than Dana Carvey's impression of me. Speaking of **the Carveymeister,** most nights my "special guest" is invariably one of my **old SNL buddies.** Like **Chris Farley.** I thank him for coming on and using my show to plug his new "road picture" with the Spadester. Or **David Spade.** I thank him for coming on and using my show to plug the remake of his previous "road picture" with the Farleycane. Farley, man! He's one funny, fat bastard, and I always loved watching him sweat over at 30 Rock. I love those guys. **I really do.** Actually, I have to say that because I'm beholden to **Lorne Michaels** to have someone from every one of his little SNL spinoff projects on to **shill away,** because they say I copped his **"Weekend Update"** and turned it into my **"Big Screen."** Which is absolutely not true. There I sat behind a desk. Here I stand in front of a big TV!

ARTIST: RICK TULKA   WRITER: RUSS COOPER

Generations come and generations go, and with each change of an era comes challenging personal and social issues, revolutions, rebellions and an idealist youth culture. The Sixties brought Vietnam, Kent State, LBJ, while the Nineties, well...let's just say the times they are a' changin' as MAD contrasts the...

60's AND THE 90's

VOICES OF A GENERATION:

60's SIMON & GARFUNKEL

90's BEAVIS & BUTT-HEAD

60's Free Love

90's $2.99-per-minute Love

60's Tune in, turn on, drop out...

90's Rent it, view it, rewind it...

WOODSTOCK THE VIDEO

15

FLOWER POWER

ARTIST: SAM VIVIANO
WRITER: DICK DEBARTOLO

I'm **Schlock Love-It**, leader of an **underwater expedition** to find **lost treasure**! Movie producers have **already** gone to the **bottom** of the **barrel** looking for **old stories** to recycle, so I'm going **deeper**! All the way to the **bottom** of the **ocean** to find a **tale** that's been told **too many times**, and a **lot better**, already! But **this time**, I have a **new gimmick**! I not only **dug** up an **old story**, I dug up an **old lady** to tell it to **you**!

Pay attention, this is **tricky**! I'm the **same Rouse** as the **young Rouse** you're about to meet, except I've **aged 85 years**! That's **how long the Trypanic** has been at the **bottom** of the **ocean**! Of course, when you see **all my wrinkles**, you'll think *I've* been at the **bottom of the ocean** for 85 years too! I'm telling **my story** in **flashbacks** which is a **big help**, because at **my age** remembering it all at once is **impossible**! Not to mention **implausible**! But I'll tell you **this**: when you're on a **sinking passenger ship**, what do you **do**? Try a **call** for **help**? Try a **last-ditched effort** to get to a **lifeboat**? Naaaaah! You...

I'm **Jerk Awesome**, and I **won tickets** on the **Trypanic** playing **poker**! I have a **feeling, though,** that the **guy I won them** from **didn't** want to go on **this ship**! He **insisted** my **pair of fives** beat his **flush**! I'm an **artist** and I have a **vivid imagination**! At least that's what **people say** when I try to sell them **my sketches**! They say: "If you think **that crap is art**, you have some **vivid imagination**!"

I'm **Rouse Blackwater**, and I'm **returning** to **America** with my **fiancé**! He's **handsome** and **rich**, but he's so **proper** and **stuffy** he wears **starched shirts**, **bow ties**, and **bowlers** — even when he **makes love**! I, On the **other hand**, I like to **sleep** in the **nude**, whether at night **in bed** or by day in a **deck chair poolside**!

I'm **Rouse's mother**, **Ruthless**! My **daughter** Rouse has many **radical ideas**, but her **wildest ones** concern **marriage**! She has this **weird notion** that people **marry** for **love**! Fortunately, I'm **teaching her** the **truth**: that you **marry** for **money**! And there's **love** in that! Love of **money**!

I'm **Callous**, Rouse's **fiancee**! Rouse has a **burning desire** to **experience** and **explore** all that **life** has to **offer**! That's **everything** I **HATE** in a **woman**! On the **other hand**, she's got **great legs** and a **great chest**! That's everything I **LOVE** in a **woman**!

There are two kinds of people in the world: those who think
there are two kinds of people and those who don't!

—Alfred E. Neuman

HEAR THE RADIO THAT WOKE UP AN ENTIRE INDUSTRY*

*To the fact that there are idiots out there willing to spend hundreds of dollars just for a radio!

Popular Audio wrote that it is "a sonic masterpiece." *Radio Magazine* wrote that it is "simply amazing…a genuine breakthrough in sound quality!" And *High Fidelity* wrote, "Sorry, but you'll have to take thousands of dollars in advertising in *our* magazine like you did in *Popular Audio and Radio Magazine* before we'll write hyped-up copy about how great your radio is." What radio are they all talking about? The Boose® Wavy radio.

HALF A MILLION PEOPLE ALREADY OWN THE BOOSE® WAVY RADIO.

In just over three years, the Wavy radio has changed the way half a million people listen to music — people like Stanley Karpinski of Staten Island, NY, who said, "It's changed the way I listen to music. I stopped listening to CDs and audiocassettes! I had to! The Wavy won't play them. It's just a damn radio!"

OUR EXCLUSIVE, AWARD-WINNING DESIGN

The secret to the Wavy radio's remarkable success lies in an exclusive, award-winning design. Our experts spent countless hours designing sleek, elegant ads for the Wavy radio, resulting in a remarkably successful ad campaign that has won numerous awards for its design. The actual design of the radio itself

Open up a Wavy radio and you'll see our exclusive acoustic waveguide speaker technology. It'll also immediately void our 30-day money back guarantee.

was a piece of cake, using the same technology found in a $9 K-Mart clock radio. The Wavy radio measures just 4 1/2" x 14" x 8 1/4" x 10"x 22 1/8" x 9". It comes with a credit card-sized remote control that will easily slip between the tightest of sofa cushions never to be seen again, six AM/FM pre-set buttons that have been permanently set at the factory to our favorite stations for your convenience, and dual alarms which can be heard up to five miles away. Is it any wonder that people who weren't smart enough to buy a stereo system with a CD player, AM/FM radio, dual cassette deck, graphic equalizer and detachable speakers (for half the price that our product costs) are now stuck using the Boose® Wavy as their primary stereo system?

This miniature remote control was lost forever right after this photo was taken.

EVEN OUR IN-HOME TRIAL SOUNDS GREAT.

Order a Wavy radio today and take advantage of our risk-free, in-home trial. If after 30 days, you aren't convinced that this is the best sounding radio you've ever heard, simply return the radio to us in its original unopened carton for a full refund. No questions asked! That's right! You have our 100% guarantee that our in-home trial sounds great, providing you don't go back and reread this last paragraph for finely-crafted legal loopholes.

CALL TODAY AND MAKE SIX INTEREST-FREE PAYMENTS.

The Wavy radio is available for $349 direct from Boose®, one of the leading names in high fidelity equipment manufacturers when listed alphabetically. And now our six-month installment payment plan lets you make six monthly payments interest free when you agree to our exclusive seventh payment of all interest! Call today and hear more about the product that has consumer groups and state attorneys general talking.

CALL BY NOVEMBER 1, 1998
and ask our operators about
FREE SHIPPING
and why we don't offer it.

CALL 1-800-BAMBOOZLED EXT. R2D2

When you call, ask about our six-month installment payment plan. (Qualifications based on a sworn affidavit that you own a valid credit card and that your call is not being traced or recorded by law enforcement officials.) Also ask about FedEx® delivery service and how it differs from the third rate carrier we'll be using to ship your radio.

Please specify your color choice:
☐ Barry White   ☐ Earl Grey

Mr./Mrs./Ms. _____
Name _____ (Please Do Not Print)
Address _____
City _____ State _____ Zip _____
Morning Phone _____
Afternoon Phone _____
Late Afternoon Phone _____
Evening Phone _____
(No Salesman will call.)

Mail to: Boose® Corporation, Dept. NOCD-RU-NUTS
The Compound on The Mountain, FramedAgain, MA 00019

BOOSE
Better sounding ads through research.

WRITER: JOHN FICARRA

A MAD AD PARODY

#371 JUL '98

WHITETAIL DEER: 4 years old. Forest creature and a member of the Nature's Revenge Association.

"Every year my peaceful woodland home is invaded by thousands of hunters who shoot at me with rifles and guns with absolutely no provocation on my part. Usually I'm just walking around, minding my own business or chewing on some berries when BANG! A bullet goes flying past my head. Now don't get me wrong, I have nothing against sportsmen, but I don't like being the target of some accountant from Scarsdale out for a weekend with his buddies. All of the bears, rabbits, racoons and other forest creatures I've spoken to feel pretty much the same way.

"That's why we formed the NRA—Nature's Revenge Association. We've learned that a hunter will have a new appreciation and respect for an animal that's armed as heavily as he is. We know that guns aren't toys… Believe me, we know. So we teach our members gun safety and train them not to shoot unless they've been shot at first … a lesson most hunters haven't learned yet.

"So this year we're ready. We've been practicing for months. We've got our permits. And we're determined to have a safe hunting season for all involved. If you want to visit our home and take our pictures, fine. But keep your guns in the cities where they belong.

No one wants to be the deer-ly departed." **I'm the NRA.**

NATURE'S REVENGE ASSOCIATION OF AMERICA
This is to certify that the creature whose hoofprints appears below is a
WILDLIFE MEMBER

The NRA Animal Firearms Program provides law abiding beasts with basic instruction in the safe handling of guns with their paws. If you are an endangered species and want more information, write to Nature's Revenge Association, Yellowstone Ntl. Park, Wyoming, 00118.

WRITERS: CHARLIE KADAU AND JOE RAIOLA   PHOTOGRAPHER: IRVING SCHILD   COMPUTER IMAGING: PETER BARN

A MAD AD HANDIY

#308 JAN '92

180

RECTORY EXAMINATION DEPT.

It has been known to happen to doctors, lawyers, athletes, politicians and high powered Wall Street Execs. But there is nothing more disturbing than...

WHEN PRIESTS GO BAD

ARTIST: JOHN CALDWELL
WRITER: MIKE MAY

SLOPPY EXORCISMS

HOLY WATER BALLOON FIGHTS

QUESTIONABLE CHARITIES

NO-WIN BINGO

BISHOP'S HAT KEEP-AWAY

PRODUCT PLACEMENT IN SERMONS

DRIVE-BY BAPTISMS

EMPLOYING "WHEEL OF ABSOLUTION" TO DETERMINE PENANCE

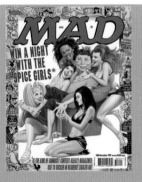

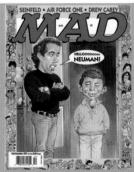

First, megalomaniac Ken Starr hounded the President, his staff, his friends, his former intern and just about every-one else in the Clinton White House, except Socks and Buddy! With that investigation in shambles, the overzealous prosecutor has turned his attention to others who, in his eyes, "threaten" the very foundation of our society! Here's a sneak peek of a confidential report sure to be illegally leaked by Starr and his thugs any day now...

THE SPECIAL PROSECUTOR'S OFFICIAL REPORT ON MISTER ROGERS

ARTIST: DREW FRIEDMAN

WRITER: DESMOND DEVLIN

INTRODUCTION:
THERE IS TROUBLE IN THE NEIGHBORHOOD

As required by United States Code Section PBS-13, Title 28, and brought to you by the letters "E" and "P," the Office of the Special Prosecutor hereby submits substantial and credible information that Fred "Mister Rogers" Rogers committed acts that may constitute grounds for immediate cancellation.

This investigation into Mister Rogers began in 1994, during the Special Prosecutor's look into President William J. Clinton and the Whitewater scandal. While no wrongdoing was discovered in Whitewater, facts from that case led to a study of the White House travel office and fundraising irregularities. Those inquiries were later closed without result, but not

before this office expanded its mission to include the Paula Jones lawsuit and the Lewinsky matter (AKA "Forni-Gate").

A remark by Lewinsky's dry cleaner indicated that President Clinton had watched part of the Ken Burns documentary on the Civil War before getting bored and switching over to the USA Network's *Silk Stalkings*. A $6 million dollar investigation into *TV Guide* subsequently revealed that the Civil War documentary had been shown on PBS television. This naturally led to a full inquiry into the entire PBS schedule. It was during this phase that the wrongdoing of Mister Rogers became virtually apparent.

This complex investigation into Mister Rogers' misdeeds cost $46 million dollars to complete, not counting free give-away tote bags. This cost, naturally, must be paid by PBS. It is suggested that PBS make up the money by expanding their on-air pledge drive from 335 days per year to 363 days per year.

SECTION ONE:
INDIVIDUAL GROUNDS AND CHARGES

There is substantial and credible information that Mister Rogers committed acts that may constitute grounds for cancellation, depending on polls and how the FCC appointments turn out.

The information obtained reveals that Mister Rogers:

- **Lied** when he claimed that all his viewers were "special." The evidence will show that even while repeating these statements, Mister Rogers knew perfectly well that human life is cheap and that most of his viewers were in fact worthless lumps;

- **Misused** his position to teach 30 years' worth of children that it's okay to watch a grown man take off his clothes;

- **Conspired** to deprive jazz composers of their rightful royalties by having the invisible piano play random notes that only occasionally go near a melody;

- **Violated** Article 1, Section 9 of the U.S. Constitution by recognizing the royal sovereignty of King Friday XIII within United States borders;

- **Failed** to pay taxes on the teeny-tiny imaginary fares collected by the Magic Trolley;

- Has **never specifically disproved** his possible role in the mysterious death of *The Joy of Painting* host Bob Ross;

- **Inserted** his fist into numerous puppets.

#379 MAR '99

When it comes to the lack of cleanliness at public urinals, it's amazing what some guys will stand for!

ARTIST AND WRITER: PETER KUPER

#370 JUN '98

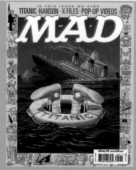

Turmoil has engulfed the movie industry as legions desperately await the next Star Bores epic. Hoping to resolve the matter, greedy director George Lucas begins filming while dispatching his lawyers to sign merchandising deals throughout the galaxy. As the geeks endlessly debate who's cooler, Darth Maul or Boba Fett, moviegoers everywhere waste hours waiting on line, only to discover that after all the hype, this story-free, poorly-acted flick's nothing more than...

I'm QuiteGone Jim, Jet-Eye Master! I am **closely attuned** to the **living Force**, but I follow a **different path** than most **Jet-Eyes**! I made sure I got **killed off** in the **FIRST** of these **three lame flicks!**

I'm the **young Oldie Von Moldie!** I've **nearly completed** all my **training** as a **Jet-Eye apprentice!** As a matter of fact, I'm so **close** to **graduating**, I've already had my **picture taken** for the **yearbook!** I was voted "**Most Likely to Succeed in Sequels**"! As part of my **Jet-Eye training**, I built this **light saber** with my **own** hands! It can **cut through anything**... except the **overblown special effects** to this **overdone story!**

I'm **Death Hideous** from the **Dark Side!** I inspire an **unsettling sense** of dread, like those "You have **performed an illegal action**" blurbs that suddenly spring up on our **super-sophisticated computer screens** when you haven't done a thing! My **lifelong dream** is to put an **end** to all **peace-loving Jet-Eye Knights!** I spread **evil** via **holographic transmissions** from my **headquarters** on **Croissant** — and to *really* annoy folks, I send 'em **COLLECT!**

ANTIQUE JUNK

MAY HIS LOSS BE WITH YOU!

MATTEL

MOTHERS AGAINST POD DRIVERS

I'm **Mannequin Skystalker**, apprentice to **Jet-Eye Master QuiteGone Jim!** Even at my **young age**, I can feel the **Force within me!** Either that, or it's **puberty kicking** in a little **early!** I'm also in **training** to be a **loyal and obedient Jet-Eye!** Already I learned how to **roll over, beg, and fetch** a **light saber!** To be a Jet-Eye, I had to **abandon my mother** so that in the **future**, I can become the **father** of **Lube Skystalker** and **Princess Laidup!** Pretty **confusing**, considering that **everybody** knows how this **cash-milking saga** ends!

I'm **Shamu**, Mannequin Sky-stalker's **mother!** I know this **sounds strange**, but Mannequin **doesn't have** a **father!** I guess you could call it an **immaculate MIS-conception!** Oh, okay, so I **did** have a **husband**, but he made me **promise** I'd **never tell anyone** who **fathered** such a **rotten little actor!**

I'm **Queen AmaDilly**, leader of the **No BooBoo Nation!** When I was **younger**, I wanted to be either a **fashion model** or the **ruler** of a **small nation!** This is the **perfect combination** — I **rule** a **small, starving nation** AND I'm **emaciated** and wear lots of **weird clothes!** My **vow** is to keep **NoBooBoo** a peace-loving place, no matter how many **battles** and **blood baths** it takes to do it!

ARTIST: MORT DRUCKER   **WRITER: DICK DEBARTOLO**

STAR BORES
EPIC LOAD I
THE FANDUMB MEGAMESS

I'm **Creepio**, a droid on the planet of **Tattoo**! Believe it or not, I was made from a **huge mess** of **wires** by **nine-year-old Mannequin Skystalker**! In effect, he was my **father**! My **mother** was a **plate** of **spaghetti**!

I'm **Death Mall**, and I wield a **double-bladed light saber**! It's not quite as good as that **triple-bladed Gillette Mach 3**, but I can give my opponents a **damn close shave** anyway! I revel in the **evil** of the **Dark Side**! My scary **tattooed face**, **glowing evil eyes** and **horned skull** mean only one thing: **KISS** just might be able to **stage** a **comeback** after all! Don't **believe me**? See **page 43**!

I'm **Har Har Blinks**, a Gungun! **Gunguns** are **extremely intelligent** beings, which is kinda **hard to believe** since we all tawlk wike **liddle baybees** wid **iwrating voices**, like **Baabaa Walters** on **speed**! Truswt mee, a **liddle Gungun** goes a **roooong waay**!!

I am **Lace Windows**, the only **black senior member** of the **Jet-Eye Council**! Actually, that **isn't bad**, when you consider that the **other members** are mostly **green**, **yellow** and **magenta**! As a **senior member** I **no longer wield** my **blue-bladed light saber** and I **don't get to say** a heck of **a lot**! But I **do enjoy** a **10% senior citizen's discount** at the **Jet-Eye commissary** and **gift shop**!

MAY THIS HORSE BE WITH YOU!

PULP SCIENCE FICTION

ATM INSERT CARD HERE

FORCE BE WITH YOU MAY THE

DRUCKER

I'm **Bar Stool**! I was a sort of **glorified garbage can** in *Star Bores IV, V, and VI*! But now it's **years earlier**, so I'm an **earlier version**! I'm **just like** the **later model**, only **without** the **driver's side airbag** and **automatic pencil sharpener**!

Yodel I am, a **senior member** of the **Jet-Eye council**! **Famous** I am for over **800 years** of **dispensing wisdom**! I was the one who **proclaimed**: "The **Dark Side** is **hard** to see in a **dim light**"! And "Why do they call it a **light saber** when it **weighs ten pounds**?" Find these **wise**, you **do not**? Well, **800 years old I am**! **Gems** they all **cannot** be!

I'm **Pikachu**! Although I'm **not in** this **movie**, I'm here to **learn** from a **master**! No, not a **Jet-Eye master**! I'm talking about **George Lucas** — a **merchandising master**!

#385 SEP '99

MAD — After Gaines

By Frank Jacobs

Although Bill Gaines ran MAD as his private protectorate until his death in 1992, he hadn't owned the magazine since 1961 when he sold it to Premier Industries. No corporate executive dared wield power over the iconoclastic publisher, however, and even when ownership changed hands twice more and MAD became part of Warner Communications (today's Time Warner), Gaines ruled supreme over his comedy kingdom.

But now Gaines was gone, and many wondered, "Wither MAD?" Would corporate suits turn the magazine upside-down? After all, sales had been slowly declining, and all magazines were feeling the first tremors of the digital revolution. Some change was inevitable. DC Comics' Jenette Kahn and Paul Levitz would, respectively, become MAD's Editor-in-Chief and Publisher. Though Gaines had always kept MAD's offices blocks away from corporate headquarters, the staff would now occupy the same building as its owners.

One of the first changes was increasing MAD's frequency from eight issues per year to twelve. To fill the 50% increase in editorial need, more new artists and writers were recruited than at any previous period in MAD's history. New features were introduced, and some discarded. One thing that remained untouched was MAD's black and white interior, printed on a cheaper, uncoated paper stock.

Despite a "relaunch" in 1997, the magazine's appearance still, as the editors often joked, "made it look like it was printed in Mexico in 1957." It was a vestige from the decade in which MAD was born, when magazines, most movies and practically all television shows were also in black and white. But now, when even daily newspapers were in color, MAD's editors lobbied for a similar upgrade. Beginning with color "inserts" like the 16-page "Entertain Me Weakly" parody in 1998, and later that year with the introduction of the annual "MAD 20 Dumbest People, Events and Things," the magazine began transitioning to full color.

But printing on the better quality paper that color required came at a price. To cover the cost of upgrading the product, MAD would have to raise its cover price to $10.00 per issue

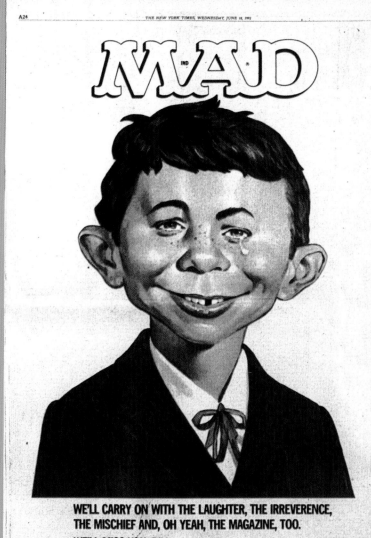

The full-page tribute published in the New York Times following Gaines' death.

(not so "cheap!") or rethink the previously unthinkable — to begin accepting advertising.

It was an idea which Gaines had long shunned. "How can we make fun of Pepsi when we're taking money from Coke?" he

The Black Spy and the White Spy bring their battle to New York's Times Square (L); the MAD-themed Double Jeopardy board in 2010; MAD on Cartoon Network.

asked Morley Safer on *60 Minutes*. Ads, Gaines believed, could convey the impression that MAD was guilty of favoritism.

But the new regime decided that advertising was essential to keep MAD contemporary and relevant. And so, the first ad, for Corn Nuts, made its appearance in issue #403 in March, 2001.

In this new era, MAD not only began accepting advertising, but also licensed its legendary name and characters, which in 1995 (ironically, from a deal Gaines had initiated years earlier), resulted in the premiere of *MADtv* on FOX, an original sketch program awash in Alfred E. Neuman imagery and animated Spy vs. Spy and Don Martin shorts. The program ran for a very respectable 14 seasons. Four years later, just in time for Y2K, one of MAD's first ventures into the digital world, "Totally MAD," a CD-ROM containing the entire contents of every issue and newsstand special from 1952-1998 was released. In 2004, Mountain Dew created ingenious live-action Spy vs. Spy TV spots and billboards.

As we commemorate the 20th anniversary of William M. Gaines' passing, his 60-year-old offspring is still very much a part of our popular culture. Besides many mentions on *The Simpsons* and other television programs, a 2010 episode of *Jeopardy!* used MAD themed "answers" in all six Double Jeopardy categories. That same year, MAD (catchy title!) premiered

on the Cartoon Network and quickly became one of the network's top-rated programs.

Now publishing six issues per year, and operating under the guidance of DC Entertainment President Diane Nelson and Co-Publishers Dan DiDio and Jim Lee, MAD has also gone digital — with the website madmagazine.com, TheIdiotical.com, a blog featuring original content, a MAD iPad app, and a digital subscription option. Imagine that, a digital magazine with no paper to buy or printers to pay! Bill would have loved it!

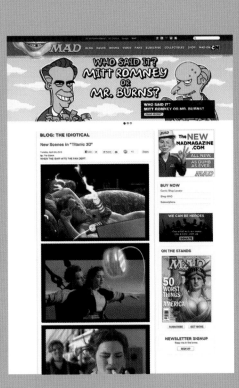

The Idiotical (L); Issue #515 available as an iPad app.

This is a series about a lovable family man — a "Godfather Knows Best" if you will! This show is on HBO! It's best viewed if you get cable — illegally! So get comfortable, sit back in your undershirt and watch...

The

ARTIST: MORT DRUCKER   WRITER: ARNIE KOGEN

Supremos

#389 JAN '00

WHAT BALL ARE
MANY PEOPLE
ANXIOUSLY WAITING
TO SEE
FINALLY DROP?

FOLD PAGE OVER LIKE THIS!

A ⟨⟩ B FOLD BACK SO THAT "A" MEETS "B"

WHAT BALL ARE
MANY PEOPLE
ANXIOUSLY WAITING
TO SEE
FINALLY DROP?

HERE WE GO WITH ANOTHER RIDICULOUS
MAD FOLD-IN

To find out what infrequent special event hundreds—no, thousands—are gathering to see, fold page in as shown.

FOLD PAGE OVER LIKE THIS!

A   FOLD PAGE OVER LEFT   B FOLD BACK SO THAT "A" MEETS "B"

TIMES SQUARE HOTEL

A FRENZIED CROWD WAITS WITH ANTICIPATION FOR THE THRILL OF THIS GREAT EVENT. TO ENJOY THIS SHOW BY SHARING IT WITH OTHERS IS SUPER GRAND AND REQUIRES NOTHING MORE THAN A GREAT SPIRIT.

A   ARTIST AND WRITER: AL JAFFEE   B

A FREE
THROW BY
SHAQ-

A ⟨⟩ B

WHAT A LONG STRANGE STRIP ITS BEEN DEPT.

We were sad to see *Peanuts* come to an end and even sadder to see its creator Charles Schulz pass away. Schulz was a warm and kind man who always let his gentleness show through in his work – right up until the very last *Peanuts* episode. Unfortunately, because of this, many readers came away without a sense of closure to the strip, a wrapping up of the various story lines that occupied Charlie Brown and friends for so long. That's where we come in, the neither warm nor kind editors of MAD, who've come up with these…

Final Episodes of PEANUTS You Never Saw

LUCY THE PSYCHIATRIST

CHARLIE BROWN AND THE KITE

SALLY AND HER SWEET BABBOO

LUCY AND SCHROEDER

CHARIE BROWN, LUCY AND THE FOOTBALL

ARTIST: JACK SYRACUSE   WRITER: J. PRETE

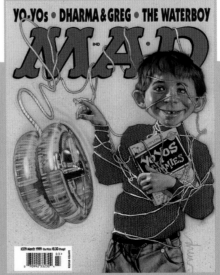

THE POSTULATION EXPLOSION DEPT.

When our nation's forefathers framed the basics of our government, they believed that a two-party system would play an integral part in the preservation of our republic. (The fools!) One wonders what Washington, Jefferson and that kite-flyin' Franklin would say if they could see how both political parties have become so blinded by special interests and hatred for the other guy that their positions have become laughable! For instance...

ONLY A REPUBLICAN DEMOCRAT COULD POSSIBLY BELIEVE...
(VOL. 2)

ARTIST: PAUL COKER
WRITER: RUSS COOPER

Only a **REPUBLICAN** Could Possibly Believe...

...a philandering President is somehow more impeachment-worthy than a senile, arms-for-hostages trading President.

Only a **DEMOCRAT** Could Possibly Believe...

...Clarence Thomas: Repulsive, woman-abusing pervert!
Bill Clinton: re-electable good ol' boy!

Only a **REPUBLICAN** Could Possibly Believe...

...the Sixties was a self-obsessed, self-indulgent decade, as opposed to, say, those selfless, altruistic Eighties.

Only a **DEMOCRAT** Could Possibly Believe...

...a purse-carrying, lavender little creature with the universal symbol for homosexuality over its head is in no way, shape or form a gay character.

STATIS-TICKLE DEPT.

A NEW MILLENNIUM UPDATE to MAD's TABLE of LITTLE KNOWN and VERY USELESS WEIGHTS, MEASURES and DISTANCES

ARTIST: BOB STAAKE   WRITER: J. PRETE

6,914 GALLONS

...is the total amount of vomit cleaned up by Times Square sanitation workers the day after New Year's Eve.

2 FEET 9 INCHES

...is the average distance of a "pick and flick" with no wind resistance.

1 FEET 3 INCHES

...is the average length of an opening day waiting line for any Woody Allen movie.

1.3 CENTIMETERS

...is how much Sam Donaldson's toupee shifts during one newscast.

22.9 YARDS

...is the furthest you can walk in any direction in any city without seeing a GAP.

19 FEET 7 INCHES

...is the minimum window clearance needed when taking the 1,000 Pound Man out of his house on a forklift.

3.4 OUNCES

...is the amount of drool you can expect to see when your 90-year old uncle blows out the candles on his birthday cake..

9.7 OUNCES

...is the amount of butter it takes to fill all the nooks but only some of the crannies in an English muffin.

2 FEET 7 INCHES

...is how much closer the average American male moved toward his TV screen when soccer player Brandi Chastain whipped off her top.

1.7 MILES

...is the distance between the target and where the "smart bomb" actually landed in the video footage the Pentagon doesn't release to the public.

2 3/4 INCHES

...is the height of the local newspaper headline when you're arrested for DWI. (1.2 centimeters is the height of the headline when you're acquitted of all charges.)

15.7 FEET

...is the diameter of the circle around a homeless guy eating in a McDonald's.

.03 CENTIMETERS

...is the depth of those little indents you get in your nose from wearing glasses all the time.

2.1 PINTS

...is the amount of blood you're likely to lose if you're a black male stopped by a New York City cop.

3.4 QUARTS

...is the amount of toilet water swallowed by a freshman pledge during initiation week.

3 FEET 7 INCHES

...is the average distance your clipped toenail careens across the bathroom floor.

"14 1/2 INCHES

...inseam, no cuffs," is Mini-Me's standing order at his tailor's.

16 INCHES

...is the length of spam in your in-box when you don't check your E-mail for a week.

14.2 INCHES

...is the average size of a "17 inch" computer screen.

2 FEET 4 INCHES

...is the airline industry's definition of "generous leg room."

4.7 INCHES

...is about how much any basketball shot by Patrick Ewing misses whenever the game is on the line.

1.3 CENTIMETERS

...is how much larger Andrew Jackson's nostrils are on that goofy new $20 bill.

9.4 GALLONS

...is the maximum amount of cellulite a team of doctors can suck out of that fat chick from *The Practice* before breaking for lunch.

.057 INCHES

...is the depth of Calista Flockhart's cleavage.

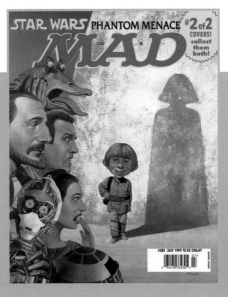

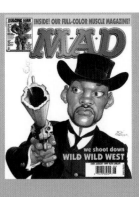

Most people's definition of a dumb person is someone who doesn't recognize their brilliance.

A DOLT'S EDUCATION DEPT.

The very fact that you take the time to read an introduction to a MAD article convinces us that your IQ hovers somewhere around your body temperature. But if you need even more convincing that you're doomed to a lifetime of wearing paper hats, offering to "super-size it" and earning minimum wage, then read on (if you can) (*without* moving your lips!) Sorry, all you brainiacs out there, but...

YOU'RE PROBABLY NOT HEADING TO COLLEGE IF...

...Your senior class project in history was a detailed account of the decades of bad blood between Hulk Hogan and Bobby "The Brain" Heenan.

...Your entry in the regional science fair was titled: "Yo, pull my finger, dude" Balloon Inflation Simplified.

...You're pinning all your academic hopes on a "Twister" scholarship.

...At the end of every session, instead of guidebooks and curriculum information, your guidance counselor gives you a different landscaping tool.

...You still can't figure out how that F#$%ing mall sign knows where you are!

...The highlight of your academic year was finally finding Waldo.

...Organizing and cataloging your ever-growing collection of urinal disinfectant cakes leaves little time for studying.

...Your basic philosophy can best be summed up as, "Who needs higher education when I'm sitting on a virtual gold mine in mint condition pogs!"

...You spend your entire Career Day wandering aimlessly around a crowded auditorium in a futile search for bait shop operators.

ARTIST AND WRITER: JOHN CALDWELL

#400 DEC '00

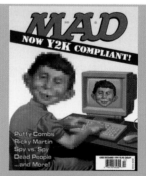

196

ARTIST AND WRITER: DUCK EDWING

#395 JUL '00

How come when it comes to doing something about Global Warming, most politicians get cold feet?
—Alfred E. Neuman

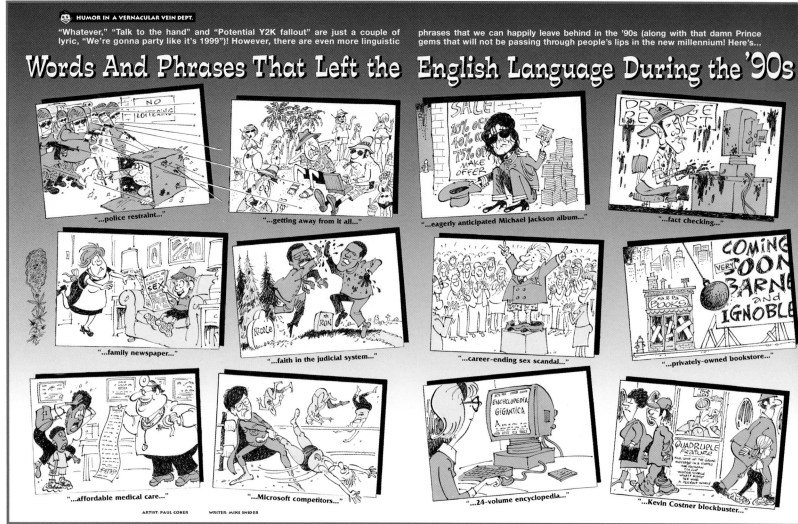

HUMOR IN A VERNACULAR VEIN DEPT.

"Whatever," "Talk to the hand" and "Potential Y2K fallout" are just a couple of lyric, "We're gonna party like it's 1999")! However, there are even more linguistic phrases that we can happily leave behind in the '90s (along with that damn Prince gems that will not be passing through people's lips in the new millennium! Here's...

Words And Phrases That Left the English Language During the '90s

...police restraint...

...getting away from it all...

...eagerly anticipated Michael Jackson album...

...fact checking...

...family newspaper...

...faith in the judicial system...

...career-ending sex scandal...

...privately-owned bookstore...

...affordable medical care...

...Microsoft competitors...

...24-volume encyclopedia...

...Kevin Costner blockbuster...

ARTIST: PAUL COKER   WRITER: MIKE SNIDER

#396 AUG '00

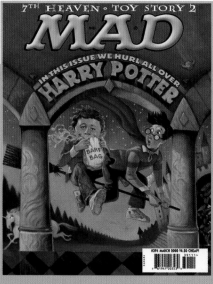

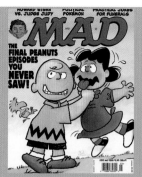

From the Makers of Cherry Garcia and Phish Food Come...

NEW "ROCK & RAP INSPIRED"

Also available! Sour McLachlan and Alanis 'SmoresSette!

Sample the world's first "sampled" ice cream! A'ight!

BEN & JERRY'S FLAVORS

Try it and help topple the corporate whore ass-kissing Praline agenda!

The favorite of convicted felons with refrigerator privileges!

Artist: Scott Bricher Writer: Arie Kaplan

A MAD AD PARODY

WHAT— MAD SELL OUT?

Most of the letters that we received after we started taking ads said, "Your founder Bill Gaines must be turning in his grave." (Note: He isn't. Gaines was cremated.) We were accused of kowtowing to the almighty buck. And to that we plead, "GUILTY AS CHARGED!!!!" We hope that our slide down the slippery slope of greedy commercialism doesn't get any worse, but ooooh, the sweet allure of crisp legal tender is so seductive. She is a powerful mistress controlling our every editorial move. Help us! Help us!

A MAD Cover We'll Soon See?

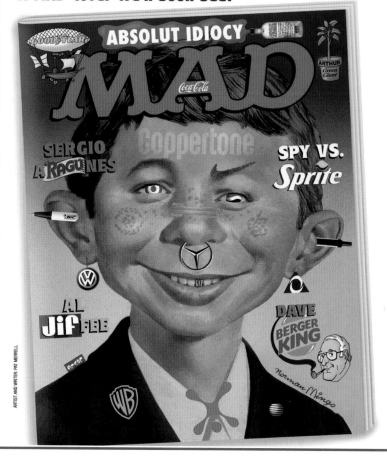

ARTIST AND WRITER: PAT MERRELL

GESUNDHEIT!

THE DISSING LINK DEPT.

It's time for a MAD writer to bring home the bacon! How? By ripping off (once again) the premise of the "Six degrees of Kevin Bacon" game. He'll be eating pork for a month off this one! Here's...

6 DEGREES OF SEPARATION BETWEEN ANYONE AND ANYTHING PART V

Can you link THE FORMER YUGOSLAVIA to MOOSEHEAD BEER?

The Former Yugoslavia → is a deadly combat zone, as is... Any U.S. High School → which produces unemployable illiterates, as does... A MAD Subscription → which costs a mere $24 a year, as does... Bill Gates' Wardrobe → which was fashionable in 1968, as was... Draft Dodging → which is one of the only two reasons to ever go to Canada, the other being... Moosehead Beer

Can you link THE VICE-PRESIDENCY to EGYPT AIR?

The Vice Presidency → is a club very few belong to, as is... MENSA ANNUAL MEETING → which is a hang-out for annoying Brainiacs, as is... Microsoft → which is inside everybody's computer, as are... Free Porno Downloads → which are shameful, but addictive, like... Cigarettes → which are a proven method of suicide, as is flying on... Egypt Air — KUR PLUNK!

Can you link THE INVASION OF POLAND to OLESTRA USERS?

The Invasion of Poland — BLITZ! → was a despicable German act, as is... Siegfried & Roy → who are a pair of phony boobs, which you'll find on... Britney Spears → who is a minor rock derivative, as is... A Meteorite → which is a falling star, as is... Ricky Martin → whose butt is never "at rest," like... Olestra Users

Can you link CELLULITE to RIGOR MORTIS?

Cellulite → strikes most women in their lives, as does... Mike Tyson → who gets checks from a guy with goofy hair, as does... Ivana Trump → who's hard to understand, as is... The Kama Sutra → which is an ancient authority on sex, as is... Hugh Hefner → who gets stiff 1 of 2 ways men his age do, the other being... Rigor Mortis

ARTIST: RICK TULKA   WRITER: MIKE SNIDER

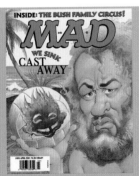

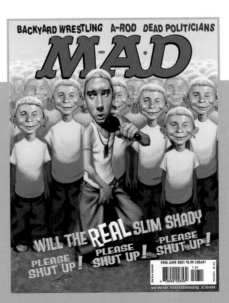

How is it that a well-rounded diet consists of three square meals?

SNIDE AND PREJUDICE DEPT.

Everyone will tell you they know what racism is — cross burnings, causing someone harm based solely on the color of their skin, terrorizing those different from themselves. They'll tell you it involves discrimination in hiring and selling real estate, and denying opportunities to people because of what they look like. Then these same people will be quick to tell you they've never done anything like that and they condemn anyone who does, and they're probably right. But what about those actions where nobody gets hurt — little, teensy actions that come and go in a flash — actions the individuals are probably not even aware they're committing — these are the actions that brand them...

UNCONSCIOUS RACISTS...

...Insist it's habit that makes them call Martin Luther King Boulevard by its former name.

...Always seem to find themselves on supermarket checkout lines manned by their own kind, no matter how much longer the wait.

...Walk right past stores that use rap songs in their advertising.

...Swear they eat at Denny's "for the food."

...Refer to *In Living Color* as "the show Jim Carrey was on."

...Often forget to pick up things at the local 7-Eleven because they're too busy staring at the clerk's "dot."

...Never wonder why there are no black people on *Friends*.

...Pulled for Mark McGwire over Sammy Sosa.

...Always just assume the white guy is in charge.

...Go to the country club and hand their keys to the first minority they see.

...Always have a perfectly logical reason why they didn't let the guy with the turban merge into their lane.

...See a Native American and assume he's got a piece of a casino somewhere.

ARTIST: PETER KUPER   WRITER: BUTCH D'AMBROSIO

#417 MAY '02

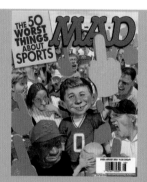

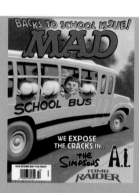
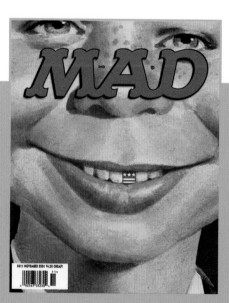

204

DEMI AND ASHTON: Dude, Where's My P.R.?
What it comes down to is this: one middle-aged woman, one boy, and a nation's entertainment media following and reporting their every move for reasons we *still* can't fathom. Please, someone tell us it's just an elaborate prank and that we've all been Punk'd!

Mademi and Child

GRIEVING LAS VEGAS DEPT.

MAD's CELEBRITY CAUSE-OF-DEATH BETTING ODDS

Our team of crack oddsmakers gives you the latest Vegas line on how one of today's biggest stars will receive his closing notice!

THIS MONTH'S FUTURE HOST TO THE GHOSTS:

JAMES LIPTON

CAUSE OF DEATH	ODDS
Caught in post-interview stampede of *Inside the Actors Studio* audience rushing up to star to beg to "put in a good word to Spielberg for me"	2:1
Dies in fawning and swooning mishap	5:1
Slips on church altar while thanking God for cable TV with its desperate need to fill 2,000 hours a week	9:1
Terminal "phone ear" from calling stars' publicists and P.R. flacks to get pre-approved questions	15:1
Gags on own vomit upon hearing himself actually call Val Kilmer "one of the greatest actors of his generation"	20:1
Suffocates when he forgets to breathe during especially long dramatic pause	25:1
Drunken fall at a party celebrating his show's ratings beating out 20-year-old Bob Vila reruns on A&E for the first time	432,000,000:1

ARTIST: HERMANN MEJIA   WRITER: MIKE SNIDER

the BUNION

a.v. club — B-list celebrity interviews! | 🛒 **store** — Wacky non-sequitur T-shirts! | **subscriptions** — Pay for stuff you get here for free! | **books** — Pay for old, free stuff!

VOLUME 38 ISSUE 43 — **AMERICA'S PHONIEST NEWS SOURCE** | [Search]

Front Page | Previous Issue | Archive

IN THE NEWS

Funny Hairdo, Muppet Reportedly Turns Otherwise Uninteresting Bush Photo "Wacky"

Above: President Bush, seen here sporting a comically oversized woman's hairdo while standing next to popular children's character Grover, was in fact standing alone and had a traditionally short, conservative men's hairstyle at the time the actual photo was taken.

NEW YORK, NY — The additions of a funny hairdo and a Muppet have turned what many referred to as an uninteresting photo of President Bush into a hilariously "wacky" image. The original photograph, released last Monday, was downloaded from the official White House website. With the use of a standard computer graphics program, a bouffant hairdo was digitally added to his head. Pasted into the photo is an image of popular Muppet character Grover, who appears to be standing next to Bush. "We made the photo so wacky that we almost didn't need to write our usual overly-long and one-note gag news story to accompany it," laughed Bunion editor Tom Koehler.

Unlikely Words, Phrases In Headline and Body of Story Make Some Articles Sorta Funny, Experts Say

ST. LOUIS, MO — A study issued by the Conference of American Journalism says that the simple act of using "a few well-chosen words can maybe turn a dry news story with, like, little humor potential, into one that's sorta funny. "It's a delicate balance," says panel spokesman Todd Aberline. "You've got to use a certain amount of standard news jargon but then every few lines, throw in a ringer." Experts note that you've totally got to watch the placement of the quotation marks as well, or you're screwed. "You definitely don't want to put your quotes around the incongruent word or phrase," Aberline explains. "That makes it look like you're quoting someone and that you, as the reporter, know the word wouldn't normally appear in that context in a standard newspaper article otherwise." According to the study, without the quotation marks, a really lame story can end up being pretty frickin' funny, and also way cool.

CRAPshot

A look at yet another rip-off of Letterman's Top Ten

The Most Overused Themes On Our Website

1. Subject of article vaguely referred to as "Some Guy" in the headline

2. Offensive, sacreligious news story featuring Christ as a normal person who just happens to live among us

3. Headline peppered with gratuitous curse words as the entire set-up and execution of a gag

4. News item about a well-known advertising character saying and doing things its corporate owners would not approve of

5. Typical advice feature attributed to an unlikely columnist who disregards the questions entirely and instead replies to each letter by expounding on his, her, or its area of expertise, literary style, or obsession

6. Thinly-veiled "humorous" take on a horrific tragedy done sooner after the actual event than good taste would dictate

TOP STORY

Area Man Finds Headline Amusing But That's About It

Above: Legal assistant Ray Jeffries often finds the headlines amusing, but the bodies of the articles lacking in substance. "The captions they run below the photos aren't much better," he says.

BETHESDA, MD — Ray Jeffries thought the headline to this story was kind of funny, but "that was about it." Jeffries, a legal assistant at a local law firm, admits to having become bored by what he describes as an "entirely predictable format." "The headline was kind of amusing, I guess. But then the article was just a rehash of the headline. What's the point?"

Jeffries noted that it's not the first time he's had this reaction and that he previously chuckled at headlines involving the aging pope, a kindergarten class's bean sprout project and the Kool-Aid Man. "But basically it's all the same," he explains. "They shoot their wad with the headline and it's a lot of nothing after that." The 36-year-old considers himself a "fairly intelligent" person with a "reasonably good" sense of humor. "It's not that I don't get it. I can grasp subtlety. And I understand satire. But what more is there to say after you've led with, say, 'Ticketed Motorist Vows To Exact Revenge On Meter Maid With Caustic Barb In Memo Line Of Check'? That's the whole gag. Anything more is mere repetition."

OPINION

Point-Counterpoint: Point-Counterpoint

We've Kind Of Run This Feature Into The Ground, If You Ask Me

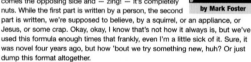

by Mark Foster

You know, these debates were funny at first. But they've become very predictable. And here's why: Generally, the first viewpoint puts forth a reasonable, logical argument in favor or in support of something, anything, whatever. Fine. All straight lines. Very dry. That's the set-up. Then comes the opposing side and — zing! — it's completely nuts. While the first part is written by a person, the second part is written, we're supposed to believe, by a squirrel, or an appliance, or Jesus, or some crap. Okay, okay, I know that's not how it always is, but we've used this formula enough times that frankly, even I'm a little sick of it. Sure, it was novel four years ago, but how 'bout we try something new, huh? Or just dump this format altogether.

Oh, Come On! I'm An Egg Separator, For God's Sake! That Right There Is Funny!

by An Egg Separator

Look, I'm an inanimate object and I'm delivering the opposing viewpoint to your argument! Don't you get it? It's frickin' hilarious! I can't really talk or think, nor do I have the physical ability to puts words on the page or computer screen. But that doesn't change the fact that here I am, arguing against your position and telling you that, yes, these debates are incredibly funny! Why? Because I'm a kitchen utensil, and not only do I have an opinion, but apparently it's such a strong opinion that I feel compelled to respond to you by totally flying off the handle! That's hilarious! A plastic doo-dad from your junk drawer actually getting upset! Instead of pitting your lame-ass argument against the rants of another person, the rebuttal is being written by me, (once again) an EGG SEPARATOR. Too damn funny!

EDITORIAL

Why Running An Editorial Attributed To Someone You Wouldn't Expect To Be Writing An Editorial On A Trivial Subject That Normally Doesn't Warrant An Editorial Is So Damn Funny Week After Week
by Nelson Mandela

ARTIST: SCOTT BRICHER   WRITER: SCOTT MAIKO
PHOTOS: IRVING SCHILD & AP/WIDE WORLD PHOTOS

OTHER NEWS

Some Guy In Mall Signs A Release To Pose For Picture To Run With Possibly Unflattering Mock News Story

Thirty Column Inches Of Text Used To Describe Fictional Middle-Class Woman In Dull Job Facing Uninteresting Dilemma, Maybe About Minor Nuisance In Break Room At Work Or Something

Ending Crazy Headline With Some Variation Of "Study Shows" Ensures Hilarity, Study Shows

Report: Starting Bizarre Headline With "Report" Apparently Even More Hilarious Than Ending With "Study Shows"

Retarded, Crippled People Head List Of Easy Targets For Zany Mock Articles For Third Consecutive Year

NEWS IN BRIEF

Inconsequential Everyday Occurrence Covered With Gravity, Detachment

BOULDER, CO — An inconsequential everyday occurrence was covered today with the gravity and detachment normally associated with a serious, substantial news item.

Jim Grout, a one-hour photo service employee, got a particularly bad static electricity shock when touching his bedroom doorknob after shuffling back from the bathroom at approximately 2:37 this morning. "Son-of-a-bee, it really woke me up," Grout, 51, told reporters. "I was half-asleep, then zap! Talk about a rude awakening."

Despite the noise of the shock seeming "very loud" to Grout, his wife, Kay, 49, slept undisturbed through the ordeal. "I had no idea anything happened until he mentioned it at breakfast," she explained as though the incident were indeed newsworthy. Experts describe this phenomenon as a form of "irony." "A 'nothing' occurrence will be written about with all the unbiased objectivity and seriousness of a major event," notes Dr. David Jeschke, a legitimate-sounding person who in fact doesn't exist, "while important news will be covered as a human interest piece or incredibly conversationally." While irony can be very effective, Jeschke notes, its overuse in some formats can become "terribly repetitious and one-note." He points to the popular online website...

Full Text »

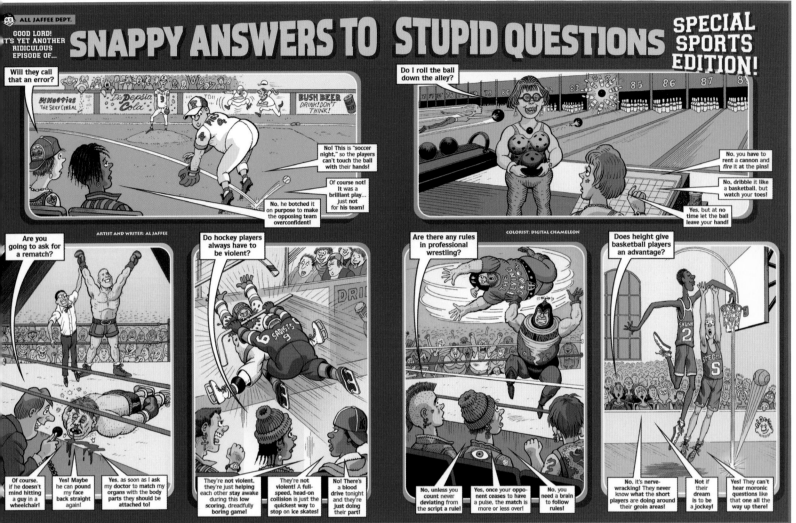

TODAY, YOU DA MAN DEPT.

Lately, Bar Mitzvahs have become big business! Families are shelling out millions of shekels for entertainment and hiring bigger and bigger stars to play the Bar Mitzvah circuit. In recent years, comedian Jackie Mason has performed at Bar Mitzvahs (go figure), but so has the rap group D12, the rock band Cake, and even the almighty 'N Sync! Which makes us wonder...

WHAT IF CHRIS ROCK PERFORMED AT A

I'm so **glad** to **be here** at **Adam Marmelstein's Bar Mitzvah!** This is a **reverent** and **sacred occasion!** Hey, Adam, **Mazel Tov, ya dumb cracker!**

Adam, I **saw you** this morning at the **temple, gettin' your prayer on!** It was like **Amateur Night** at the **Apollo!** When your **voice cracked,** I thought **Sandman** was gonna **sweep your ass** off the **stage!** Hey! You're a **man** now! You're **supposed** to sound like **Barry White,** not **Barry Manilow!**

When they **told me** I was **booked** at a **Jewish religious ceremony,** I thought it was a **circumcision!** Then I thought, **that can't be right,** 'cause you **old White folks** would **NEVER** let a **Black man** in a **room** with a **knife!**

I wanna thank **Rabbi Katz** for **introducing me!** Rabbis are a **lot like pimps,** don't you know; they both wear **fuzzy hats** and **hold positions of power** in their **community!** But the **difference** is, you **won't** ever hear a **rabbi** say, **"Man, I wish** these **ho's** would **just back** the **f**k** up off me!"** At least **not** in **public!**

BAR MITZVAH?

I notice the chefs here have **killed** your **chicken dinner them-selves**! If you **really** wanted to **kill that chicken**, you should've just **sent it** to the **'hood** with a **wad of cash under its wing**! There's a **lotta crime** in the **'hood**! I think all the **Black-on-Black crime** has **got to stop**. You **Jews** don't have no **Jew-on-Jew crime**; the **closest thing** you've **got** is Richard Lewis ripping off **Woody Allen's** "I'm depressed" act!

I like how **y'all open the door** every **Passover** for Elijah! Up on **Fordham Road**, we **don't open** the **door** for **nobody** unless they **have** a **search warrant**!

Before we started, **Adam's grandfather** was **talking to me** in **Yiddish**! Yiddish! That's like the **Jewish jive talk**, or as **I** call it, **"Hebonics"**!

Here I am, a **Black man** at a **restricted club**. Not only **couldn't** I be **a member** of this place, I **couldn't flag down** a **cab** to **take me here**!

To **finish things up**, the **band** is now **going to play Havah Nagilah**! Havah Nagilah — That's a **catchy song**! I'm **waitin'** for the **P. Diddy remix**! Now **that'd** be a **switch** — Imagine a **Black record producer making money** off a **Jewish songwriter**!

When **I got here** today, **Rabbi Katz** gave me a **yarmulke** and **told me** to **put it on**! At first, I was **shocked**; I thought it was **one** of **Lil' Kim's pasties**!

You know, I got **really excited** 'cause I **heard someone say** that **Ol' Dirty Bastard** was **in the house**! Then I **realized** that it was **just Mrs. Goldfarb talking** about her **ex-husband**!

ARTIST: DREW FRIEDMAN
WRITERS: ARIE KAPLAN AND JOSH MALINOW

#419 JUL '02

9 QUESTIONS WE'D LIKE TO ASK SADDAM HUSSEIN

To your knowledge, did Michael Jackson ever try anything funny with Uday or Qusay?

Can you believe Steinbrenner let Pettitte sign with Houston?

It's been said that you put a million people to death — were you trying to beat Bush's record as Governor of Texas?

Your Minister of Information reports that you're currently living it up in Aruba — any comment?

Weren't you just copying Al Gore when you decided to grow a beard after you lost?

While you were in hiding, did you TiVo anything?

Do you have any advice for aspiring young dictators who want to annihilate, maim and torture their countrymen and threaten the international community with weapons of mass destruction?

For the elite Republican Guard's uniforms — boxers or briefs?

So, what's next for Saddam?

THE COVER WE *DIDN'T* USE

MAD

IN THIS ISSUE WE PROBE "THE SIMPLE LIFE"

BITTERMAN

I don't know why you waste your time playing these stupid video games. It's just another of Corporate America's insidious plots to turn you and your entire generation into uncreative, mindless drones, perfectly content to sit glassy-eyed, like freakin' zombies, in front of a computer monitor all week, crunching meaningless data and processing useless information for THE MAN!

Did you just rip off that guy's arm and beat him with it?

Yep.

I got winner.

PAGES

VIDEOGAME CORNER
HOW THE TOP GAME CONSOLES COMPARE: A CONSUMER'S GUIDE

XBOX   PLAYSTATION 2   GAMECUBE

	XBOX	PLAYSTATION 2	GAMECUBE
Big green "X" on unit	YES	NO	NO
Plays Xbox game cartridges	YES	NO	NO
Provides Bill Gates with R&D money to create new, kickin' games	YES	NO	NO
Headquarters near Seattle, which was named for renowned Native American prophet	YES	NO	NO
Based in Japan, which didn't send soldiers to help topple Saddam Hussein's evil regime	NO	YES	YES

CLEARLY, XBOX IS THE SUPERIOR GAME SYSTEM!
(Special thanks to Microsoft for research assistance in preparing this feature)

CELEBRITY CAUSE-OF-DEATH BETTING ODDS

OUR TEAM OF CRACK ODDSMAKERS GIVES YOU THE LATEST VEGAS LINE ON HOW ONE OF TODAY'S BIGGEST STARS WILL MEET HER DEMISE!

This month: JESSICA SIMPSON

CAUSE OF DEATH	ODDS
Brain aneurysm while staring for hours at frozen orange juice can marked "Concentrate"	5:1
First-ever "contract hit" put out by MENSA	12:1
Starvation after locking herself inside car	16:1
Slapfight with Mandy Moore over which of them is #3 behind Britney and Christina	20:1
Fatal "repetitive-pouting" injury	25:1

THE GODFREY REPORT

IN	FIVE MINUTES AGO	OUT
Satchels	Valises	Steamer Trunks
Ointments	Salves	Balms
Incontinence	Holding It In	Going Behind the Garage

MONKEYS ARE ALWAYS FUNNY

MELVIN & JENKINS' GUIDE TO WINTER FROLIC

Jenkins salts the sidewalk to make it safer for passersby to go about their daily business.

Melvin used up all his rock salt months ago while torturing garden snails.

OSCAR BY THE NUMBERS

$6,850: Combined worth of all Oscars presented in the non-televised day-time portion of the Award ceremony, held a week or so prior to the actual Oscar telecast. Also, the total amount the Academy spends on this ceremony, plus maybe another $45 for a party platter from Subway.

February 24th, 5:00 p.m.: Deadline for all Academy members to submit their ballots for voting. Also, the deadline for all aged Academy members in declining health to pass away if they want to be included in the ceremony's "In Memoriam" reel.

.03 cm: Thickness of the gold-plating on an Oscar statuette. Also, the length the ends of Russell Crowe's mouth extend in that infectious grin of his when he wins one.

972 bubbles per minute: Amount of fizz rising to the surface in an average glass of Dom Perignon served at Elton John's annual after-party. Also, the amount of frothing at Tom Cruise's mouth after it's clear another year has passed him by with no Oscar.

$2.95: Cover price of *Us Weekly*'s Oscar coverage issue featuring perennial "Oscar Night's Best- & Worst-Dressed" article. Also, the value of any formerly $10,000+ gown that had the misfortune to wind up in the "Worst" column.

Be wary of anyone who gives you advice that begins with, "Be wary of..."

Yet another self-portrait by someone who doesn't realize that cameras held at arm's length never yield flattering pictures.

The catering hall's "deluxe" beef sirloin and an Altoid to compare size with.

A waitress walking in front of what would have been a great shot of the groom feeding the bride.

The bride after vomiting in the women's room, before her bridesmaids have a chance to freshen her up.

PRINTS UN-CHARMING DEPT.

The latest "in" thing to do at weddings and other social events is to place a cheap, disposable camera on each table so guests can take their own candid pictures at the reception — beautiful, emotion-packed, artistic masterpieces that could only be captured on a $5.99 Kodak throwaway. Well, unless your drunken Uncle is Ansel Adams and your Aunt is Annie Leibovitz, it ain't gonna happen! For proof, look at this recent collection of...

Disposable Camera Wedding Photos
THAT DIDN'T MAKE THE ALBUM

Five favorite family members from the neck down.

The garter belt after it was tossed to the single men, before the do-over.

Table Seven posing for another camera.

The person whose cell phone rang during the best man's toast.

The bride, her father, and more ceiling tiles than anyone ever has good reason to look at.

ARTIST: TIMOTHY SHAMEY   WRITER: BUTCH D'AMBROSIO

#428 APR '03

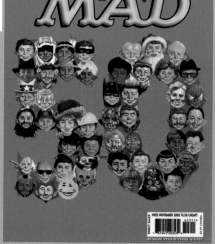

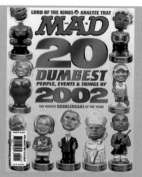

THE BUSH CAMPAIGN'S TV COMMERCIAL IF HE WAS RUNNING AGAINST JESUS

Jesus of Nazareth says, "Give to him who begs from you, and do not refuse him who would borrow from you."

Jesus favors more government handouts for welfare cheats.

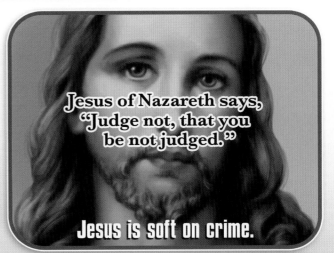

Jesus of Nazareth says, "Judge not, that you be not judged."

Jesus is soft on crime.

Jesus of Nazareth says, "Render therefore unto Caesar the things which are Caesar's."

Jesus will raise your taxes.

Jesus of Nazareth says, "Do not resist one who is evil. But if anyone strikes you on the right cheek, turn to him the other."

Can we trust Jesus to fight the War on Terror?

Jesus — Wrong on social services. Wrong on crime. Wrong on defense. Wrong for America.

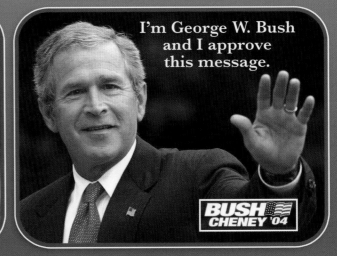

I'm George W. Bush and I approve this message.

BUSH CHENEY '04

ARTIST: SCOTT BRICHER   WRITER: DON VAUGHAN   BUSH PHOTO: AP/WIDE WORLD PHOTOS

#446 OCT '04

KEVIN CAN WAIT DEPT.

By now, everyone's familiar with "Six Degrees Of Kevin Bacon," the game where you begin with the name of any movie actor and move through a chain of associations until, in six steps or less, you end up at the star of *Footloose*. But we were thinking: who needs actors? Who needs six degrees? And for that matter, who needs Kevin? That's how we came up with the new lean, mean game we call...

FIVE DEGREES OF BACON

EMINEM
is a white rapper, as was...

GEORGE W. BUSH
runs the country with...

BRITNEY SPEARS
was married for about five minutes to a guy named...

BATMAN
has a sidekick named...

SADDAM HUSSEIN
is the former leader of...

KEVIN BACON
appears in Mystic River with...

VANILLA ICE
who shares part of his name with the sport of...

DICK CHENEY
who has had several...

JASON ALEXANDER
which is also the name of the Seinfeld star who did commercials for...

ROBIN
as does...

IRAQ
which is a country that borders...

SEAN PENN
who was in The Thin Red Line with...

ICE HOCKEY
which is the national pastime of...

HEART ATTACKS
which are the result of...

KFC
where you can order your chicken...

HOWARD STERN
who frequently encourages his guests to...

TURKEY
which shares its name with a key ingredient of a...

JOHN TRAVOLTA
who was the star of...

CANADA
which has its own famous style of...

CLOGGED ARTERIES
which are often caused by consuming too much...

EXTRA CRISPY
which is also how many people like their...

STRIP
which is what you call a serving of...

CLUB SANDWICH
which also includes lots of...

GREASE
which is what's left in the pan after you fry up some...

BACON

WRITER: MICHAEL RODMAN
BACON/CLUB SANDWICH PHOTOS: IRVING SCHILD
PHOTOS:
AP/WIDE WORLD PHOTOS
CORBIS • IMAGE SOURCE
PHOTODISC • RUBBER BALL

MAD thanks the Bacon Council for its invaluable assistance in preparing this article.

#446 OCT '04

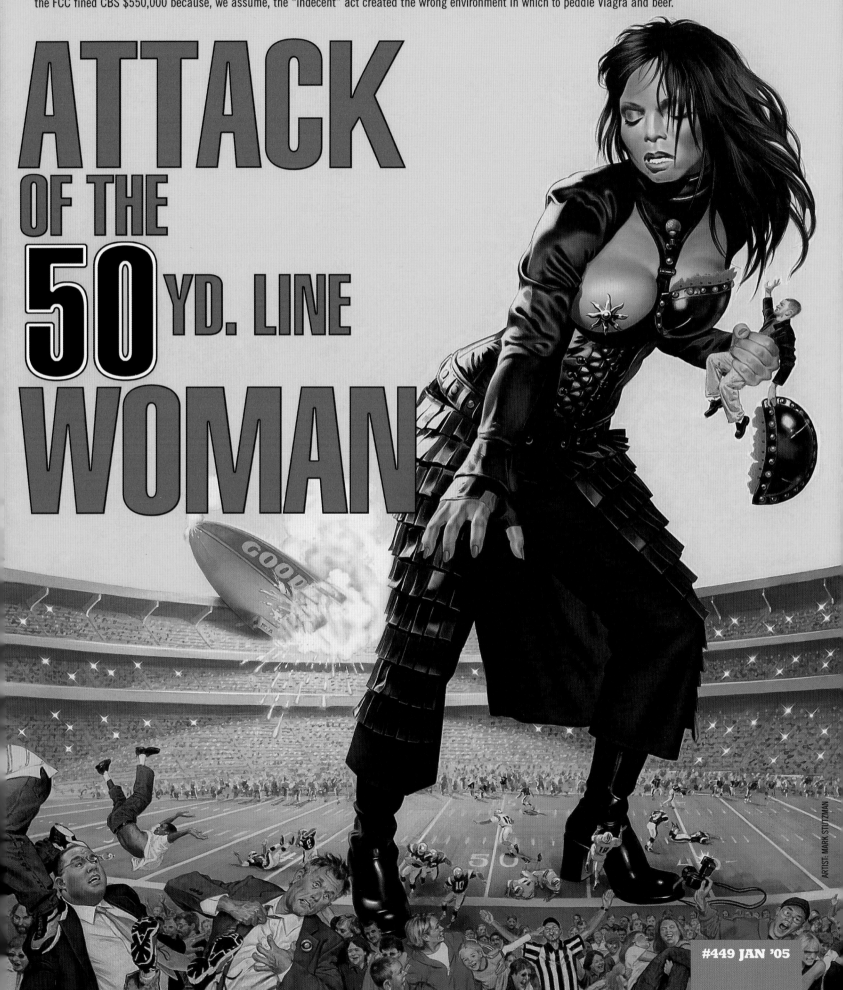

JANET JACKSON'S "WARDROBE MALFUNCTION"
TEMPEST IN A C-CUP

February 1, 2004: Superbowl Sunday. America tunes in for a wholesome evening of sports violence. Instead, at halftime, the country is subjected to a fleeting glimpse of a mammary gland, a glance that would shake the very foundation of our democracy. The NFL blamed CBS, CBS blamed producers MTV, MTV blamed Janet and Justin, and Janet and Justin blamed that ever-pesky "wardrobe malfunction." Inexplicably, it created the kind of panic and frenzy usually only seen in 1950s horror flicks. Ultimately, the FCC fined CBS $550,000 because, we assume, the "indecent" act created the wrong environment in which to peddle Viagra and beer.

ATTACK
OF THE
50 YD. LINE
WOMAN

ARTIST: MARK STUTZMAN

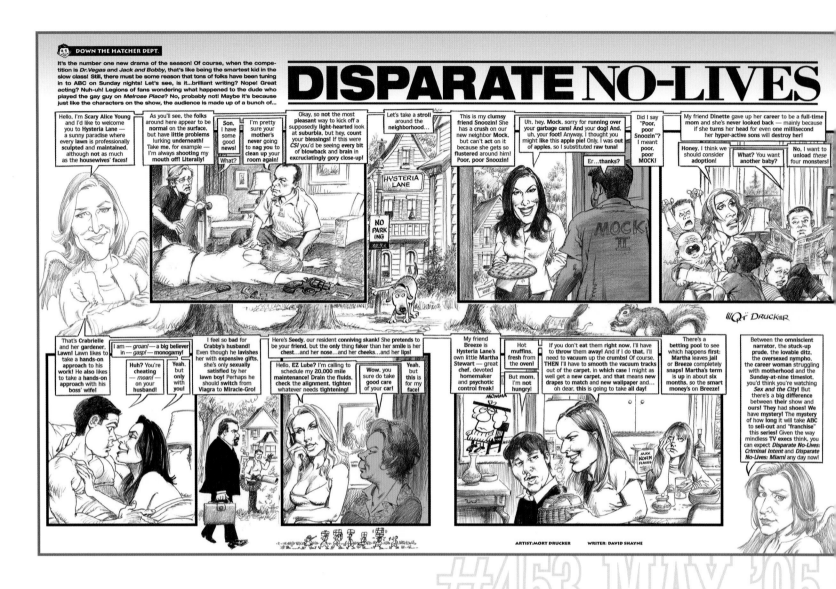

DEAN'S SCREAM

After coming in a distant third in the Iowa Caucuses, closer to the fourth-place, eyebrow-challenged Dick Gephardt than second-place pretty boy John Edwards, Democratic candidate Howard Dean concluded his "victory" rally with a freakish and disturbing yell, his now infamous, "YAAAAAAAAAAAAARRRRHHHHHH!!!!!!!!" (Perhaps you saw it — the network and cable news programs repeated it about eight *billion* times.) The only scream that would have been more widely heard is the one that would have erupted around the world had this irrational lunatic actually been elected President.

DONALD TRUMP THE ART OF THE HEEL

He's an arrogant, self-important douche-bag — yet he's one of the biggest stars on television. His hotel and casino empire is facing bankruptcy — yet he's still perceived as a business guru. He's had two messy, obscenely expensive divorces — yet he's about to marry another amazingly attractive, albeit temporary, trophy wife. Yes, it's safe to say that Donald Trump has had a lucky and improbable life, so much so that he reminds us of another idiot savant with an annoying catchphrase.

He was a retard
with a stupid haircut.
But he had a knack
for making
millions. **Forrest Trump**

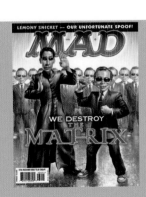

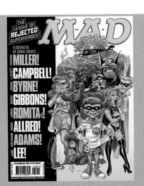

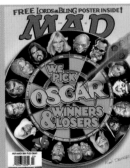

The Las
CIRC

Supper
004

#444 AUG '04

If you put someone on a pedestal, it just makes it easier for them to look down on you.

WHEN ADVERTISING TAKES OVER THE PLEDGE OF ALLEGIANCE

WRITER: DARREN JOHNSON   ARTIST: TIMOTHY SHAMEY   113

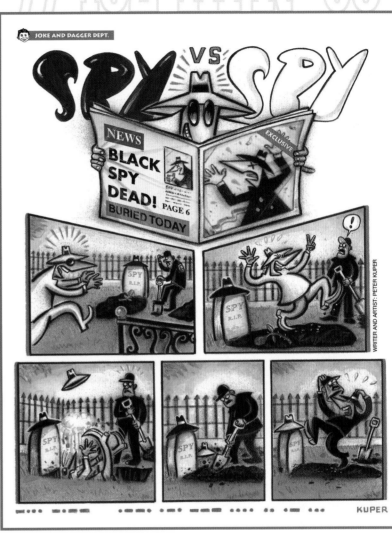

JOKE AND DAGGER DEPT.

SPY vs SPY

WRITER AND ARTIST: PETER KUPER

KUPER

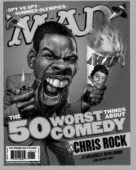

...DONALD TRUMP YOU'RE

Every week *The Apprentice* ends with a contestant getting pink-slipped and told why he or she doesn't measure up business-wise — but never the one person who, week after week, consistently shows bad business judgement, makes embarrassing corporate decisions and, frankly, has one of the worst résumés in corporate history! This is an easy one. We're sorry, but...

For starting every season with 16 or 18 varied, multicultural contestants of both genders, only to pick as the winner another boring, corporate, brown-nosing white guy... **...Donald Trump, YOU'RE FIRED!**

For pretending on network TV that any real businessman in his right mind would hand over the reins of a major building project to some guy who won the job by selling four cups of lemonade in the middle of a city street... **...Donald Trump, YOU'RE FIRED!**

For being a dude with a zillion divorces, bankruptcies and/or mistresses who lectures contestants on "ethical behavior"... **...Donald Trump, YOU'RE FIRED!**

For continually claiming your show is the highest-rated show on TV, except for the seven other shows that consistently and inconveniently out-viewer you... **...Donald Trump, YOU'RE FIRED!**

For wasting sixteen weeks to impart such rare gems of Trump business wisdom as "Think big"..."Work well with others" and "Love what you do"... **...Donald Trump, YOU'RE FIRED!**

For subjecting America week after week to that moronic, gravity-defying, architecturally-unsound, can't-be-mocked-enough hairdo from no known period in coiffing history... **...Donald Trump, YOU'RE FIRED!**

FIRED!!!

For encouraging every other annoying, charisma-deprived *Benefactor* and *Rebel Billionaire* to clog the airways with their own lame-o business reality shows... ...Donald Trump, **YOU'RE FIRED!**

For being the only human in the history of planet Earth to own a casino that *LOST MONEY*... ...Donald Trump, **YOU'RE FIRED!**

For picking female contestants with pouty lips, do-me hair and big boobs and then chastising them for using sex to get ahead... ...Donald Trump, **YOU'RE FIRED!**

For somehow convincing the world your nickname should be "The Donald" instead of more appropriate monikers like "The Dickwad," "The Deadbeat," or "The Debt-Ridden-Diddler-of-Beauty-Pageant-Rejects..." ...Donald Trump, **YOU'RE FIRED!**

For criticizing others about "not thinking outside the box" when your sum-total marketing strategy involves pathologically slapping the word "Trump" on everything in sight... ...Donald Trump, **YOU'RE FIRED!**

For mentally ruining that hip-cool "Money, Money, Money" song by forever linking it to slow-motion images of a certain white, middle-aged, bloated, funk-free, lard-ass pucker-squinting his way out of a gold-plated helicopter... ...Donald Trump, **YOU'RE FIRED!**

For somehow making *Joey* the SECOND most embarrassing show on NBC Thursday... ...Donald Trump, **YOU'RE FIRED!**

For unironically coming to the conclusion that it's perfectly reasonable for a bankruptcy-skirting, junk-bond-peddling, deal-reneging, contract-welching business-weasel to be the spokesman for Visa credit cards... ...Donald Trump, **YOU'RE FIRED!**

ARTIST: SAM SISCO
WRITER: RUSS COOPER

#453 MAY '05

Put together one very run-down house, a deserving family, a guy with a bullhorn who you'd like to choke, hundreds of construction workers and a bunch of designers who do the same kind of renovation over and over, and over and over, and over and over, and what do you get?

Extreme ONCE-OVER HOME REPITITION

HAIR GEL FROM BEBALD SOSOON

BLEACH JOB BY L'ORÉHELL

PROVIDED BY BEST CRY (AT OUR SERVICE)

SHIRT AVAILABLE AK CRAP

I'm **Trying Bragington**, as if you didn't **know** that! This week's *Extreme Once-Over* involves a **man**. A **very special man**. Not as **special** as me, but still a **little bit special**. Marvin's had **more** than his share of **bad luck**, as you'll see by the **video** he sent us!

I want to do **something** very **special** for this **family**! **Something** they can **point out** and say: "**Wow**, look at this **very special thing** Trying did for me!" Of course the **first thing** I'll do is make a **plaque** with **my picture** and signature so it can be part of the **foundation**!

I know you like to take **credit** for everything **yourself, Trying**, but **others** help, too! As an **interior designer**, I like to **ask the kids** what **they** would like to **see** in their **own rooms**! And if I **don't like** what I **hear**, I **strongly suggest** that what they **really** want is something I designed **already**! I mean, **what** am I supposed to **do**? Really **design** and **build** a kid's theme room in **less than a week**? Let's get **real**! I'm telling you **right now** — one of those **kids** is getting a room with a **boating motif**, even if a picture of a **lake** makes him **puke**!

HOVEL SWEET HOVEL

Good morning, Lakely Family! Wake up and **come out** here! Or should I say, "**wake up** and *roll* out here"? Your annoying *Extreme Once-Over* team has **arrived**!

When we saw your moving **video**, the whole **design team** agreed that we had to **do something** to help you get **ahead**. I'm sorry. I mean you *have* a **head**, but we're going to make life **easier** for you and your **five kids**!

Five? I only have **two kids!**

BULLHORN EMPORIUM

Yes, **five!** You **had two** when we came here, but our **producer** felt **two kids** in **your situation** was merely **daunting**, but he thought **five kids** would make your situation **truly frightening**! So he **adopted three more** for you to care for! It makes for a **better reality show**!

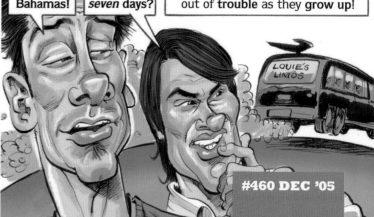

WHAT IS THE LEADING CAUSE OF HEART ATTACKS AMONG AMERICANS?

HERE WE GO WITH ANOTHER RIDICULOUS
MAD FOLD-IN

Even though it's hurting them in the long run, Americans are still clamoring to get their fill. Despite the health risks, they're determined to get what they want. There is one culprit, however, that can cause real harm to these gluttons for punishment. To find out what it is, fold page in as shown.

FOLD PAGE OVER THIS!

A ◄ FOLD PAGE OVER LEFT   B ► FOLD BACK SO THAT "A" MEETS "B"

Mini-Mart

$$$SAVINGS ON EVERYTHING! THERE ARE 3 GREAT DAYS OF BARGAINS THAT ARE REAL.

ONE DAY ONLY 2 for $1

OUR RETURN POLICY

PORK RINDS   BEEF JERKY   LUNCHABLES

CIGARETTES   COLD BEER   LIQUOR

NO CHECKS CREDIT PETS PROFANITY BARE FEET BODILY FUNCTIONS ANYTHING

HOME OF THE WHOPPER

SALE ITEMS

NOTICE! NEW ROAD TO TOWN CENTER

YOU ARE HERE

TODAY'S SPECIALS
★ TRIPLE CHEESEBURGER
★ MOUNTAIN of FRIES
★ BACON WRAPPED SAUSAGE
★ LARD SANDWICH
★ BUTTERBALL SOUP

CHICKEN FAT   HOG FAT

SOME PEOPLE ARE UNAWARE OF THEIR RISKY HEART-THREATENING BEHAVIOR. THEY WEIGH GOOD HABITS AGAINST BAD ONES AND ACT AS IF IT'S OK TO IGNORE THE GOOD. IT'S A PRETTY FOOLISH WAY TO INDULGE ONE'S VICES

ARTIST AND WRITER: AL JAFFEE

A◄► B

WHAT IS THE LEADING CAUSE OF HEART ATTACKS AMONG AMERICANS?

FOLD PAGE OVER LIKE THIS!

A ◄ ► B   FOLD BACK SO THAT "A" MEETS "B"

ONE DAY ONLY 2 for $1

$3 GAL.

OUR RETURN POLICY NO NO NO NO NO NO

NO CHECKS CREDIT PETS PROFANITY BARE FEET BODILY FUNCTIONS ANYTHING

SALE ITEMS

NOTICE! NEW ROAD TO TOWN CENTER

YOU ARE HERE

SKY HIGH GAS

PRICES

A◄► B

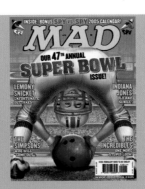

FACTS THAT SOUND FOR A SECOND LIKE THEY MIGHT BE TRUE... BUT AREN'T

MAD Presents...

WRITER: JUSTIN HEIMBERG   ARTIST: KEVIN POPE

One Fine Morning In Fallujah

ARTIST: PAUL COKER   IDEA: L.P. FERRANTE

The Iraq War Mish-mosh Accomplished

For four years the Bush war mantra was to "stay the course" in Iraq. Now, with roughly 3,000 Americans dead and tens of thousands injured, the new Bush war mantra is "we won't leave short of victory." But our delusional Commander-in-Chief can't tell us what victory is and how we achieve it. So American G.I.s slog onward, like pawns in some never-ending sick game. That the War in Iraq is the dumbest thing of the year is painfully obvious. The only question remaining is whether or not it proves to be the dumbest thing of the century.

THE IRAQI QUAGMIRE CHESS SET

From the makers of THE 'NAM CHESS SET!

Now you can experience the bumbling American mission in Iraq, but without the constant hassle of having to pick hot shrapnel out of your ass. With the Quagmire Chess™ set you'll feel like you're in the middle of all the unpredictable action from the comfort of your living room! And you can do what the Pentagon *never* has: apply and implement a **strategy to win the war!** But it won't be easy! By combining the rules of traditional chess with the anarchy of the Sunni Triangle, Quagmire Chess™ replicates "Bush's Blunder" with amazing (and frustrating!) accuracy.

The Battlefield

Unlike conventional chess boards, the Quagmire Chess™ board is actually shaped like Iraq, giving a nearly **insurmountable advantage** to the Iraqi player who is familiar with the "terrain." Further hindering the American side is that conventional chess strategies **don't work** in this game. In fact, most American players will soon realize that the game *itself* makes no sense.

HAND-CRAFTED QUALITY!

The Fighters

Quagmire Chess™ pits a undermanned battalion of exhausted, homesick Americans, some on their third or fourth tour of duty, against a ragtag army of furious Sunni militants and rabid foreign jihadists. (Fun!) Play the Iraqi side and you're a "winner" as long as the fight rages on. In fact, a mere stalemate is a **major victory!** Play the American side, however, and "winning" — since it's **not clearly defined** in the rules — is *impossible*. It's a debilitating battle with no clear objective or end in sight. That's why it's called **Quagmire Chess™**!

DICK CHENEY
(AMERICAN BISHOP)

PENTAGON
(AMERICAN ROOK)

HILARY CLINTON
(AMERICAN KNIGHT)

DONALD RUMSFELD
(AMERICAN BISHOP)

CONDOLEEZZA RICE
(AMERICAN QUEEN)

GEORGE W. BUSH
(AMERICAN KING)

JOSEPH LIEBERMAN
(AMERICAN KNIGHT)

LIMITED EDITION!

SADDAM'S PALACE
(IRAQI ROOK)

ABU-MUSAB AL-ZARQAWI
(IRAQI QUEEN)

MOSQUE
(IRAQI ROOK)

MUQTADA AL-SADR
(IRAQI KNIGHT)

QUSAY HUSSEIN
(IRAQI BISHOP)

SADDAM HUSSEIN
(IRAQI KING)

UDAY HUSSEIN
(IRAQI BISHOP)

ABU HAMZA AL-MASRI
(IRAQI KNIGHT)

SUICIDE BOMBER
(IRAQI PAWN)

The Rules

U.S. troops must fan out from the relative safety of Baghdad's "Green Zone" into a vast, unconquerable desert that's teeming with insurgents hell-bent on forcing the American military completely off the board. Just like in the real war, this is **no fair fight!** Should an American capture a suicide bomber before he strikes, he'll be replaced by two more desperate fanatics ready to blow themselves and everyone around them to smithereens. "Staying the course" has never felt so counter-productive!

OUR GUARANTEE

With Quagmire Chess™ "the violent last throes" will go on forever. And pretty soon the American player will throw up his hands in disgust and realize that he probably shouldn't have played in the first place!

NATIONAL GUARDSMAN
(AMERICAN PAWN)

CAPITOL
(AMERICAN ROOK)

THE IRAQI QUAGMIRE CHESS SET

Yes, I want to invest my money, time and energy in a quagmire! Send me the limited edition, hand-crafted Quagmire Chess™ set! I understand that the game will go on far longer than I want it to and that I'll soon come to believe that the price I've paid is too high.

Name _____ Address _____

City _____ State _____ Zip _____

SS # (for government spying purposes only) _____

WRITER: JACOB LAMBERT   SCULPTOR: HERMANN MEJIA   PHOTOGRAPHER: IRVING SCHILD

Success is achieved by those who are more or less confident, kind of specific, and take a relatively firm stand.

—Alfred E. Neuman

PAINT MISBEHAVIN' DEPT.

This July, the National Portrait Gallery in Washington D.C. will reopen with a new high-profile addition — a portrait of former President and Cassanova-in-Chief Bill Clinton. The portrait has raised some eyebrows for the rather sassy pose struck by Mr. Clinton. What has not been widely reported is that this was not the only painting Billy-Boy posed for and submitted to the museum. So begin walking as the MAD docent leads you on a tour of the...

BILL CLINTON ~~REJECTED~~ PORTRAITS

ARTIST: RICHARD WILLIAMS

#468 AUG '06

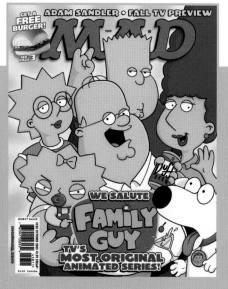

A-HOLE FOODS MARKET

Fancy-Shmancy Food
Unbelievably High Prices

WEAKLY BUYS

Apples

At our secret quality testing centers all our apples are tested for firmness, taste, visual appeal, stem-rotation, intelligence, and juiciness.

2 for **$7.00**

80% MORE Expensive Than Supermarkets.

Cranberries

Our award-winning cranberries are grown locally on a 400-acre plot cultivated solely by its owner, 76-year-old Jane Fertlandan, and her dyslexic son, Jeffy. Both always wash their hands after going to the bathroom.

1 lb. for **$16.00**

BUY ONE GET ONE for the Same Price

Blueberries

Each berry is individually wrapped in three layers of UV-blocking, organically-produced nickel foil to ensure long-lasting freshness.

1 lb. for **$27.00**

SAVE $20 Just Grow Your Own

Bananas

Bananas are dirty and unnatural, and we don't sell them at A-Hole Foods®.

Broccoli

Before being shelved, each broccoli stalk is treated to a free weekend spa treatment and polished to an eye-catching sheen with a combination of Turtle Wax and vinegar distilled by blind Nordic monks.

2 lbs. for **$72.99**

plus cost of Turtle Wax

Asparagus

Our asparagus is a good source of vitamin C (like its cousins: leeks and onions), and a fine garnish (like its fraternal grandfather: garlic). Our asparagus is untouched by human hands and kept in hermetically-sealed jars that cannot be opened.

$15.99

Buy 21 JARS get the 22nd for $15.00

Chicken

All chickens sold at A-Hole Foods® are free-range and raised to hold basic Christian beliefs. Their feed is antibiotic-free and composed of the finest of imported Italian grains. Every coop is ocean-front and temperature-controlled. Monkeys serve as butlers.

1 lb. for **$86.99**

WRITER: KIERNAN P. SCHMITT

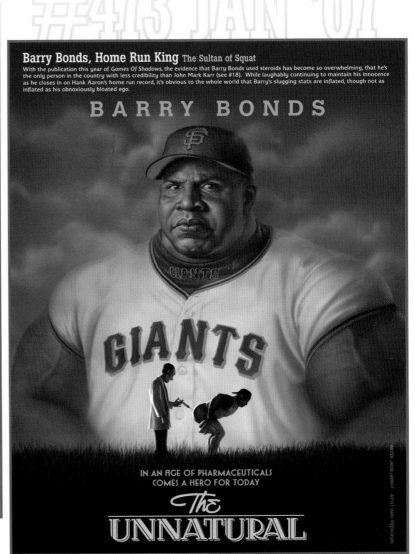

Barry Bonds, Home Run King The Sultan of Squat

With the publication this year of *Games Of Shadows*, the evidence that Barry Bonds used steroids has become so overwhelming, that he's the only person in the country with less credibility than John Mark Karr (see #18). While laughably continuing to maintain his innocence as he closes in on Hank Aaron's home run record, it's obvious to the whole world that Barry's slugging stats are inflated, though not as inflated as his obnoxiously bloated ego.

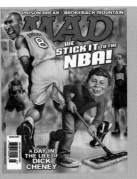

235

Every dog has its day — but that day
still consists largely of sniffing butts.

—Alfred E. Neuman

HILLARY'S CAMPAIGN FOR THE WHITE HOUSE:
Thar She Blows It

Going into the 2008 presidential campaign, the only thing bigger than Hillary Clinton's ambition was her grating sense of entitlement to the Democratic nomination for President. More heavily favored than the Patriots were in the last Super Bowl, Hil found a way to snatch defeat from the jaws of victory just like the losers from New England. But at least they had the sense to stop playing when the game was over. Confusing determination with delusion, Madame Clinton pressed on in the primaries until the awful truth finally sank in: Monica Lewinsky was no longer the only one in Bill's life who "blew it"!

Artist: Mark Stutzman

CELEBRITY SEX SCANDALS: Adultery Swim

It all begins with the collective delusion of a handful of would-be heroes — that their sins will go unnoticed and the price will never have to be paid. Are they deluded, or have they in fact figured out a way to have secret extramarital sex? Oops, turns out they're deluded! Dodging their wives and the press, these fallen heroes desperately try to maintain their reputations while still getting their rocks off. Instead, they are all caught with their capes down, shocking their families to their core and changing the way the world looks at them forever! Follow these seven sex-obsessed celebrities from Hollywood to Detroit to Staten Island in this vow-breaking story of cosmically stupid infidelity — the story of...The Crotchmen!

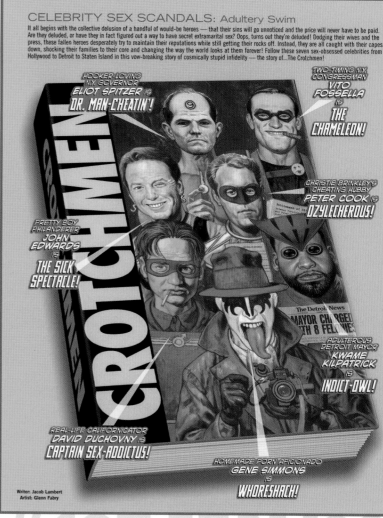

Writer: Jacob Lambert
Artist: Glenn Fabry

#497 JAN '09

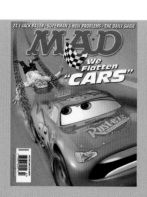

236

ALL FAT AND NO COWBOY DEPT.

THESE DAYS we hear a lot of alarming reports about overweight people. America, it seems, is a nation of fatties getting fatter all the time. But like most alarming reports from the media, you probably shouldn't believe them. The truth is, we've always been a country of overeating heifers, we just didn't have talking heads with hours of television airtime to get us all excited about them. Too bad! If we had TV back in the old West, we could have seen some pretty entertaining special reports, such as...

THE HARDSHIPS FACED BY THE SUPER OBESE OF AMERICA'S WILD WEST

Even the best-made chaps were never slimming

Square dancing wasn't so much fun, ever

Yours was always the last wagon to pull into camp

You were never, ever picked for the posse

Support groups were hard to come by

The seldom-won quick-draw showdowns

Long, harsh winters left you feeling less like a person and more like a commodity

No matter that they swung wide, saloon doors were a constant struggle

Being the only one to survive an Indian attack was pretty embarrassing

46

WRITER AND ARTIST: TERESA BURNS PARKHURST

47

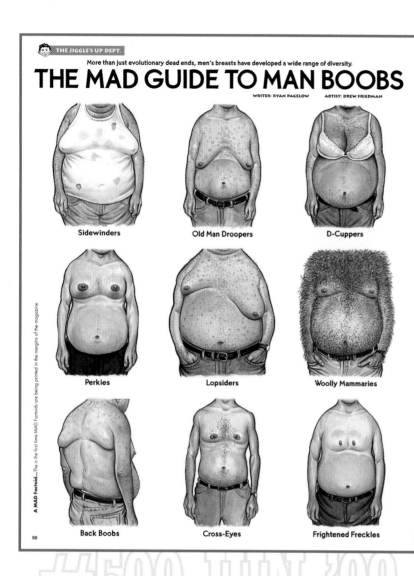

#500 JUN '09

#476 APR '07

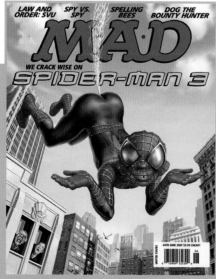

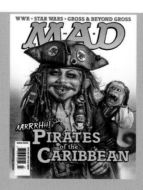

#476 APR '07

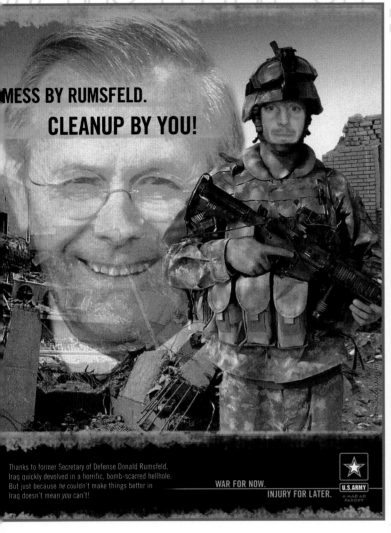

MESS BY RUMSFELD.
CLEANUP BY YOU!

Thanks to former Secretary of Defense Donald Rumsfeld.
Iraq quickly devolved in a horrific, bomb-scarred hellhole.
But just because *he* couldn't make things better in
Iraq doesn't mean *you* can't!

WAR FOR NOW.

INJURY FOR LATER.

U.S. ARMY
A MAD AD
PARODY

WRITER: JACOB LAMBERT

THE U.S. ARMY:
YOU'RE *NEVER* TOO OLD.

Instead of reliving old war stories from 'Nam, why not make
some new ones? We're so desperate for troops, we may just
increase the maximum recruitment age from 44 to 65!
So enlist now — there's prune juice in the mess hall!

WAR FOR NOW.

COMMON SENSE FOR LATER.

U.S. ARMY
A MAD AD
PARODY

WRITER: JACOB LAMBERT

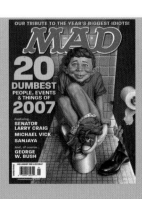

Genius is rarely recognized in its lifetime, but
fortunately, neither is gross incompetence.

—Alfred E. Neuman

A MAD PUBLIC SERVICE ANNOUNCEMENT

#505 OCT '10

#508 APR '11

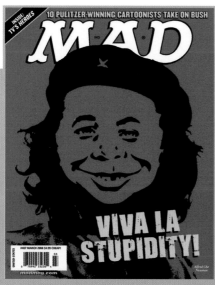

VIVA LA STUPIDITY!

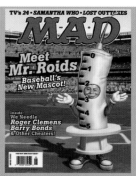

SERGE-IN GENERAL DEPT.

SERGIO ARAGONÉS

Presents A MAD LOOK AT AVATAR

WRITER AND ARTIST: SERGIO ARAGONÉS   COLORIST: TOM LUTH

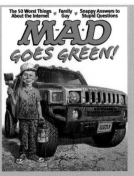

A gambler who thinks he has a "can't lose" system for winning at blackjack isn't playing with a full deck.
—Alfred E. Neuman

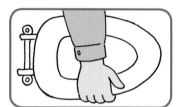

STOP THE SPREAD OF GERMS!
FOLLOW THESE SIMPLE RULES

IN THE WORKPLACE

1. Avoid bare skin-to-skin contact! Shake hands using a stick.

2. Don't sneeze into your hands: whenever possible, sneeze into the back pocket of a co-worker.

3. Do not touch vending machines. Insert coins with your mouth.

IN THE RESTROOM

1. Avoid contact with the faucet. Wash hands wearing gloves.

2. Toilet seats breed germs. Carry your own toilet seat with you wherever you go.

3. Never flush using your hands. Push the handle with your foot. Then wash your foot thoroughly.

A MAD HEALTHY LIVING POSTER

WRITER: DICK DEBARTOLO   ARTIST: GARY HALLGREN

#503 MAY '10

WHAT COULD POSSIBLY TOP OUR **DOUBLE DOWN?** INTRODUCING OUR NEWEST SANDWICH...

THE KFC® TRIPLE! BY-PASS!

Three Original Recipe Triple-Fried 100% Chicken* Filets!
(*Yes our filets are 100% Chicken! White meat, dark meat, legs, thighs, wings, breasts, feet, feathers & beaks ground to perfection! Breaded to conceal!)

And between those three fried Chicken Filets? Two more Chicken Filets!

We take each one of the five filets & deep-fry 'em once, slit 'em open & stuff 'em with a buttery-type filling** and deep-fry 'em again!
(**We do not use fillers in our fillings, only 100% pure and natural lard!)

Between the first two Chicken Filets we pile on bacon, sausage and a slab of pork-roll!
(Lightly cooked to bring out the flavor.)

Next, we slide in two fried eggs!

Then we add cheese — American, Swiss, Cheddar and our famous Pepper Jack Cheese! And we deep-fry it again!

To make our new food sensation a healthy choice, we add a leaf of lettuce. Yes, it's deep-fried too!

How do you hold the new Triple By-Pass?
(Don't worry, we still didn't add bread...)

We added three MORE deep-fried Chicken Filets!

It's like nothing you've ever tasted — and nothing you'll ever digest!

$12.95

Stop into KFC and ask for a Triple By-Pass then stop at the hospital and ask for the same!

If your appetite's especially inhuman, get the KFC Triple By-Pass Combo Meal! Includes a full pound of our triple-fried Tater Gobs and a 2-liter cup of our exclusive deep-fried soda (regular or diet)!

WRITER: DICK DEBARTOLO   PHOTOGRAPHER: IRVING SCHILD   A MAD AD PARODY

#504 AUG '10

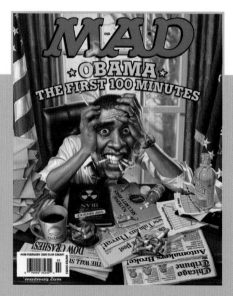

244

PEN AND STINK DEPT.

THE STRIP CLUB

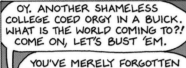
it only hurts when I laugh

OY. ANOTHER SHAMELESS COLLEGE COED ORGY IN A BUICK. WHAT IS THE WORLD COMING TO?! COME ON, LET'S BUST 'EM.

YOU'VE MERELY FORGOTTEN WHAT IT'S LIKE TO BE YOUNG. ME? I'M HAPPY FOR THEM.

WHUMPA WHUMPA WHUMPA

IT WAS DIFFERENT WHEN WE WERE YOUNG.

IT WAS NOT! YOU JUST FEEL LEFT OUT. IF YOU'RE GONNA BE SUCH A PARTY POOPER, WHY DON'T YOU GO BACK TO THE CAR TO EAT DONUTS AND SULK? THE REST OF US ARE HAVING FUN OUT HERE AND YOU'RE SPOILING IT.

THIS MORAL DEPRAVITY MAKES ME WANT TO VOMIT. THIS COULD BE ONE OF OUR DAUGHTERS, YOU KNOW!

THERE! HAPPY?! NOT OUR DAUGHTERS. NOW, WILL YOU JUST SMILE FOR ONCE AND GET OVER BEING LEFT OUT?!

MAYBE YOU'RE RIGHT. MAYBE I AM BEING SELF-CENTERED. JUST BECAUSE I'M NOT HAVING FUN, DOESN'T MEAN OTHERS SHOULDN'T.

WHY DON'T YOU JOIN US, THEN, AND HAVE SOME FUN?

WELL, SURE. OKAY.

SORRY, YOU'RE NOT MY TYPE.

SLAM!

WHUMPA WHUMPA WHUMPA

WHUMPA WHUMPA

CHRISTOPHER BALDWIN

#503 MAY '10

THE DORK SIDE

...THE THIRD KIND IS AN ENCOUNTER. THE FOURTH KIND IS AN ABDUCTION. AND THE **FIFTH** KIND IS WHERE YOU AND I MAKE A SEX TAPE.

SCOTT NICKEL

HELP! I CAN'T SWIM!!

FEGGO

JUST BELOW THE SURFACE

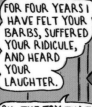

DOUGLAS PASZKIEWICZ

THE *JERSEY SHORE* CAST THE LEAGUE OF EXTRAORDINARY SIMPLETONS

Just when you thought the New Jersey Nets were the biggest bunch of losers to come out of the Garden State, MTV debuted *Jersey Shore*! Even more amazing, it became the network's top-rated show! People are obsessed with the inarticulate, emotionally-stunted, orange-skinned, black-out drunks and their…"unique" looks. And viewers couldn't get enough of Snooki's poof, The Situation's abs, J-Woww's boobs, Pauly D's hair and Angelina's…uh, actually, no one gave a crap about Angelina. Still, if we're going to dissect the lives of these idiots, we might as well dissect the idiots themselves! Usually, this is only done when the people are dead – but in this case, "brain dead" is close enough.

"Pauly D"
Did you know that the human heart pumps more than 100,000 times every day? And every night, a guido pumps his fist twice that much!

"Snooki"
You'll see all the muscles, veins, bones and fat deposits… but no brains!

"J-Woww"
Enjoy a rare chance to examine the human body's natural — and unnatural — wonders!

BODIES THE EXHIBITION **JERSEY SHORE** EDITION

"The Situation"
Now "GTL" stands for Guts, Tendons, Ligaments!

ARTIST: HERMANN MEJIA

> Understatement is a zillion times more effective than exaggeration!
> —Alfred E. Neuman

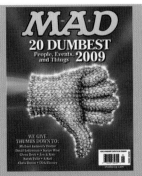

People who live in glass houses are a reality TV producer's dream come true.

And now we shine a bright light on an all-new installment of a favorite MAD feature...

THE SHADOW KNOWS

WRITER AND ARTIST: SERGIO ARAGONÉS   COLORIST: TOM LUTH

54

55

#510 AUG '11

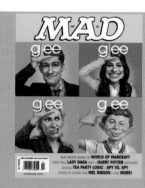

250

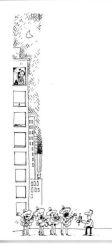

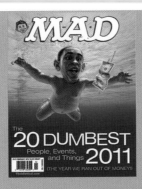

WRITER AND ARTIST: PETER KUPER

KUPER

SPY VS SPY

Afterword By John Ficarra

ne of the things that inevitably happens when I meet a MAD reader is that they tell me their all-time favorite MAD article. Usually they can quote large portions of it verbatim and usually the article is from the point in their life when they first started reading MAD.

Oh, and one more odd thing, it's never, ever been the same article. Everybody's favorite is different.

Sometimes it's a Don Martin cartoon, other times it's a song parody, a strip from The Lighter Side of..., an ad takeoff, or some obscure article that I don't even remember, even though I may have written it.

So it was something of an impossible task when it came to selecting the material that would appear in this book. With over 60 years worth of MAD to fit into 256 pages, no matter what I chose, some readers would be disappointed. If you are among the disappointed, I can only say one thing – too bad! I tried. And besides, we already have your money and I call "no backsies!"

But to be serious, I want the experience of reading this book to be like curling up in a big, old comfy chair. I want this book to transport you back to the time when you first discovered MAD. Maybe it was at summer camp. Maybe it was an older brother's copy. Maybe it was under the covers with a flashlight because your parents forbade you from reading such trash. I want to shake loose from the cobwebs articles you may not have seen, or even thought

about, in years. To remember the gags of the writers and art styles of the artists that made you laugh and maybe even opened your eyes to the world. I want you to discover the new generation of writers and artists that make up today's "Usual Gang of Idiots." But most of all, I want you to forget the whole big, old comfy chair analogy which, in retrospect, makes no sense whatsoever.

Putting out an issue of MAD has always been a highly collaborative effort. A small editorial staff works with freelance writers and artists from all over the world. Scripts are written and rewritten. Gags are added. Layouts are created. Artists submit initial sketches ("pencils") which are tinkered with and then returned to the artist for inking. Final layouts are finessed. And it is then and only then that we realize that the entire article was a bad idea from the start, but it's too late into the process to scrap it, so we just publish it and hope for the best.

As I said, trying to whittle down what articles made it into this book was not easy. I tried to represent the work of as many artists and writers as possible, and also to include as many of the recurring features that have appeared in the pages of MAD over the years. I couldn't include everyone's work, but hopefully I can include everyone's name. Here, with a big thanks to MAD historian Doug Gilford, is a complete listing of everyone who has ever contributed to MAD over the past 60 years. If nothing else, at least now you know who to blame.

John Ficarra, Editor
May 2012